THE POLICEM

The Story of Hull Police Force
1836 to 1974

by

A. A. Clarke

To Malcolm
Love
Arthur, Paula
and Paul.
x x x

HUTTON PRESS
1992

See Page 179.
famous again.

Published by the Hutton Press Ltd.
130 Canada Drive, Cherry Burton, Beverley
East Yorkshire HU17 7SB

Printed and bound by

Clifford Ward & Co. (Bridlington) Ltd.
55a West Street, Bridlington, East Yorkshire
YO15 3DZ

ISBN 1 872167 39 X

This book is dedicated to

Kathy, Sarah, Susan and Penny
who cheerfully accepted all the trials and tribulations
of having a policeman for husband and father respectively.

ACKNOWLEDGEMENTS

The author wishes to express his gratitude for the help and assistance he has received from so many different people and organisations during the preparation of this book.

Many who served in Hull Police, and many others who had relatives in the force, were kind enough to give, not only their time, but information and photographs together with other items which were most useful.

Particular thanks must go to David Hall CBE, QPM, former Chief Constable of Humberside, for his ever ready assistance and, to Norman Woollons, without whose careful preservation of many records of the force no book would have been possible. My thanks go also to the staffs of the Hull City Record Office, the Local History Library Humberside Libraries and Beverley Library.

A special word of thanks must go to Mrs. Patricia Lewis who kindly gave me the research done on Hull police by her late father, James 'Jock' Ferrier, a Chief Superintendent in the force.

CONTENTS

PREFACE

Winter still held the town of Kingston upon Hull in its icy grip as a group of well dressed young men made their way from the town hall in Lowgate to the Humber pier. Although well before 6 am on a raw, end of February morning in 1836, men women and children, their faces pinched with the cold, were already emerging from the warren-like houses and scurrying about their business.

Caricature of 18th Century Yorkshire Watchman
(Courtesy of Chief Constable of North Yorkshire)

Despite the frost, a heavy acrid smell of stale refuse, human and animal excrement, all mixed with strong industrial odours, hung over streets and buildings as the top-hatted party picked their way fastidiously round the pools of foul brownish liquid on the road. The night soil men were just finishing their messy business as people wakened and allowed them access to the small one-door dwellings packed tightly into courts and alleys.

The leaders of the group, William Woolley and Boswell Middleton Jalland, exchanged glances as a shuffling figure appeared with flickering lantern in one hand and a large rattle in the other. "Six o'clock and all's well", an old man's voice quavered from the depths of a tattered cloak.

The two men received the well-wishes of their companions as they boarded the first ferry for New Holland. Both were lawyers, town councillors, and, members of the town's newly formed Watch Committee. Untiring and uncompromising advocates of reform they had been two of those primarily responsible for the decision to form a force of 'new police' in the borough and, to seek an experienced man from London to be its head. Woolley in particular, as chairman of the Committee, had convinced his colleagues they should seek professional advice before embarking on their own force and to this end he was going to London.

All day they travelled south via Brigg, Lincoln and onwards down the Great North road, to the capital. An appointment had been arranged with Colonel Rowan, veteran of Waterloo and one of the two joint Commissioners of the London police force since its inception some seven years previously. His office was at 4, Whitehall Place, the rear entry to which was in Scotland Yard.

Well-received by the Colonel, Woolley and Jalland were delighted with the outcome of their meeting. They had obtained an offer of the services of Alexander McManus who had entered the London force at its commencement in 1829 and had risen rapidly to the rank of Inspector. Not only did he have Rowan's recommendation, but also that of J. S. Little, chief magistrate of Kensington. A further impressive reference came in the form of a note from none other than HRH The Duchess of Kent who wrote that, "from her own personal observation McManus was an admirable officer". He had in fact served for a period at Kensington Palace while she had been in residence.

Three days after leaving, the two envoys returned to Hull confident their visit had been extremely worthwhile. Their confidence was to be fully vindicated by future events.

CHAPTER 1

BEFORE THE NEW POLICE

Like other towns in England at the beginning of the nineteenth century, Hull had a system of policing little changed since the Middle Ages. By the time the industrial revolution arrived, with exploding urban populations, it was becoming less and less effective.

The two main arms of law enforcement were the parish constable and the watchman. The former was an age old function with origins dating back at least to Norman times. A constable was elected annually in each parish and, unpaid, he had a duty to arrest offenders and take them before the magistrates while, at the same time, somehow coping with his normal means of making a living. Likewise, it was every citizen's duty to maintain the peace and, if a crime was committed and a hue and cry raised, everyone was expected to join in the chase to apprehend the offender.

As time went on, wealthier merchants and others become very disenchanted with having to serve their year in this troublesome and unpaid post and the practice of paying deputies crept in. The deputies soon began paying their own deputies and the job often ended up in the hands of the otherwise unemployable.

The country's second arm of policing was the system of Watch and Ward started in 1285 to supplement the parish constables in towns. In Hull it is assumed watchmen would have manned the town gates between sunset and sunrise and been subject to instruction by the parish constables. Watchmen were put on a proper footing in the town as a result of Improvement Acts secured by both Hull, Myton and Sculcoates in the eighteenth century which authorised Commissioners, among other things, to appoint watchmen for duty at nights. They would usually do this job in addition to any normal daytime work.

A rather vague post of High Constable also existed under the system, this official usually being drawn from the ranks of prosperous townsmen and having a loose form of control over both parish constables and watchmen.

Certainly neither the system nor the quality of the men filling the posts within it was such that it could ever have coped with the changes occurring in society as it moved into the nineteenth century.

Conflicting accounts are found both of the numbers of constables and watchmen and the state of law and order in Hull prior to 1836. At the beginning of the eighteenth century one high or chief constable and twelve petty constables apparently kept the town in good order and were only supplemented by extra men for the really exciting spectacles such as pillorying or public whipping! One visitor in 1717 described Hull as "not large but very populous, but as free from noise and disturbance as any country village." Only once is it recorded that police failed to quell trouble when, in 1780, the magistrates were forced to pay the Suffolk Militia and troops from Hull Garrison to help suppress riots. In fact the reputation of Hull's efficient thirteen guardians of the law is seen in the remarks of one incredulous observer in the late eighteenth century who wrote, "they even had the temerity to arrest press gangs and their officers."

This situation was not to last and, despite more deaths than births occurring in the town, a tremendous influx of newcomers to the Hull and Sculcoates areas meant that the population increased sixfold between 1700 and 1830.

By the early nineteenth century the number of police had been increased to 1 chief and 39 constables and by 1833 Hull's Town Clerk was telling Commissioners enquiring into the state of the Corporation that there were 44 constables and 72 watchmen for Hull and Sculcoates. The town's lock-up keeper was included in the constables and, in addition, 10 of the dock company's labourers were sworn in as constables.

Criminal activity and disorder had increased and a general lack of respect for the law existed in all sections of society. One eminent witness recalled that "the streets at night were hideous with noise and drunkenness and it was the fashion for young men to remove the door knockers from houses. *Old Charleys* (as the elderley watchmen were known), who were simply walking barometers covered in long coats, a huge wood rattle carried in front of them and an old lantern in hand, walked the steets, shouting at the top of their voice, 'past twelve o'clock and a cloudy morning!' Magistrates and others returning home after dining out would, by way of diversion, if they caught a watchman napping in his sentry box, gently roll him in his box, down the road and make off. So far had respect for the law fallen."

Another growing problem was the effect that new police methods elsewhere in the country were having on Hull and similar places where systems had not changed. London had introduced the new police in 1829 and towns like Liverpool had taken steps to modernise their forces. Criminals began to leave such areas where their lives were becoming more difficult and move to areas like Hull where crime was easier. At the time whereas Hull and Sculcoates had some sort of police-cover, Holderness was completely unprotected and Councillor Woolley forcefully pointed out "the area was a refuge for thieves and villains of every description from where they travelled to carry out their crimes".

Throughout the country reformers had been making their views heard but, despite the obvious need for changes in policing, opposition to any moves in that direction remained strong. Many considered the proposals put forward would lead to gross infringements of personal liberty and to a form of military rule from London. Nowhere was the opposition to change stronger than in the counties and, in the East Riding area surrounding Hull the gentlemen magistrates remained obdurate in their resistance long after most areas had established new police forces.

The boroughs, however, were generally more enlightened and Hull was blessed with a number of progressive men in positions of power at the time. Pragmatic merchants and traders ran the council and many of them supported

Hull's eighteenth century gaol and lock-up.

reform. The feeling in the town was summed up in the *Hull Advertiser* as early as 1829 when it greeted the new London police with a leader;

> "The reign of Dogberry in the Metropolis is nearly over. The antiquated system of watch boxes and hour calling is on the wane. But the new plan has excited considerable jealousy. Some fear the introduction of military rule, others are alarmed at cries of fear for the constitution and individual liberty. The system may be unpopular for a time but we see nothing objectionable in the new police or the rules for their behaviour."

The need for action was further demonstrated when a Royal Commission, which was established in 1833 to enquire into the state of municipal corporations, included the newly created Parliamentary Borough of Kingston upon Hull, including Sculcoates , in its deliberations. The Commission visted the town for ten days in December, and among other things, concluded there was no effective policing in the borough, and they were particularly concerned that military had been called in during elections in 1832 to maintain order.

In 1835 Parliament passed legislation which empowered municipal boroughs to appoint watch committees and form new style police forces. Hull was quick to seize the opportunity and early in 1836, a committee of the council was established under William Woolley to fully examine the situation and make recommendations for an efficient police force. The Commissioners of the various parish watches, childishly piqued that their power was to be eroded, sullenly refused to supply any figures to the sub-committee and threatened to discipline any staff who talked to them. Nevertheless it was established there were around 96 parish constables, 102 watchmen plus 9 dock constables and 15 dock watchmen c overing the borough. Ten of the watchmen were over 60 years of age, 48 were over 50 and at least half were totally unfit for duty. Only 4 of the parish constables were fully active.

The sub-committee also reported that a large number of criminals had been driven to Hull by improved policing in other places and were not only committing crime in the town but using it as a headquarters for raids on other nearby towns. The overcrowded cobbled streets and courts saw frequent robberies and stabbings and women were too frightened to go out at night. Even men made up parties before venturing on to the streets after darkness had fallen. During daylight, gangs of boys, run by older men, flagrantly picked pockets in the market place. Houses were regularly broken into — one had been attacked four times in two years. The only policing took place at night, by watchmen who were paid a mere seven shillings a week in winter, reduced to five shillings and threepence in summer when the shorter nights required less work. Much criminal activity was believed to take place in evenings and early mornings when, although it was dark, the watch had either not started or had finished their duties.

Even when they were patrolling most watchmen were of such poor quality they served very little purpose. The committee claimed "it had been usual for the Commissioners to appoint to the office of watchmen, paupers unable to earn a livelihood elsewhere, recommended by the Parish Officers". It went on,

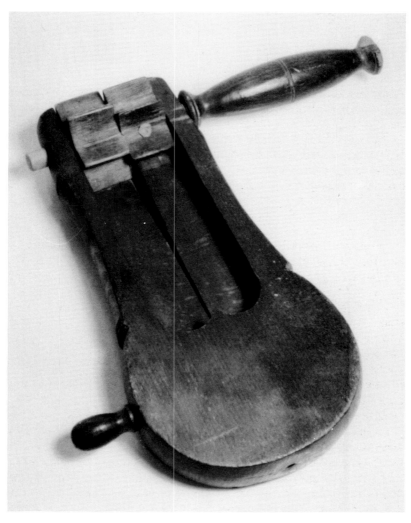

An early 19th Century watchman's rattle as would have been used by watchmen in Hull
(Courtesy of Hornsea Folk Museum).

"Many are too old for the performance of their duties, one was tried and sentenced to transportation for committing a burglary at a house on his beat, when on duty; and another has been a watchman twenty years in a populous district, and has never been known to signalize his valour by the capture of a single prisoner!"

The report continued by again drawing attention to the Holderness side of the town which had no watchmen and, together with South Myton, "was infested with thieves to an alarming rate." Those constables who operated only got paid for actual work done and were often being reimbursed by the victims of robberies.

The sub-committee considered that other towns had police operating on a 24 hour basis and Hull should do likewise. To achieve this they recommended the town be divided into four irregular sections which would, in turn, be divided into beats. These beats should be carefully measured by surveyors to be 1 mile square. It had been calculated that beats of this size would allow a patrolling policeman, walking at an average 2 m.p.h. to pass his colleagues on adjoining beats once every half hour. These precise calculations allowed the committee to suggest a force of 110 men with 10 reserves and 10 places for vacancies, would be suitable for Hull.

In the light of other forces' experience the committee were also able to estimate the annual cost of such a force as being:

	£	s	d
1 Superintendent at £3 p.w.	156.	0	0
8 Inspectors at £1.50 p.w.	520.	0	0
Clothing for above	60.	0	0
110 Privates at 18s. p.w.	5148.	0	0
Clothing for above	715.	0	0
1 Clerk at £1.1s p.w.	54.	12	0
Expenses of 4 lock ups	150.	0	0
Incidentals	200.	0	0
Total	7003.	12	0

In February the council appointed William Woolley as chairman of a newly formed watch committee. The clerk of the council was instructed to write to Leicester, Liverpool and Newcastle for copies of the rules of their own committees and immediate steps were sanctioned to seek a suitable Superintendent from London or elsewhere, to take charge of the Hull force. The new Hull committee were instructed to study the report of the earlier sub-committee and in particular the salaries recommended. These were to be altered if necessary to keep expenditure as moderate as possible compatible with efficiency.

Advertisements were placed in the local press for Inspectors and a Clerk and placards were printed and distributed, not only in the town but throughout the surrounding county areas, for lower ranks. By March applicants were flooding in. Twenty-four men applied to be clerk and 74 applied for the 8 Inspectors' posts.

The day Messrs. Woolley and Jalland set off to London, four Inspectors were appointed, a Mr. George Freeman of 12, St. Joseph's Square, Witham, having been appointed the Clerk a few days earlier. Once started, the borough elders were letting no grass grow under their feet — the stage was set for the start of a police force, which was to serve Hull until the second half of the twentieth century.

CHAPTER 2

THE CHIEF CONSTABLES OF HULL

Twelve men were to command Hull's police in the years from 1836 to 1974 the post initially being designated Superintendent but upgraded to Chief Constable after the first few years. The men came from a variety of backgrounds and made a varying degree of impact on the force they commanded. Many completed their period in office with distinction, some made little impression and a few gave way to temptation and left ignominiously.

McManus

Alexander McManus, first of the twelve, had arguably the most difficult task and the fact he and the force remained together until his death some thirty years after his arrival in Hull is an indication of the considerable dedication he showed to his work throughout.

Inspector McManus had been second-in-line for a Superintendent's post in the London force when he accepted the job as Superintendent in Hull. He came on twelve months trial with both sides having the right to terminate with no penalty and his salary was agreed at £150 per annum for the first year, £175 for the second and, £200 after the third anniversary of his appointment. So impressed were the watch committee with his early performance they rewarded him with a £25 bonus and moved him on to the top rate of £200 a mere six months after his arrival.

Little is known of his early background prior to joining the London police in 1829. He was a Roman Catholic and had served in the Connaught Rangers, an Irish regiment. He apparently did nothing to dispel the misconception among leading citizens of Hull that he held a commission in the army.

In many ways McManus was an ideal man for the job. He was experienced, a firm disciplinarian when required but always a fair leader who had the welfare of his men at heart. More importantly he was uncorrupted by local connections and was soon able to secure the confidence not only of the force but of the citizens and corporation of the borough. In November 1839 the Council officially raised his status to that of Chief Constable of Hull.

His standing with the watch committee became such that he easily survived what could have been a potentially damaging allegation made against him in 1848. One of his constables complained that McManus had taken liberties with his wife. A full watch committee was drawn up to hear the matter which naturally excited an unusually heavily attended meeting. Local speculation was rife but, to the chagrin of the local Press, they and the general public were barred from the hearing. After an hour and a half the committee dismissed the allegation with a brusque statement that the evidence was too contradictory.

Mr. Andrew McManus, First Chief Officer, Hull Police Force, 1836-66.

Chief Constable Cook

The Press considered this a bizarre decision, particularly as it transpired McManus had not even been called to give evidence.

Further examples of the borough's confidence in their Chief Constable appear elsewhere but the attitude of the councillors can best be summed up in the glowing tribute paid by the Mayor in 1863 when he proclaimed that, "in no town in England could a man retire 'to bed' with greater assurance that his property was secure than in Hull".

This came a mere three years after the Mayor, in the presence of the whole corporation, had presented their Chief Constable with a massive gold watch, bought with a collection from the men in the force. It was in gratitude for his support in opposing legislation which would have increased the length of service necessary for a pension to ten years.

Thirty years is a long time to spend as Chief Constable of any force and there is little doubt that by the end of his days the original self-confidence of the young McManus had matured to a self-satisfaction with his own position and the police force.

A commentator of the time described him as, "having a very good opinion of himself and the force he helped to create. He was a plethoric, choleric man with a very red face, extensive corporation and large appetite".

When he died at his son's home in Withernsea in 1866, only four months after the death of his wife, he was sixty-eight and had played a significant part in the foundation and development of modern policing in Hull. Thousands turned out to pay their respects on his last journey to Hull's cemetery.

So impressed were the watch committee by the service they had received from him, they looked no further than their own force for a successor.

T. Cooke

Thomas Cooke, who joined Hull police in December 1843, was first of only two men ever to rise from the ranks of the force to be its Chief Constable. The other was Thomas Howden.

Cooke had been senior Inspector and Clerk in the force and was physically a very impressive figure with a full beard. The stipendiary magistrate of the time — T. H. Travis said, "With regard to Mr. Cooke's appointment, if experience, if knowledge of his duties, if the various qualities which are indispensable in the character of a constable and particularly that of a Chief Constable, are guarantee that the gentleman will be a satisfactory substitute for Mr. McManus, I am sure that the Corporation may congratulate themselves on the appointment of Mr. Cooke."

Unfortunately the borough's faith and pride in their new Chief Constable was to be shattered by subsequent events. Cooke had served for nearly a decade when growing suspicions about him came to a head. Questions were initially raised by Her Majesty's Inspector of Constabulary after a visit to the force in 1875. He expressed considerable disquiet about the Chief Constable's handling of certain money for which he had responsibility and, in particular about money received by him in respect of pedlars' certificates, sweeps' certificates, the police band fund and the superannuation and library funds.

Cooke was asked by the watch committee to report on certain specific matters raised and, although he claimed to have done so, no report was ever received. When questioned further Cooke admitted retaining some of the money but alleged he was entitled to do so.

An already disturbed watch committee began to be thoroughly alarmed when yet another aspect arose in connection with monies paid by parents of children committed to reformatories, which Cooke was responsible for collecting as agent for the Home Secretary. Cooke agreed he had retained 10% of all such receipts since his appointment and again claimed it was his entitlement.

The watch committee were most unhappy with the situation and rightly felt a Chief Constable's salary should be his sole income. This was what members of the committee had understood his terms and conditions of service had laid down. A stern direction was given to Cooke to submit a full report at once.

This time he complied with the order and reported he had received a total of £8. 6. 0d commission between 1870 and 1880 and some £129 previously. He also admitted receiving about £14 from sweeps' and pedlars' certificates.

On 16th August 1880 Cooke sent what he no doubt hoped would be a placatory letter to the committee in which he admitted there had been a "certain laxity in police book-keeping" and went on, "by inadvertance I owe the superannuation fund the sum of £1. 9s. 6d, the band fund £9. 5. 0d and the borough fund 9s. 0d. I was totally unaware these accounts had not been paid. As far as the £20 per annum I deducted from the pedlars' certificates money, I did nothing wrong except deducting the money myself instead of recouping it from the Treasurer. I gave up taking this commission in 1876. I considered commission on reformatory fees a personal matter but I shall give it up forthwith."

Justifiably disturbed by the position they found and, by their Chief Constable's rather arrogant reaction the watch committee arranged for a comprehensive enquiry on all aspects of the affair to be carried out by the Clerk of the Council. The resulting report pulled no punches and was quite damning. It spoke of Cooke's conduct being reprehensible, creating great distrust and, that he was clearly blameable.

On the 18th August Cooke resigned and asked for a pension. The watch committee accepted his resignation but deferred a decision on the pension aspect. The full town council, however, were not prepared to let their Chief Constable slip away scot-free. They considered the watch committee's treatment of the unfortunate Cooke far too lenient and ordered the acceptance of his resignation be withdrawn. They were hoping for some disciplinary action against him.

The situation became very confused and it is not clear what further action was taken in the matter. Suffice to say that by September a ridiculous situation existed where a short list of six candidates for the Chief Constable's post had been drawn up while Cooke remained technically in office but suspended. How the matter was finally resolved is unclear except that Cooke left the force and was ordered to pay back a sum of money to the Council.

A rather pathetic footnote to the affair occurred at the November 1882 meeting of the watch committee when it was reported a request had been received from relatives of the then late Thomas Cooke, asking to be released from a bond entered into by the ex-Chief Constable, as they themselves were in very straitened circumstances.

J. Campbell

After their unfortunate experience with a home-grown Chief Constable the watch committee were taking no chances and looked elsewhere for his successor. From their short list of six contenders they chose Mr. J. Campbell, then a police Superintendent employed by the North-East Railway Company at York.

The black-bearded Campbell came with something of a fearsome reputation as a strong personality who enforced the law without fear or favour. He soon put his reputation to test by tackling Hull's thieves and wrongdoers and achieving considerable results, much to the delight of the general population.

Campbell was also extremely firm with members of the force whose standards fell below those he considered appropriate. Not only were policemen constantly being found the worse for drink but Superintendents and Inspectors in the force were often guilty of quite serious misconduct. The Chief Constable adopted a firm line in such cases despite the watch committee's tendency to show great leniency, particularly when senior ranks were involved. There is no doubt he often made himself unpopular with some members of the committee by publicly challenging their decisions in disciplinary cases.

He was similarly unpopular with local editors as was seen in 1884 when one paper snidely reported, "The Chief Constable is obviously seeking pastures new. He is on the short list for the post of Chief Constable of Hove in Sussex. I hope he is successful!"

Considerable public concern was being expressed at the time about morality in the town, particularly the widespread juvenile prostitution. Legislation had recently been passed giving police greater powers in this area and there were demands they should start to be seen to use them. The Chief Constable was expected to adopt his usual resolute attitude to the problem when, he himself became involved in the most unsavoury controversy. It was in November 1884 and the town was in the middle of election fever, when the first extraordinary rumours began to circulate about him.

A startled Mayor received an application in his capacity as a magistrate alleging impropriety by Mr. Campbell with a young girl at 1, St. Thomas's Place, Portland Street, which was not one of the town's best addresses. It was thought the girl's mother had approached the magistrate more for advice than to prosecute and, when Campbell got to hear of the rumours, he immediately instructed his solicitor, a Mr. Laverack, to deny the allegations.

The matter was referred to a surprised watch committee who had no option but to investigate it. Campbell immediately wrote them a letter and re-emphasised his denial, indicating he was quite confident to leave the matter to the committee's sense of justice.

Still smarting from heavy criticism they had received about the secrecy

Chief Constable J. Campbell

Chief Constable Major Gilbert

surrounding previous disciplinary hearings the committee decided to hear the case in public and, on Wednesday 2nd December 1885 they gathered in front of an excited and expectant crowd of reporters and members of the public.

As usual, the Chief Constable was perfectly self-assured and confident the hearing would exonerate him. He sat impassively in the room as the complainants, 14 year old Edith Creighton and her mother entered. They were from a poor but apparently honest family.

At the Mayor's request the clerk read a report by the sub-committee which had carried out an initial investigation. The allegations he read were that approximately three weeks previously, on Friday 13th November, Edith had been at home, alone. Her father was at sea, her brother at work and mother had gone to a meeting of teetotallers. At about 7pm the Chief Constable, whom she knew, arrived. He asked if her mother was in but declined the girl's offer to go and fetch her. He entered the dwelling and asked if anyone could see through the blinds. The girl claimed she went out and put the shutters up. When she returned Mr. Campbell had sat down and pulled her on to his knee. She alleged he kissed her and then asking to see her leg, pulled her clothes up. He kissed her on the cheek and on the mouth and pushed his tongue into her mouth. "Has anyone kissed you like that before?", he enquired. When the girl said no he released her and started to unbutton his trousers. Then, apparently having second thoughts, he gave her sixpence and told her not to tell her mother he had called. When the girl refused to agree to this he said, "You can tell her I called and that I will assist her if I can".

When he left Edith locked the door and told two women about the incident when she went to work the next day. On their advice she told her mother.

The clerk continued that the Chief Constable had strongly cross-examined the girl but failed to shake her story in any way. He had then admitted paying the visit in question saying he was a frequent visitor to the house. He also admitted having the girl on his knee and remarking "my, what a fine girl you've grown to" and giving her a paternal kiss on the cheek. He had admired her legs and patted her shins but nothing else.

The sub-committee concluded their report with the view that any criminal charges would fail for want of corroboration and, that in any case the mother did not wish to press charges. Both the Chief Constable and the girl were then requested to withdraw while the committee considered their dilemma.

Alderman Stuart, the chairman, opened the discussion in surprisingly dogmatic fashion by saying that both he and the vice-chairman saw no option but for the Chief Constable to resign. Others pointed out that Campbell would be losing his job on the word of a young girl and would have been exonerated if the case had been heard in a criminal court. Alderman Symonds expressed considerable concern at the effect the resignation would have on Mrs. Campbell and the Chief Constable's nine children and asked if it would not be possible to re-employ him in some more junior capacity. The chairman retorted there was no vacancy except in the lowest rank and the feeling of the public was such it would be better for him to go.

Campbell was recalled and given an opportunity to address the committee. He took full advantage of this and put forward a very robust defence. Claiming

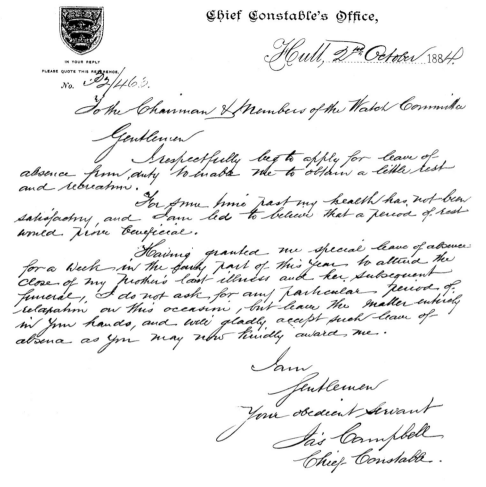

Letter from Chief Constable Campbell to Watch Committee one month before the scandal broke around him.

he had been visiting the girl's father for some time on confidential police business, he denied having done anything he had not done previously when the girl's mother had been present. Shaken by this powerful performance the committee recalled the girl and re-questioned her. She would not budge from her story. Finally the Chief Constable was recalled and asked if would resign. Reluctantly and possibly sensing he had no option, he agreed to do so but asked if he could have three month's salary as he was penniless. The committee, relieved to have obtained his resignation, agreed.

Two weeks later the committee were forced to call Campbell before them again in relation to a number of letters about a gun-powder plot which were missing from his office. Campbell returned them with some pages torn up and claimed they had been taken in error when clearing his office. He said he had been in such a state he hadn't known what he was doing.

Whether Campbell received justice or not is perhaps best summed up by Richard Cooke who wrote of him in the *Hull Critic*:

> *His defence may be quite as true as the girl's story. Mr. Campbell's friends will no doubt think it hard that he should lose his situation especially as serious faults in Superintendents and Inspectors have been condoned or lightly punished by the committee and council. For some time past the Chief and his committee have not worked harmoniously together. In the force matters have gone awry. Recently a serious complaint as to its management was made by Mr. Justice Hawkins, and it is possible that some persons may look upon the incident as a lucky termination to an unfortunate appointment. Meanwhile every disreputable character in the town is rejoicing over Mr. Campbell's downfall, for he was in truth a terror to evil-doers.*

A number of influential people in Hull took a charitable view of the affair and were much concerned over the effect his resignation could have on his large family. Headed by the Rev. John Warren, vicar of All Saints, a fund was started which eventually raised the fare for Campbell and his family to emigrate to Australia. He was never heard of in Hull again.

Gilbert, Gurney and Malcolm

Chief Constable Campbell's indiscretions brought an end to a genuinely professional attempt to sort out many of the problems besetting Hull and its police force at the end of the nineteeth century. He had resolutely determined to end indiscipline and corruption in the force and to deal particularly with the rampant problems of vice and drink-related offences in the town.

The search for his successor became a battle between those who favoured a continuation of his policies and those who, for whatever reason, preferred a more relaxed regime.

One section of the community felt strongly that long serving Deputy-Chief Constable — Superintendent Jones — should have the job. Petitions were raised from householders and ratepayers who wanted a Hull appointee but, despite the furore, the short list of nine drawn up from 74 applicants failed to include a Hull name.

The *Hull Critic* sarcastically reported

> "It is calculated that the number of applications for the post of Chief Constable are so numerous, that it will take the next fifty years to go through their various merits and demerits. In that case Superintendent Jones has got a good spell as Acting-Chief Constable before him. The following are some of the applicants:
>
> > First Colonels and the Majors
> > Seek to terrify the thief
> > And Young and old swell stagers,
> > Yearn to be our Peeler Chief.
> > The Captains from the Navy

Come and join our glorious throng
And say they'll take their davy
To 'Come Down' on all that's wrong.
King Theebaw is applying,
And the Pasha Ara-bi
All anxiously are trying
To obtain the post so high.
Maharajahs and Mahdis
Next upon the scene appear
And other la-da-dahdies
Follow closely in the rear.
The Kings of many a nation
Are resigning stately thrones
For the Parliament Street station
Hip hurrah for 'Charlie' Jones."

To their credit the watch committee opted for a candidate with no Hull connections and, for the first time, turned to the proven ability of ex-soldiers in such posts and chose a Major Gilbert for the job.

Thirty-nine years old, Deputy-Chief Constable of Norfolk and previously commissioned in the 37th Regiment of Foot, he immediately impressed the locals and, as one paper reported, "Major Gilbert is a fine man in every respect. He has a handsome countenance, a splendid physique, and is only about 38 years of age, so that, if he isn't married already, I shouldn't wonder if he has every young lady in the town setting her cap at him". Hull's watch committee were also impressed but more with his sound and far-sighted views on policing than his physical attributes and they were taken aback when, in August the same year, he announced he had been offered a District Superintendent's post in the London Metropolitan Police, provided he could start the following Friday!. Magnanimously, the committee gave him their blessing and once again started on the search for a chief. In the interim they did agree Superintendent Jones could act in the post but, for no longer than three months.

There were 48 applicants this time and, sticking to the military, the committee appointed Captain Francis Prescod Gurney. A rather dour and solemn figure — he had been commissioned in the 53rd Regiment and subsequently promoted Captain in the 91st Highlanders. Retiring in 1878 after thirteen years in the army, he became a Superintendent in the Monmouthshire Constabulary. In Hull he was an unspectacular incumbent for the next seven years.

The appointment of Major Pulteney Malcolm as his replacement was again heavily criticised in the *Hull Daily Mail* on the grounds it was time a professional policeman rather than a soldier got the job. Written large between the lines was the message that a man from the local force should have been appointed.

Although no local, Major Malcolm could hardly have been better connected. Son of General Sir George Malcolm and privately educated before Sandhurst, he served with distinction in India and, prior to taking up the Hull

Captain Gurney, Chief Constable of Hull.

Major Malcolm, Chief Constable of Hull.

appointment, claimed to have "studied police work under the Chief Constable of Buckinghamshire and the Chief Commissioner of the City of London, in addition to attending the courts of the stipendiary magistrates in London".

Notwithstanding this rather superficial police experience he at once took over where Campbell had left off some eight years previously. A high principled, practising churchman he began vigorously tackling the twin problems of vice and drink in the town and in doing so soon ran foul of the vested interests in those areas. Such were the problems he encountered that in 1910 he successfully applied for the post of Chief Constable of Cheshire at a £200 reduction in salary.

A furore erupted inside and outside the council when his resignation was announced. Watch committee member W. C. Dawson JP spoke for many when he said, "If the members of the committee would compare the city of Hull of seven years ago with its condition today, they must admit that the Chief Constable had rendered excellent service. The members present were aware that seven years ago there were public houses in the Old Town which were neither more nor less than houses of assignation and others which were even worse. As a result of the Chief Constable's efforts, many of the worst conducted houses had their licences confiscated."

"Seven years ago there were houses of ill-fame in the city which were allowed to go on unchecked and in one case there was a house with no less than thirty bedrooms and the proprietress of which owned six cabs and had made a fortune out of the business. When Major Malcolm arrived she was prosecuted, convicted and deported as an undesirable alien. Before ever the Children's Act of 1908 was thought of Major Malcolm had introduced a system for dealing with child offenders which preserved such children from the influences of the Police Court."

Acrimony was increasing at the meeting of the watch committee when Major Malcolm added fuel to the fire himself in his resignation speech in which he said, "One thing is on my mind to say and I must say it. There are a number of men in the city, not by any means devoid of money or influence, who met periodically and conspired together to thwart all the forces which made for righteousness in the city. I feel that all my efforts for the improvement of the social conditions of the city have been opposed — not openly, but by methods which the committee well understands. I have not been afraid of these men, I have not been influenced by them, I have tried to do my duty and I thank the committee for their kindnesses".

Some members tried to persuade the Chief Constable to withdraw his resignation but it was too late, he had accepted the Cheshire post.

The circumstances surrounding Malcolm's departure became public knowledge when details of the watch committee's proceedings were leaked to the *Eastern Morning News*. Piqued at this scoop by their rival the *Hull Daily Mail* launched a vigorous defence of the citizens of the city who, the paper felt, were being libelled by the allegations.

Morley, Woods & Howden

Wednesday 27th July 1910 saw a well attended meeting of the watch committee to select yet another Chief Constable. The chairman, Alderman

Mr. G. Morley, Chief Constable of Hull.

Captain Woods, Chief Constable of Hull.

Cooke, told press representatives the meeting would be in private and, once interested members of the Corporation had been allowed in, the door was locked. The five candidates awaiting interview in the banqueting room were Major W. A. C. Denny of the Army Service Corps; Cedric V. Godfrey, Chief Constable of Salford; Captain J. G. Mignon the Superintendent of Physical Training for Surrey; Mr. G. Morley, District Inspector in the Royal Irish Constabulary at Kenmore and Captain The Honorable Eric Thesiger, on the headquarters staff of the Commissioner of the Metropolitan Police.

After a long and difficult meeting District Inspector Morley was appointed. He was 37 years old, a former Oxford open scholar, a barrister and had eleven years police service. He appeared a most suitable choice to receive the salary of £700 per annum and a horse and carriage allowance of £50 and, so it transpired. He remained for twelve years, including the 1914-1918 War and the industrial unrest immediately afterwards, before taking up the post of Chief Constable of Durham County where he was later knighted.

Once again Hull reverted to the military for a successor, this time in the figure of Captain W. A. Woods. Aged 36 and a native of Scarborough he had initially considered a career in the civil service before entering the army.

Conscientious to a fault, Captain Woods attended a fire in Boots shop in King Edward Street on New Year's eve 1925 when he was not in the best of health. Thought to have been as a result of this action, he was taken seriously ill shortly afterwards and, despite two major operations his condition continued to deteriorate. His gallant efforts to continue in his post finally ended when he died in 1928.

The funeral was large and impressive. Some 200 police processed behind a fire-engine carrying the cortège with the Chief Constable's helmet and sword on top. Starting in Anlaby Road it wound through crowded streets with the police band playing the funeral march, on through Walton Street and Chanterlands Avenue and finally to the northern cemetery. Hull had lost a good, steady Chief Constable.

The watch committee chose the man who marched at the head of Captain Wood's funeral procession to be his successor. Superintendent Thomas E. Howden, the Deputy-Chief Constable, had been forced to act in the capacity of Chief Constable for lengthy periods during Captain Wood's illness. Born in Breighton near Selby he had joined Hull police in 1898 and had seen comparatively rapid progress in the force. Progressing from Sergeant to Deputy-Chief Constable in only twelve years he nevertheless had a wide range of experience including being head of the force C.I.D. and having responsibility for policing the 1926 General Strike in Hull.

He was generally well liked and well-connected in the city and his performance as Chief Constable could perhaps best be described as adequate. Knowing the area and its inhabitants as he did may have made it difficult for him to tread a perfectly impartial line in all things. Certainly he was not averse to savouring the good things that came his way by virtue of his job. His driver was often called upon to render discreet assistance to his master in the early hours of the morning after some particularly generous hospitality somewhere in the city. Although such incidents received no publicity and, had little or no apparent effect on the running of the force, it can only be surmised whether it was under his command, or earlier, that the canker which was eventually to blossom in the force, was sown. The difficulties which face men appointed to command small forces in which they have continually served were recognised by Home Office years later when such appointments were banned nationally.

T. E. Howden retired during the early years of the war, apparently due to ill health. Certainly it was in a year that saw the war's worst air attacks on the city but, after retirement, Mr. Howden managed to undertake another, perhaps less onerous job, as a Ministry of Food Inspector!

Thomas (Tosh) Wells

Howden's replacement as Chief Constable of Hull was the Chief Constable of Chesterfield in Derbyshire, Thomas (Tosh) Wells who had started his police career in Brighton in 1911. He was a highly unusual personality. Gregarious, extrovert, he came to have a reputation which can best be described by a police officer who knew him well, "he was like the church spire of the borough he had come from!". He brought two henchmen from Chesterfield with him, Archer his driver and Middleyard who later became Hull's road safety officer.

Wells soon gained a reputation as one who was very well versed in the less savoury practicalities of policing and who carried out his duties with the flair of one who was part showman and part con-man. He quickly established a circle of friends in the city which tended towards the sleazier side of Hull's society. He was particularly involved with many of the boxing fraternity and on one occasion personally organised a boxing show for charity in which the British heavyweight champion Bruce Woodcock took part. Stories about him are legion and still circulating over four decades after he left the force.

In fairness it must be said that on his arrival the problems of corruption which were faced by his predecessors Campbell and Malcolm at the turn of the century still lingered. Professionally competent though he undoubtedly was, Morley had been too busy with the war and its aftermath and Captain Woods never really got to grips with the job. Both the city and hierarchy and its police force were well tainted. Members of the force were convinced it was *who*, rather than *what*, one knew that was important in the promotion race. Clubs abounded and it was strongly rumoured many were in league with certain police officers. Allegations were rife that these were raided and closed in connivance with the owners who, when they lost their licences, were able to apply for new ones for the same premises which would be unopposed by police. So many clubs were named "The new ....." or "The Second ....." it became a standing joke in the city. Tales circulated about a small rather nondescript individual, Ken McKenzie. A bachelor living in a small house in Westcott Street he was believed to have cultivated a special relationship with Alderman Stark, chairman of the watch committee who, it was claimed he had helped in the past. A typical McKenzie anecdote related to an occasion when he was having difficulty wheeling his pedal cycle, laden with bales of cloth, across one of the city's bridges. A passing constable good naturedly gave him a friendly hand and McKenzie enquired his name. The officer is alleged to have received rapid promotion thereafter but whether due to McKenzie's influence must remain conjecture. It was, however, all symptomatic of the unfortunate atmosphere which existed in police and council circles in the city at the time of Well's appointment.

It is almost certainly true that Mckenzie was responsible for collecting rationed food from suppliers in Hull to distribute among senior officials, including police, up to very high levels. In return information was passed to the suppliers of pending visits from food inspectors.

Although Wells had considerable ability as a practical policeman his attributes were heavily outweighed by his greed and personal eccentricities. The force was virtually held together while under his command by the fussily conscientious Deputy-Chief — Harry Jarram. On one well remembered occasion, after a particularly good rehearsal for a parade to be held in front of Her Majesty's Inspector of Constabulary, Wells was so impressed he stood up at the end and told the assembled force, "everyone take tomorrow off!".

His alleged forays into neighbouring counties to collect scarce goods in wartime were well known and it was claimed he never returned without supplies of dairy produce, any surplus of which he generously distributed to his staff. For a period he upset his patrol inspectors and pleased his constables by ordering the former to deliver hot drinks of 'Beetox' to constables on night patrol. He felt it would help them withstand the cold! It subsequently transpired this generous gesture had been facilitated by the Chief Constable's discovery of a quantity of this beverage, in the local A.R.P. stores!

On one occasion he wanted a Christmas tree but was disappointed when the wood in the East Riding his driver had taken him to had only large trees. The story is recounted that a surprised gamekeeper came across the Chief Constable of the city of Hull, standing on the shoulders of his driver, busily sawing the top from one of the trees!

Unfortunately for Wells he eventually crossed swords with a veteran local politician, Councillor A. K. (Kyno) Jacobs. A self-made business man with interests which included Triangle Garages and a number of taxi licences, there developed what can only be described as a deadly feud between the two. Things came to a head when the war ended, slander writs flew between them and finally Jacobs complained officially about the Chief Constable and his alleged activities. It was strongly suspected at the time that Jacobs had a source of information from within the force and suspicion fell upon a particular Sergeant who lived close to the politician's home.

Nothing was ever proved in this regard but the allegations were passed to Home Office and an enquiry was instituted. The complaint was first made by Jacobs, in the city council, early in 1946 and the Home Office enquiry took place at the end of that year. It was in mid-1947 that the matter really came to the boil. In July a Councillor Atkinson said, "Ever since the Chief Constable's appointment in 1941, all sorts of allegations have been made against him both inside and outside the council. All sorts of rumours have circulated alleging misuse of petrol and police cars, persecution and misrepresentation to the police authority."

Then came allegations that there was an unacceptable delay in framing charges against Wells and that the city fathers were engaged in a cover up.

This, the chairman of the watch committee, Alderman Fairbotham, angrily denied.

It was known the Home Office had concluded its investigation, written a report and sent a copy to Hull Council. Demands grew for this to be published. Uproar ensued when Home Office refused point blank to allow its release claiming privilege in that the report technically concerned the efficiency of the force rather than the conduct of its Chief Constable. In fact the report was, very exceptionally, made subject to an eighty years disclosure ban which is double the normal time for a public document. Not until the year 2027 will it be released into the public domain.

With an enraged Councillor Atkinson threatening to hire Queen's Hall and read the report himself and, under extreme pressure from all sides, the city council instructed their clerk to frame disciplinary charges against Wells. By the time these were prepared, however, the Chief Constable had retired to 'Baselow', his house in Hessle and was apparently too ill to accept service of the charges. In July the watch committee received a medical certificate signed by Dr. Philip Science, the long-standing police surgeon, confirming that Wells was ill, confined to bed and unable to attend to any official business.

Those in Council who wanted the matter fully aired were far from satisfied and were even less so when three Hull surgeons certified the Chief Constable was not likely to be able to give further efficient service to the city! The certificate said he was suffering from psycho-neurotic changes coupled with cardio-vascular and renal degeneration. Despite the heavy inference he should be retired on medical grounds many sections of the council strongly resisted this and on a seven to six vote in the watch committee, a medical pension was refused. Many councillors were astonished the Chief Constable was not prepared to fight what seemed to be comparatively trivial charges.

Although the report by Home Office was never published, it was reliably understood at the time the allegations did relate particularly to the misuse of cars for private purposes and the misuse of official petrol. Small instances of such misuse were well-known in the force. Wells always used to call at the transport garage after an evening out, often the worse for drink, to get a car to take him home. On one such occasion no-one was present when he called so he just climbed into one of the cars and drove himself home. When the vehicle's disappearance was discovered next morning a great hue and cry was raised until Wells himself rang up and said, "I understand you have a car missing —well come and collect it from my drive!"

On another day the chairman of the watch committee was going to Blackpool on holiday. He missed his coach, contacted the Chief Constable and a police car was sent to pick him up and chase the coach.

The situation dragged on to the end of the year with the council and watch committee resolutely refusing to grant a medical pension. Ultimately, however, in face of consistent medical evidence from independent specialists they were forced to yield and Thomas Wells retired in an atmosphere of acrimony.

If the matters which brought about Well's downfall were really only indiscretions regarding use of police vehicles and petrol, the eighty-year ban on publication of the Home Office report on the subject seems a grotesque over-reaction! An intriguing mystery awaits some future historian!

Lawrence & Walton

Even after the influence of Thomas Wells the force still contained very many officers of the highest quality and integrity who had remained loyal to their oaths as constables, but there is little doubt the spectre of corruption and malpractice had tainted many of their fellows. Wells had done nothing to cleanse a force which was already infected when he arrived and in fact he could hardly have been a worse choice to lead them because he actively and quite openly indulged in unacceptable conduct himself. When he went the city watch committee were given little option by a very concerned Home Office, with the selection of a successor. They could not have made a wiser choice than the man they picked — Sidney Lawrence.

Forty-three years old, Lawrence had started his police career in the borough of Salford, rising to the rank of Deputy Chief Constable there. He then became Chief Constable of Reading before moving to Hull where he was selected from a short list of candidates which included the long-suffering Assistant-Chief, Harry Jarram. No doubt the latter's inclusion in the list was sufficient to dampen criticism from those who constantly favoured local men but it is doubtful if the Home Office would have given the necessary seal of approval to any appointment connected with the previous chief.

From the outset and throughout his period in office, Lawrence had the absolute confidence and support of his chairman, Alderman Fairbotham with whom he eventually became a great personal friend. His arrival provided a tremendous, albeit beneficial, shock to the Hull force. Charming to outsiders he was an absolute martinet to his staff. He immediately removed all the discretion which had been allowed to Divisional Superintendents and everything fell under iron control from central headquarters and his own office.

Rules were imposed that all correspondence had to be answered within 24 hours of receipt or, an immediate acknowledgement sent and a full reply despatched within 3 days. If this was impossible a letter explaining the reasons was to be sent and a full reply made within the week. All correspondence was sent via headquarters to avoid any suggestion of maladministration.

If an officer appeared before him on a disciplinary charge Lawrence would leave the man who proffered the charge in no doubt that it was he, the who was really on trial for allowing the offence to occur

One man who recalls him well is Ronald Joyce who became Assistant-Chief Constable of the force. Soon after Lawrence's arrival, Joyce, who was then working in the headquarters administration, was told the Chief Constable was going away next day and any mail for him was to be sent to his home. This Joyce did. At 3 am the following morning he was awakened by loud knocking at his door. A policeman told him the Chief was highly displeased that the mail had not reached him before he left home the previous day. Joyce was to report for beat duty at Crowle Street at 6 am that day!! The shattered Joyce did as instructed and, it was not until 48 hours had passed that he was allowed

Robert Walton O.B.E. – last Chief Constable of Kingston upon Hull.

to return to his normal duty. He had received one of Lawrence's sharp and most salutory warnings.

One Christmas Lawrence discovered the C.I.D. had run a seasonal raffle and three senior officers in the department had won the major prizes. He immediately called for a meeting of all senior officers of the force — to be held on the morning of Christmas Day!!

Witch hunts became the order of the day and the new Chief Constable would leave no stone unturned to get to the bottom of anything which seemed anything other than absolutely correct.

On his arrival he strongly suspected the author of his predecessor's downfall, A. K. Jacobs, to be anything but the paragon of virtue he made himself out to be and arranged for him to be placed under surveillance for a considerable period. No evidence of wrongdoing being forthcoming he reluctantly cancelled the operation.

While the force knew Lawrence as an extremely hard and demanding taskmaster with a famous temper — the public of Hull thought he was marvellous. They received a service second to none and when, in 1962, he left to become one of Her Majesty's Inspectors of Constabulary he had transformed the city police from an organisation with some dubious apsects into one of the finest forces in the country.

On his departure, Robert Walton was appointed as his replacement and, unknown to anyone at the time, was to become the last Chief Constable to command the city force. A professional policeman who had started his career in Newcastle-upon-Tyne, Bob Walton had spent a considerable part of his service in the training field. In 1958 he was appointed Chief Constable of Gateshead.

A large and likeable man, he was almost bound to be a more relaxed figure than his predecessor and, during his tenure, much of the day-to-day running and disciplining of the force was left to his capable Deputy — Jim Cocksworth and the Assistant-Chief, Ronald Joyce. Robert Walton was still serving when the force was amalgamated and went on to be the first Chief Constable of Humberside County.

CHAPTER 3

THE FIRST THIRTY YEARS

Let us now return once more to the earliest days of the new force with the watch committee duly impressed by chairman Woolley's achievements and his ideas on the new style policing. When their chairman and Jalland returned from the visit to London the committee quickly agreed to appoint McManus for a trial period and, on his arrival they were at once taken by his obvious professionalism. All the committee members, and Woolley in particular, struck an immediate rapport with the new Superintendent which overcame many of the initial problems. No-one could have foreseen the length of time McManus was to serve the town but, unfortunately both for him personally, and for Hull, William Woolley was not to last so long. He was to die, after a short illness, in 1837, at the age of 38.

Having first dealt with the pressing matter of agreeing the sum of £35 2s 0d be reimbursed to Woolley and Jalland for the costs of their visit to the capital the new watch committee wasted no time in carrying on their new work. They were extremely conscious of the quite revolutionary powers over policing which were now vested in them as councillors by the legislators and were determined to sever links with what had become a useless system and provide Hull with a new and properly efficient police force.

The town, already large with a population of over 25,000 and growing all the time, needed proper policing. No longer was it sufficient to have a system which creaked slowly and often futilely into action after a crime had occurred. The new arrangements would be designed not only to apprehend offenders but to prevent offences taking place in the first instance. This would be in the city's interests and it was something the Home Office in London now required to know about at quarterly intervals. The reputation of the town and its council was on the line!

Having wisely swallowed municipal pride, they were willing to seek help from those with more expertise in such matters and, besides appointing a professional competent Chief Officer, they contacted many authorities where new police already existed to learn from their experiences.

McManus arrived in the second week in March and the tempo began to quicken — there was so much to be done. During three days he and members of the committee interviewed 296 candidates for the lower rank of 'privates' as the committee initially referred to them.

The potential recruits came not only from Hull but from a wide area around the town. Many were tradesmen and farmworkers for whom the pay, while deliberately not set too high lest ex-army officers should be attracted, was marginally better than they could get at their existing calling. A free uniform added to the attraction. Men were sought who could read and write,

Constable (later Inspector) Patrick Coulehan first man to be sworn in to Hull's new police force in 1836.

Painting by unknown artist of Constable 101 in the Hull police force c. 1840.

were not less than 5' 7" in height and who were between 21 and 35 years of age. While ex-army officers would have had the good character and discipline required it was feared they would have introduced an element of elitism in an organisation which needed above all else to be democratic. There was to be no accelerated promotion!

Having finally gathered together a force of 4 Inspectors, 2 Acting Inspectors, 9 Sergeants and 71 Constables, who, according to one observer of the time "Looking a very motley lot", McManus realising the task expected of such utterly inexperienced men, decided to give them some instruction. From 25th April to 1st May he, and a Sergeant he had brought with him from London, taught the new men the rudiments of their job. For this first week's work they were each given the princely sum of 12 shillings. It subsequently transpired this was to be the only formal, pre-service training given to any new recruits in Hull for the next 44 years. In the intervening period new entrants had to make do with an attachment to an existing officer for 'on the job' training.

Hull's new police force was officially inaugurated on 2nd May 1836 when all the men were drawn up, looking nothing like the 'motley lot' of a few days before but resplendent in their new uniform, in the Court of Requests. Each man was sworn in before the Mayor and whole council, and then, signed the book which, from that day forward, was to contain the signatures of every person who subsequently joined the Hull force. First man to sign was 31 year old Constable Patrick Coulehan.

After an oration by the Mayor, the force was marched off through streets filled with crowds who were variously impressed or derisive. Reaching the town gaol the new policemen were lined up while the embarrassed prisoners were paraded before them to assist in future identification.

Meanwhile a rather poignant little ceremony was taking place in the room they had just left. The Mayor had summoned before him Mr. Lee, the old Chief Constable and a dozen of the old watchmen. Some ten days previously McManus had visited them himself and been appalled by what he had seen. "A bunch of unkempt, untidy, ill-disciplined men who in themselves appeared to have little respect for law and order." Ruthlessly he sacked the lot and although offering to consider any found suitable for enrolment in the new force it is doubtful if he ever anticipated any of them joining him. So, this rather shabby and crestfallen little group were told kindly but firmly by the Mayor that from that moment their duties as custodians of the law in Hull had ceased, a new force had been sworn in. They were given the grateful thanks of the borough for their past services. Some weeks later the watch committee agreed to requests from the remaining watchmen that they should be allowed to retain their old coats!

UNIFORM

Much of the initial impression created by the new policemen when they marched on duty, was due to the smart new uniform. Preparation for equipping each man in an identical fashion had been one of the watch committee's earliest tasks and, realising how touchy public opinion was about any police uniform looking military in appearance, their eyes had been naturally drawn to London again. There, a new uniform had by now been tried and tested for seven years and the Hull committee sensibly decided to dress and equip their men in similar fashion.

Accordingly, an approach was made to Charles Hibbert, well-known London tailor and supplier of uniform to the Metropolitan Police. Time was pressing if the deadline of a May inauguration was to be met. He replied with alacrity in a letter received in Hull on 28th March:-

"Sir,

I have the pleasure of forwarding to your address by the express coach of the day, a box containing patterns of the several articles of clothing and equipment that are supplied to each constable of the Metropolitan Police force. Enclosed in the box is a list of the prices of each article and I shall be grateful if they may lead to my being favoured with an order for the supplies that will be required for the service of the Hull City Police.

The cloth of which the clothing is made is of a quality that has been greatly approved of and is the same as had been worn by the Metropolitan Police force since the establishment of that force in 1829 and, I undertake to make the clothing to the individual measurement of each constable and I have to add that the supplies that may be ordered of me shall be punctually delivered before 2nd May and that I will allow for each coat from 4/- to 4/6d after it shall have been in wear for a prescribed period which is an advantage that might either be placed as a set-off to the original costs or be carried forward to a fund to be created for the purpose of enabling the committee to grant pensions at a future period to meritorious constables who may have grown old and enfeebled in the Service. Savings of this nature and arising from other sources, amount annually in connection with the Metropolitan Police to several thousand pounds and they will soon be appropriated for the ulterior benefit of the constables under the authority of a new Bill that will soon be obtained for that purpose."

True to his word, the box of samples arrived next day and the committee, pleading shortage of time but doubtless with one eye on economy, put the samples on display in the Town Hall so that local suppliers also could tender.

Realising that while local traders could probably do the tailoring but might have more difficulty with accoutrements, the chairman wrote urgently to Parkers of Holborn to enquire the price of button sticks, truncheons, rattles, lanterns, leather girdles, swords and sword belts.

Meanwhile the local outfitters were up to the challenge and tenders were being received at the Town Hall within days of the display. By 8th April, contracts had been placed for uniform with John Saner of Whitefriargate, Hull and for boots with Matthew Tate of Charlotte Street. As anticipated, more specialised equipment had to be ordered from London and, on the 14th April, in addition to ordering belts, lanterns and truncheons from Parkers, the chairman also acquired 12 cutlasses and belts and five pistols together with

A reconstruction of Hull's first police showing Constable and Inspector on patrol.
(Courtesy Hull Daily Mail)

A brass tipstave believed to have been issued to a senior officer in Hull's new police.

brass pocket staves for the Superintendent and Inspectors. The latter were more in the form of a tipstave or badge of office than to use as a weapon and there is no record of the pistols ever being used in anger.

Having placed the orders it was realised no enquiry had been made to establish what, if any, equipment was in possession of the old constables. Mr. Lee, Chief Constable and keeper of the lock-up was asked to report and subsequently truncheons and handcuffs were handed over for further use.

The inexperience of the local tailors in uniform making and the short time available inevitably caused problems. Promised by the last week in April there was no sign by the 29th. Urgent messages were sent to Mr. Saner who promised delivery within 24 hours. The harrassed man produced sufficient uniform on the 30th to equip each man in a basic fashion but had been unable to make capes, great coats or armlets in the time available. The committee was highly displeased by this failure of the local tradesman on whom they had bestowed their favours. They told him so in no uncertain terms and further increased the poor fellow's misery by inferring it would be his fault if there was much sickness in the force because of lack of greatcoats.

This genuine if naive concern that the policemen had proper clothing as a way to maintain good health was further exemplified some years later when the force surgeon recommended all men should be instructed to wear flannel drawers in the interest of keeping fit!

Notwithstanding all the problems, on the day of the inaugural parade every man was smartly dressed in dark-blue swallow tailed coat, a pair of white duck trousers, (soon to be changed to blue colour to match the coat) a glazed black top hat with strengthened leather crown, and Wellington boots. They carried a rattle and had a short truncheon fitted in a pocket in the tail of their coats. Each man had 'H' and his number embroidered on the collar, Sergeants had plated buttons on their cuffs, constables' buttons being cloth covered. Inspectors had embroidered silver lace on their collars and silver-plated buttons decorated with the arms of the town and encircled with the words 'Hull Police'.

This was the uniform the men were instructed to wear forthwith at all times except when they were in bed. Not until 1871 was permission given for the men to wear plain clothes when off duty.

The *Hull Advertiser* reporting the first parade, rather pompously described the uniform as being:

> "remarkably neat, that of the Inspectors particularly so — it is nearly the same as the dress of the Metropolitan Police and we are glad to observe that the watch committee has not fallen into the error committed by some other boroughs of imputing to the men the appearance of livery by facing or turning up the collars or cuffs with gaudy colours..."

One unusual aspect of the uniform was that policemen were allowed to carry and use umbrellas until 1859.

As one might have been expected, however, not everyone was impressed by the smart turn out of the new force. The *Hull Packet* printed a bitter article strongly defending the old system and complaining that not one of the old constables had been appointed to the new force, no doubt because they had been appointed by the old corporation — "which was indeed sin enough in these days of reform".

STATIONS & HOUSING

While recruiting and equipping men was a first essential in setting up the force another, equally urgent, task was to ensure suitable buildings were available to operate from.

The legislation authorising new police forces provided that any existing building being used for policing should be handed over for use by the new force. There were two such places within the borough of Hull's boundary, the Fetter Lane House of Correction and the Sculcoates watch office on the corner of Jarratt and Worship streets. There was no problem with the handing over of Fetter Lane, but Woolley and his committee realised immediately it was in no fit state for further use. Situated at the south-east end of the highly congested and dirty lane, named after the old felons' fetters hung outside the lockup, it formed part of the horrible little building. It had been described earlier by John Howard, a celebrated philanthropist as having:- "two rooms below and two upstairs about 12' square, very offensive, no fireplace and the court only 22' x 10', the prisoners are not permitted to go to the pump. There is no (food) allowance and no straw. The prisoners pound tile sherds and mix in mortar and pick oakum."

The energetic chairman lost no time tackling the problems and soon came up with a solution in the shape of slightly more commodious premises in much better condition. Situated in Blanket Row and recently vacated by Downes and Thorpe, tobacco manufacturers and owned by a Mr. S. Kirkwood, the building was secured on an initial seven year lease at a rental of £60 per annum. It was felt there would be no need to exceed £50 on alterations and the building was hastily converted to provide an Inspectors' room, three cells and a large room to accommodate 25 constables.

The premises at Jarratt Street provided problems of a different kind for the watch committee and the new Superintendent when he arrived. Owned by the Commissioners of Sculcoates and used as a court room by the East Riding magistrates, two rooms had been utilised by the old watch at nights but there was not a great deal of co-operation forthcoming from magistrates or Commissioners towards the new police force in Hull. Totally against such reforms themselves, they considered the whole idea to be an unacceptable imposition by a hostile Parliament.

It was with great reluctance that they eventually agreed to part with that section of the building which contained cells and had housed the watch. Even more reluctantly McManus put his men into the building which it became obvious was quite inadequate. Inspector Craven in charge soon reported he could not cope. He had a small sitting room for himself and the constable which had only one small window which could not be opened because it was 14 feet from the ground! There were no windows at all in the sleeping room and the only ventilation in the accommodation was if the front door was left open. This was a door which was strangely designed to bolt on the outside! Prisoners, seated on stools were chained to the walls of the same room used by police and

Artist's impression of entrance to the old House of Correction, used for petty offenders for locking up vagrants and the poor, at Fetter Lane, in use prior to 1836.

The Parliament Street entrance to the building which served as the headquarters and main station for Hull Police from 1852-1904.

the Inspector was forced to go outside if he wished to have discussions with his men in confidence.

Pedestrians going by complained bitterly about the smell from the building and, when the Mayor visited he confessed he had been in hound kennels where the stench had been less offensive than in Sculcoates Police Station! Finally McManus took the bull by the horns and announced he would no longer keep prisoners there as it was too dangerous and he moved them all to Blanket Row.

Pressure was put on the Commissioners by the Mayor and the indefatigable Woolley who pointed out that the law now directed the area should be policed as part of Hull and that being unco-operative would get nowhere. Eventually, and with great reluctance, the commissioners gave way and handed over the bulk of the building. It remained in police and fire service hands thereafter.

Surprisingly, despite the energetic approach by the watch committee and McManus to acquire suitable properties, it appears they did not always care for them properly afterwards. In 1847 they were acutely embarrassed when taken to task by the chairman of the borough property committee who announced that Blanket Row Police Station was in a filthy state. Immediate steps were taken for the building to be white washed and cleaned inside and toilets were provided for the cells.

As years went by it became apparent that the Blanket Row premises, originally taken on a temporary basis, together with Jarratt Street, were becoming increasingly cramped and unsuitable for an expanding force. In 1850, Hull Incorporation for the Poor indicated they were looking for larger premises as the Charity Hall, otherwise known as the Workhouse in Whitefriargate, had become too small for their purposes.

The watch committee, having already concluded that, despite various alterations and improvements made to existing premises, a new station house was esssential, were immediately interested. In 1852 they bought the workhouse buildings which stood on the site of the old cloth hall for £7,500. True to their merchant traditions they immediately recouped a substantial part of this investment by agreeing the main police entrance should be in Parliament Street, so releasing the front in Whitefriargate for use by the Bank of England.

Alterations were put in hand and on 3rd August 1853 the committee inspected their new building and declared official business would commence forthwith.

The Chief Constable's private room was on the left of the main entrance and the charge room with its enormous iron bound dock on the opposite side of the doorway. Detectives had accommodation on the first floor. Initially, the original paupers' accommodation at the rear was converted into accommodation for ten married officers and all the single men in the force. Later this was condemned as unsuitable for such use and all the force were made to seek lodgings outside.

At the time, local papers enthusiastically described the new station as "the best in England, very commodious with all cells fit for human beings and not the filthy dens at the old station houses. They are moreover, warmed by hot air pipes!!"

At last McManus had got a station he felt his force deserved. The Blanket Row premises were given up but Jarratt Street was retained with an increasing emphasis on providing a response to fire calls.

COSTS & EFFICIENCY

From the inception of the force, the thrifty businessmen responsible for Hull's affairs were determined not only to have the best but also the most cost-effective police force in the land. Their zeal in economising is seen by the arrangements they made with the police surgeon. He was allowed to charge 1/- for every recruit examined but the committee insisted the recruits themselves paid this fee, whether or not they passed the examination!

Delighted to discover the new force was only to cost an estimated £5,777 4s 0d, which was over £1200 less than the estimate provided by the Local Acts Committee, they continued to practise frugality wherever they could. As years went by however, added commitments meant that both the strength and cost of the force increased until in 1853 the original 90 men had grown to 120.

An abortive pay strike in 1853, which is dealt with elsewhere, resulted in an arbitrary cut-back in strength to 100, the action being decided after a most rudimentary local enquiry into the town's policing requirements. The fact that efficiency was generally equated in numbers rather than by any standards of professionalism was shown by the lack of qualms which accompanied the committee's decision to replace a large part of the force overnight under threat of the pay strike. As one councillor put it at the time, "The amount of intelligence required (in a policeman) is not of very high order, reading and writing being the only test in that respect."

Among local Press and Magistrates the efficiency of the force and its impact on the town, had become generally acknowledged during the formative years of the new police. Criticism was never absent however as when the Secretary of Hull's dock board wrote in 1854. "The inadequacy of the police in Hull is now a matter of notoriety". While this observation may have revealed a genuine grievance, a smouldering resentment had existed in the minds of those running the docks since 1844 when legislation had finally placed them under police supervision.

In 1857 a major development occurred which affected all policing in the country. Since its inception some 21 years previously, Hull's watch committee, through the town council, had been responsible for reporting certain matters to the Home Office, but that apart had no form of central control or other constraints placed upon it. New legislation, not only compelled reluctant magistrates in some counties, including Hull's neighbours in the East Riding, to form their own police forces, it also appointed Inspectors of Constabulary. Their function was, as the name implies, to inspect all forces at least once per year and to certify them as sufficiently efficient to qualify for the government grant towards the cost of policing.

Colonel Woodford, ex-Chief Constable of Lancashire had been appointed to inspect the northern forces including Hull. On his first visit he reported the force to be in a high state of efficiency with uniform and accoutrements good except that capes were badly worn. The Parliament Street station he considered was excellent with not only 12 clean cells and accommodation for 12 married and 60 single constables, it even had the unusual advantage of a small library for use by the men.

In his letter to the watch committee via the Home Office following the inspection the colonel did however raise the question of the strength of the force. Pointing out there had been more men in 1853 (pre-pay strike) than in 1857, he suggested it should be increased to the former strength. Hull watch committee replied by referring to decisions taken at the time of the pay strike and their acceptance by the Home Secretary of the day, Lord Palmerston.

Woodford, having sufficient problems already on his plate elsewhere at the time and not wishing to cross swords with a town where policing was basically sound, especially on his first visit, replied in a placatory vein. He pointed out that some beats had little or no cover and that the inhabitants of such areas had little protection day or night. However he was content to leave the matter to the good judgement of the council to decide how many police were needed. The implied flattery had the effect Woodford had hoped for. Basking in his otherwise glowing tributes about their force the committee set about recruiting extra men.

Over the next five years the numbers increased to 142 constables and, after four annual inspections with little or no criticism the colonel was to write after his 1862 visit, "The force is in a high state of efficiency. At the time of my visit only 1 man was sick and this is a tribute to the borough authorities who have always manifested an unusually warm and lively interest in the comfort and general welfare of the force. The fact that an extra 20 men have been added since my last inspection and as a result of my suggestions, is excellent!"

Andrew McManus and the watch committee had nurtured the town's fledgling police force through the trials and tribulations of its first thirty years to a position of recognition and acceptance both locally and nationally.

DUTIES OF THE EARLY POLICEMEN

The early policeman's lot, though not unusual for the times, was certainly a hard one. Provided he behaved he had a job, regular pay, a uniform and a small pension when he finished his service. In return he was expected to work, nearly always outside, at all hours, in all weather, for at least eight hours every day and with no break. Applications for leave were viewed with suspicion and even when off duty he was expected at all times to be in his uniform and ready to be recalled at a moment's notice. For this he received a modest weekly salary on a level similar to other working folk of tradesman standard. They however had few if any restrictions placed upon their private lives.

When parading for duty he would be inspected by the Sergeant for sobriety, cleanliness and to ensure he was carrying the proper equipment. Next he would be given a card with the number of the beat he was to work and detailing the streets included in that particular beat. With his rudimentary training he was then marched with the rest of his shift to their beats and dropped off the end of the column as his area was reached.

Usually this would be a collection of narrow streets with streams and pools of filth erupting around the squalid housing which crowded into every inch of space. Often the hovels would be part of Hull's famous courts which rambled, one within the other seemingly for ever, each one filled to overflowing with the wretched poor of the town. In the age of the footpad and the garrotter the streets were often poorly lit even if gas lamps had been fitted. Crowds of ragged urchins, thieves and prostitutes, roamed abroad at all hours. Amidst all this squalor the patrolling constable had firm instructions to talk to no-one unless in the line of duty.

Temptations were ever present for the unwary policeman and, knowing they were viewed with distrust and suspicion, if not outright hostility, it took brave men simply to enter some areas, let alone carry out their function of passing every part of the beat each ten or fifteen minutes. He was excused this last requirement only if he was detained watching a suspicious person or carrying out some other lawful function. Each man was also reminded not to fall into the ways of his watchmen predecessors by calling the hour.

Should he have occasion to make an arrest the constable was instructed to take his prisoner to the nearest appointed place where other constables would eventually pass and wait to be relieved before removing the prisoner to the station. There were a number of secure rooms throughout the town provided for temporary detention of prisoners if, for instance, the officer had to make other arrests.

If assistance was required he was to 'spring' his rattle but only as a last resort lest it had the effect of summoning a hostile crowd which would defeat the object. On many occasions the sound of the rattle resulted in the early police being attacked and their prisoners released.

No constable was allowed to leave his beat until the relief man had been marched out to him. He would then be marched back to the station, inspected and dismissed.

Such twenty-four hour comprehensive policing, so different from the old system, was bound to have an effect and, by October 1836 it was being reported that criminals who had come to seek refuge in the streets and alleys of Hull were being dealt with in courts in Beverley, York, Leeds, Sheffield and as far away as London, where they had been wanted for various offences. At the first Hull Fair after the inauguration of the new police, the authorities were delighted that not a single robbery was reported.

In 1839, the first figures available showed the force had made 2611 arrests, one third of them for drunkenness.

The borough was luckier than some areas in that it suffered few effects from the Chartist unrest evident elsewhere in the country. One missionary from that movement did have the temerity to enter Hull in 1843. He came from Birmingham and was eloquently addressing a crowd of some 400 by King Billy's statue in Market Square when, as the local paper reported, a "force of the local constabulary, headed by their Superintendent, marched upon the orator who, finding his eloquence lost upon the gentlemen in the glazed hats, was forced to scamper off."

The first two men to be formally charged by the new police were carefully recorded in the massive new 24" x 12" charge book specially printed for the purpose. At 10pm on 2nd May 1836, James Tarr, a gunner in the Royal Artillery was charged by Sergeant Abraham Codsworth with being drunk and

In replying, quote the following
Initial Letter

N

Admiralty, S.W.

10 Sept. 1861.

Sir,

In reference to the description return of William Hodge —— committed to confinement and sent for as a Deserter from the Deal Depot ~~Division~~ of Royal Marines, I am commanded by my Lords Commissioners of the Admiralty to transmit to you herewith an order to the Accountant-General of the Navy to pay the usual reward of Twenty Shillings to be delivered to Police Constable W Chapman by whom the said Deserter was apprehended.

I am,

Sir,

Your very humble Servant,

W. G. Romaine

J. H. Travis Esq
Police Court
Hull

Letter forwarding reward to a Hull policeman for arresting a Royal Marine deserter.

disorderly and, at the same time. James Twelves of 11 High Street was detained for assaulting a John Graham of North Street. Inspector William Lang accepted the charges.

Despite these two rather mundane offences all sorts of crime was rife in Hull, much of it going unreported. Many young boys left home at an early age and drifted into criminal activity. Errand boys caught pilfering were usually sacked but not prosecuted. Unable to get further work they too generally resorted to full-time thieving. Local papers reported the existence of Fagin-type schools in the town where youngsters opperated together under the guidance of older, more experienced thieves.

Cruelty was common place, especially amongst seamen and, in 1850 a constable was called to a fishing smack having been told a boy was near to death on board. He found the ship's boy, Isaac Nill, had displeased the boat's master. During a period of unbelievable torture, Nill had been dragged round the deck, dropped into the hold, stabbed with a herring knife, hung on the windlass and allowed to drop to the deck. He was kicked in the ribs and constantly doused with sea water. The constable reported finding the boy lying on the deck "shaking like a dog."

Statistics produced by the force in those early days are probably of doubtful veracity as an indication of crime in the borough. Much went unreported and only people arrested were recorded. Judging by the eventual outcome of cases many apprehensions would seem to have been made on the flimsiest evidence or, perhaps more likely, were presented to the courts without adequate supporting facts.

In 1849 a total of 3700 people were charged and 1080 were under 25 years of age. One in five of the prisoners was female. By 1852 the total number had fallen to 2473. Over half of these were discharged by the magistrates and, of 178 committed for trial 46 were acquitted. For those who did get convicted before the higher courts the penalties could be harsh. In 1852 one person was transported for life, 14 for ten years, 9 for seven years and 2 for three years. Four prisoners received two years imprisonment, 44 got twelve months and 31 six months. Fifty of those sentenced to prison were women.

Although the police were possibly at fault for the large proportion of acquittals the magistrates themselves were not above criticism. Jonas Brown of 30 George Street was one of the eccentrics on the bench. He is described as usually wearing nankeen pantaloons tied at the ankles with ribbons. They fitted him very tightly and, "being affected with the malady of hernia, the tightness made it appear much worse". His regular cry from the bench to constable Pearson Fox the court officer whenever a defendant displeased him was, "Commit him, commit him!!" One Irish defendant said he was a sailor by trade. "Commit him," squealed Brown, "I doubt if you have ever seen the sea". "Then y'r worship, how d'ye reckon I got here from Ireland?" "By wagon?" was the rejoinder.

Offences dealt with by police ranged through the whole gamut of crime including murder, rape, sacrilege, arson, forgery and coining but, there is no doubt what the major policing problem was at the time — it was drunkenness. There were no licensing laws and dram shops and gin houses were open as early as 4 am and only closed when demand ceased. Children were plied with gin from their early years.

Reports in contemporary newspapers illustrate the problems. The *Hull Rockingham* of 11th March 1837 reported the case of William North.

> "one of the most disorderly, outrageous fellows we ever saw in a Court of Law was charged by Mrs. Coates with the shameful exposure of his person and with using language which no christian could tolerate.
> Policeman 45 was called in and took him into custody during which the prisoner struck him several times. North, in his defence, said that the policeman dragged him along without ceremony and he therefore turned 'distropulous'. They put a pair of handcuffs upon him which prevented him sleeping all the blessed night so he kept singing, to pass away the time like, as there was nothing else for him to do. Inspector O'Hara said they had never had such a crazy man in the station house before.
> North:- "O, Thou'll tell ony lees at all!"

He was fined £5 or one month in prison.

On 24th November 1837 the *Hull Advertiser* reported:-

> John Howell was brought up in Court by Sergeant Tracey who said prisoner and his wife were warbling most melodiously in Lowgate at 7 o'clock on Saturday night to the great obstruction of all His Majesty's lieges."

He was discharged by the Magistrates with a warning.

One of the perennial problems faced by police in Hull was that of vice in all its forms. Despite the puritanical outlook of many of the town's citizens in the nineteenth century licentious behaviour was widespread and, in his report for 1855, the Chief Constable set out some facts under the heading of 'Vice'.

> "....shows a most disreputable state of things. It exhibits in all its naked deformity the extent to which the crime of prostitution prevails in our midst. The police know 423 prostitutes in Hull of whom:
> 79 are under 20 years of age.
> 175 are above 20 and under 25 years of age.
> 78 are above 25 and below 30 years of age.
> 91 are above 30 years of age.
> There are no less than 244 known brothels which are classified under two heads:
> Houses in which prostitutes are kept — 196.
> Houses frequented by prostitutes — 48.
> Each of these classes is divided into three classes:
> (1) Well conducted, the girls not being street walkers.
> (2) Well conducted, frequented by middle class and youths.
> (3) Disorderly houses, frequented by lower orders and thieves.

Looking at the wide range of criminal activity it is not known exactly when detectives, working in plain clothes, were first used in Hull but it was certainly quite early in the history of the force. It is not until Brown's guide to Hull of 1890 that a figure of 11 detectives is mentioned. That they existed a long time prior to that can be seen from individual mentions in press reports.

The "Trial of a Gang of Female Pickpockets" was reported in the *Hull Advertiser* on 20th December 1856. The case concerned the actions of Detective Sergeant Cooke and Detective Constable Clark who arrested five London women pickpockets within an hour or two of their arrival in Hull. Initially four were arrested and the fifth woman apprehended after the Sergeant had seen her send a telegram to the 'Gang boss' in London. The telegram was in cockney rhyming slang, hence the unusual language used in the newspaper report:-

> "A case of a very strange character was tried at Hull Police Court before Mr. Travis Stipendiary Magistrate.
>
> There had been great talk of late about their being sundry importations of the Metropolitan 'swell mob' into this town and if the present batch be a part of the first lot, we would have the rest to take the hint. There is no quarter given to 'swell mobs' or any such dwindling communities in Hull for we pride ourselves upon possession of a few 'traps' who are always on the 'fly' and whose local provincial experience in these matters will defy all the sagacity of the 'shalers' and the 'fancy bloaks' who dare to come, for if they venture here they will be sure to 'get the clench!'"

Interpretations: Traps = constables; Fly = alert; Shalers = young women; fancy bloaks = fancy men; get the clench = locked up.

DISCIPLINE IN THE FORCE

When Andrew McManus became the head of Hull's new police force one of his most serious and long-lasting difficulties was created, not by the criminals and troublemakers of the town but by behaviour of policemen themselves. Control and discipline of men in a British style police force has always been a uniquely difficult problem. The nature of their work dictates they usually operate alone for considerable periods among the general public. Their behaviour becomes very much a matter of training and self-discipline as opposed to the direct control which can be exercised over a body of men such as operates in the armed services.

Hull's hastily recruited force of untried and virtually untrained men was quite unused to the unusual situation, even those with previous military service had never been in such a position before. Problems were bound to occur, and they did!

Many were the temptations facing the young men, often just arrived from rural areas and unused to town life. Both rich and poor alike in the town were often happy to lure the new and unsuspecting guardians of the law from their proper duties. Sometimes it was simply to discredit the new force or, more often, to escape retribution for their own misdeeds. Usually the bait was strong drink which unfortunately few of the policemen seemed able to resist.

The watch committee found themselves in the position of sole arbiters in

REPORT of CHARGES coming under the Cognizance of the HULL POLICE FORCE,

May ~ ~ and Eleven ~ ~ ~ o'Clock in the Morning of the

between the Hours of Eleven o'Clock in the Morning of the Second

Fourth of May 1836

Number of Charge	Hour when brought to Station House	Age	Persons Charged. Name and Address.	Charge.	Persons Charging, Name, Address, and Occupation.	Witnesses, Name and Address.	Taken into Custody by.	Property Found on Person or Persons charged.	Charge, How disposed of at Station House	Signature of Police Officer taking the Charge.	Magistrate, Name of, before whom the Charge is brought.	Charge, How disposed of by Magistrate.	Number of Charge.	Remarks by Magistrate.
1	10 · 57 · P.M.		James Tarr Gunner Royal Artillery	Being Drunk & disorderly in Lurgits in the Town	Henry Mark P.L. N.o 3			Not Searched	Detained	William Jang the Major Aikin, Supt. Night watch cochran House	Discharged —	1	
2	10 · 20 · P.M.		James Larton N.o 11, High Street	Assaulting & beating his father North Street —	Wm Cudworth P.C. N.o 22 ·			None —	Detained Afterwards bailed acting Supt. at 3 past 12 O.M. 5 May	William Jang a — a — Fined Twenty , Shillings	2	

disciplinary matters. They had to decide whether an officer had transgressed and, if so, what punishment to inflict. There was no appeal against their decision. They found themselves torn between a desire, on one hand, to support the men, while not being seen to tolerate any falling from the high standards they desired in the force.

McManus himself, while appreciating men's weaknesses, was not prepared to tolerate indiscipline and knew a hard line would have to be taken with defaulters from the start. This resolution was soon to be tested. Only one day had passed since the inauguration before the Superintendent placed the case of constable 79 George Audus before the committee. He had been found drunk and incapable on his beat on his first day of duty! Determined to stamp out such behaviour from the start the committee dismissed him from the force forthwith hoping, futilely as it transpired, this would serve as a warning to his fellows.

Discipline could not be instilled over night and it would take many generations of policemen before the problem was contained. Meanwhile the committee dismissed Sergeant Sampson for drunkenness on 16th May and reduced another Sergeant to constable for disobedience. Two days later Sergeant Kirkwood was reprimanded and reduced to constable for being found asleep on duty at 5 am. The next day another constable was fined for being drunk and, on 23rd May, constable Bower was seen attending Beverley Races in uniform and without permission. He was fined one day's pay for this error. The last day of the first month saw this sorry procession of defaulters ended with yet another constable being dismissed for being drunk and disorderly and two of his colleagues were dealt with for talking together while on neighbouring beats. They were fined and reprimanded respectively.

By the end of June 1836 no less than seventeen of the original seventy-one constables had been dismissed and replaced, mostly for offences connected with drink.

Throughout his thirty years as head of the force McManus and his committee were to struggle to deal with the problem of erring policemen. Variously trying severity and leniency they achieved little except to create resentment among the men because of their inconsistency in dealing with disciplinary cases. Instances of over-reaction and sometimes blatant injustice occurred.

When young constable Freeman appeared before them on 24th June 1836 he had only seven week's experience as a policeman. He had been sent to a house where a disturbance between two women was taking place. One woman was outside on his arrival and left at his request. The other continued to howl abuse and obscenities at all and sundry from inside the dwelling and, despite all his pleas, the young officer was unable to quieten her, much to the deight of the ever-present crowd. Humiliated by their taunts the young policeman entered the house and arrested the woman. This was beyond his powers. The magistrates' court cautioned him when the case came before them but when they heard about it, the watch committee immediately dismissed him. McManus pleaded for him and said he showed excellent promise but the committee refused to budge and persisted in their ridiculous over-reaction.

On the other hand and, to their credit, the committee did on occasions stoutly support men they felt had been wrongly accused. A councillor Westdale complained that on a Sunday afternoon there had been no constable to arrest a drunk. The committee defended police by explaining that at the time they were attending the churches and chapels and that in any event the man had been arrested later.

In another case the committee went as far as taking legal action. This was when constable Hiram Wright was charged before the Magistrates by a George Weddel Headley Whitesmith, "with violently assaulting him....and stealing from him a pocket book containing two ten pound notes and a canvas bag containing four or five sovereigns." They instructed a solicitor, George Thompson, "in order that the police may be protected from unfounded attacks of the nature reported". Somewhat surprisingly the committee tenaciously continued their prosecution of Mr. Whitesmith for more than a year and eventually, in November 1849 received a letter of apology which acknowledged Whitesmith had made an error. It was decided the letter should be printed in the Press to exonerate the reputation of the force.

The committee could show equally sensible firmness against members of the force as in the case of a petition received in June 1836, from some of the constables in south section, complaining about the promotion of constable Thomas Botwood to Sergeant. Investigations revealed that a constable James Smith was the instigator and he was immediately dismissed. Other signatories were fined two days pay. The day following this decision constables Thomas Codd and Thomas Stephenson complained about the committee's decision when they reported for duty and tried to cause a disturbance on the parade. On hearing of this the committee dismissed them also. This was a salutory lesson to any others who felt that indiscipline might frighten the authorities.

Somewhat surprisingly, once having dealt with a man, even if he had been dismissed, the committee was usually willing to reconsider the decision, especially if the offender showed contrition and, if this took the form of a letter of apology. This practice of reinstating or showing leniency after receiving an appeal from the man concerned was to continue for many years as will be seen later and a suitably worded letter to the committee prior to the hearing often appeared to mollify the members and resulted in a lenient outcome.

While punishment obviously had its place there was also the bestowal of rewards available to encourage men to behave. The reward of promotion was the highest enticement and the sanction of demotion always hung over those who had made progress. In fact the records of early members of the force show alarmingly erratic paths as they received successive rewards and punishments. Patrick Coulehan, first man to be sworn in is a case in point and his record reads as follows:

2nd May 1836	Promoted to Sergeant.
1st Sept 1936	Reduced from Sergeant to constable.
16th Feb 1837	Promoted to Sergeant.
6th Oct 1838	Promoted to Acting-Inspector.
8th June 1839	Promoted to Inspector.

2nd Nov 1843	Advanced 1 sovereign for good conduct.
4th Nov 1847	Advanced £2 4s 0d for good conduct.
19th Sep 1849	Severe reprimand and caution by Watch Committee for trying to borrow money.
15th May 1850	Reduced to Sergeant for neglect.
5th Mar 1851	Severe reprimand by Watch Committee for not reporting being in house where robbery had been committed.
1st June 1857	Retired on pension.

Policemen were not only eligible for financial advancement for good work, they were also allowed to retain rewards given by appreciative members of the public in the early days of the force. One such reward was accompanied by a letter from the donor:-

August 25th 1853   2, Engineer Street, Hull.
Dear Sir,
    I shall be greatly obliged to you for causing the enclosed sovereign to be given in equal proportions to the four following officers:- John Smith (47), Wilkinson (57), Pollard (61) and Harper (40). I have witnessed their efficiency as police officers and observed with pleasure their uniform civil behaviour and I conceive it to be my duty to show, by some means my approbation of their conduct as I am fully persuaded that tradesmen in my line of business (pawnbrokers) are benefiting from the unremitting vigilance they have displayed. Allow me to add that in speaking approvingly of those under your direction I must say I am persuaded that the superintendence must be excellent where the efficiency of the corps under its care is so apparent as in the Hull police.
Believe me to be, dear sir
Your obedient servant,
Thomas Cowham.
    A. McManus.

At their meeting on 18th October 1836 however, the committee were forced to put on a brave face when publicly reporting the problems they had experienced with discipline. They primly announced that while they had been forced to dispose of a number of the original men, "who had entered the force with erroneous notions of the work expected from them", they had experienced no trouble in replacing them. This was quite true as there was always a pool of enthusiastic recruits waiting to join Hull's police.

It was not only in the ranks of policemen themselves that temptation manifested itself. On 3rd September 1847 McManus arrived at his office to find a letter on his table. On opening it he was startled to find it was from George Freeman, the clerk of the force. He had been the first person after McManus himself to be employed by the new police force in 1836 and had been a key figure in the organisation. McManus, knowing Freeman's wife had died some months previously, was nevertheless astounded to read he had left the force to go to Gainsborough in Lincolnshire. He indicated he was heavily in debt to a number of policemen and others and had gone to raise money to repay the loans. Further enquiries revealed he had not only left the force but was believed to have travelled to America. Nothing more was heard of him.

Despite all these tribulations the watch committee seldom lost its initial pride in the force it had created and on the 5th May 1843 they celebrated the seventh anniversary with a parade at which the Mayor gave fulsome praise to McManus and the whole force. The gathering ended with everyone giving three cheers for the Queen, three for Prince Albert, three for the royal children and the rest of the royal family and, last but not least, three hearty cheers for the Mayor, after which "they filed off in good order and proceeded to the Victoria Room where, through the liberality of the Mayor and gentlemen present at the Review, they had ample refreshments provided."

Alas, but a few weeks after this tribute, the Mayor of Beverley complained about men from Hull who were lodging in his borough while attending Quarter Sessions. McManus personally went to Beverley to investigate and found all but one of the men safe in their lodgings. Sergeant Jackson was absent and discovered with a crowd of ruffians breaking windows in the Town! He was summarily dismissed.

THE PAY STRIKE

Arguably the most serious disciplinary situation ever to face the Hull watch committee was that which confronted them in 1853 because of growing dissatisfaction in the lower ranks of the force about pay. In 1836 a constable's wage was set at a standard 18/- per week. In 1841 the committee had adopted a two tier system of first and second class constables to give some incentive to those failing to reach Sergeant rank. The differential was achieved by raising the pay of the first class man to 19/- but, for those whose misfortune it was to be placed in the second category, pay was actually reduced by 1/- to 17/- per week. By 1853 no further changes had been made in pay and those unfortunate enough to have been made second class in 1841 had taken a cut in their income for twelve years.

The constables felt very strongly that something should be done and decided to put in an application for an all-round increase of 3/- per week. They instructed local solicitors, Richardson and Lee to act for them. The demand was submitted in mid-June and received considerable publicity together with a degree of support from both Press and public. The *Hull Advertiser* felt the increase "was fully justified for a body of men in the prime of their lives who didn't get a Sabbath. There was not a better force in the country", they declared, proudly. However this support and a petition from ratepayers was derisively dismissed by the watch committee with the remark that the support consisted of only one newspaper and 93 ratepayers out of a population of 86,000!

Matters came to a head in July when the watch committee, enraged at being faced with such an impertinent demand, rejected it out of hand. The constables were determined, however, and for the first time recorded in any British police force, threatened to strike. An ultimatum was received by Chief Constable

McManus, from the solicitors, on 22nd July, that unless their demands were met, the men would resign at 8 pm the following day. London papers spoke of insurrection in Hull and reported other forces in West Yorkshire and Lancashire were showing signs of following Hull's lead.

The watch committee, embarrassed and outraged by this public challenge to their authority, were in no mood to concede anything. They reported the situation to the Home Secretary Lord Palmerston, describing the men's demands as quite preposterous. Angrily they searched for a solution which would not only quell the mutinous conduct but also restore their own credibility. When urgent enquiries revealed that Hull men were better paid than most forces they decided peremptorily not only to refuse the demands but to immediately reduce the size of the force to cut costs. They gave as justification for this decision the fact that while the population to police ratio in Hull was 672 - 1 and the cost of each officer £57 9s 0d, in Manchester the relevant figures were 681 - 1 and £57 2s 5d, while in Leeds the ratio was a massive 1188 - 1 and the cost only £53 6s 0d for each man., Clearly they felt Hull had been too generous by far in the money it spent on police.

But, the threatened strike had to be dealt with first. The possible consequences of total removal of police from the town were too serious to contemplate and there was also apprehension the men might march on the town Hall and cause trouble. Urgent action was required and the committee was in almost constant session from 22nd July.

They decided to call the militants' bluff, hoping at the same time to persuade the waverers to remain loyal. They announced that immediate steps were being taken to recruit fresh men to fill any vacancies. Six applicants on the waiting list were notified to attend for recruitment and a Mr. Dunn of Patrington was contacted by the clerk and asked to send for the committee's approval, any willing, respectable men over 21 years of age. Adverts and placards were hastily circulated asking for recruits.

Apprehension grew when the rumour again circulated that the men wanted to march on the Town Hall and to appear before the committee in a body to make their demands. Determined to forestall such a move and to take a strong line the committee ordered each man to appear before them individually. They were asked if they intended to resign if their wages were not raised by 3/-. If the answer was in the affirmative they were immediately dismissed and ordered to hand in their uniform. Out of 116 men, 47 left the force and 69 opted to stay at work.

To the relief of McManus and the committee the weekend which followed passed off peacefully. Neither trouble-makers in the town nor the dismissed men, created any disorder and the watch committee's strong line had been vindicated.

Twenty-seven of the dismissed men applied for reinstatement, but the committee decided to fill only eleven vacancies.

Knowing Lord Palmerston fully supported the action taken and noting a change of opinion in the local Press which had been shocked by the men's threat to strike, the watch committee, still smarting from the indignity they had suffered, set out to teach the force a lesson.

Already reduced in numbers, a sub-committee was established to carry out a review of other aspects of the borough's policing. They looked at duties, general efficiency, areas where improvements might be made and of course pay.

Losing no time they interviewed men from a variety of ranks and no-one was spared when they came to make their recommendations. It was considered the Chief Constable himself should be required to be in his office and among the force more than previously. In future he was to be in his office daily from 10 am to 11 am; return there as soon as the court had retired and stay until his dinner at 3 pm. He should then return at 6 pm and stay until 8.30 pm each evening!

The Sergeants were considered by the sub-committee to be "a useful body of men but, there were too many of them." Detectives were also thought to be useful but great care was to be taken before increasing their numbers. Of the 82 constables and 18 officers, the sub-committee felt the former were too few and the latter too many!

Everyone in the force was given a pay rise of 1/- per week from the 10th September, the cost of which was to be recouped by the reduction in the strength of the force.

PUBLIC DISORDER 1836 — 1866

Although the Chartist movement did not cause the disturbance in Hull it did elsewhere in the country, the first of the new police had to contend with considerable public disorder of a nature seldom seen in the force's later years. The mobs were ever ready to disgorge from the squalid, gardenless, slums in which they lived their mundane and poverty-stricken lives and to fight. It was a welcome diversion from the dark, airless rooms. Large crowds would magically appear at any incident and riotous situations developed very easily. Areas existed where police always patrolled in pairs and they viewed crowds of any sort with deep suspicion and considerable apprehension. It was still the age of the outlawed dog and prize fight and many were the deceptions used by crowds and organisers to prevent police from discovering the locations of such events which themselves often ended in mob violence and mayhem.

Often, the violent confrontations which took place were between police and soldiers or sailors. A military garrison was stationed at The Citadel and ships of the Royal Navy were often in port acting as guardships or just visiting. The sailors were intent on having a good time which generally consisted of three elements drink, women and a good fight to end the day! The new police, in their efforts to keep order, were the obvious adversaries for the last of these diversions and many a bloody battle took place on the streets of the town. Local mobs, not wishing to miss "the fun" would often join the mêlée with considerable gusto, always siding with those fighting the police.

In April 1856 some soldiers were arrested for being drunk and disorderly in Queen Street on a Sunday afternoon. In no time at all the police were surrounded by a huge mob, estimated to be 5000 strong, who allowed the soldiers to escape. They were chased to High Street but vanished. Three civilians were arrested and charged with obstruction.

Only a month afterwards, on the 18th May, one of the most serious of such incidents occurred and in unexpected circumstances.

Hull police had traditionally been responsible, not only for maintaining law and order, but also for dealing with fires and, for that purpose, were equipped with hoses and ladders. Invariably, if a major fire broke out, and a naval ship was available, the seaman, or blue jackets as they were known, were allowed ashore to assist with its subjugation.

On this particular day a fire broke out in Blanket Row at the premises of the wholesale druggists, Smith and Young. The area was heavily congested with housing and business premises and a large amount of gunpowder was stored there. Aware of the perils of the situation, McManus personally marched a body of his men to tackle the blaze. They were smartly followed by a company of men from HMS *Cornwallis* under the command of a Captain Randolph.

Arriving first, policemen set up hoses and started to fight the blaze. The usual large crowd of noisy townfolk had gathered to witness the exciting event.

When the sailors arrived they stood by the crowd waiting to help with the firefighting. In the event no-one apparently bothered to enlist their aid and they grew increasingly impatient at their forced inactivity, particularly as it seemd the policemen's efforts were having little effect on the smoke and flames. Whether out of sheer frustration or, following orders from their exasperated officers has never become clear, but, the sailors suddenly rushed forward and began tackling the fire themselves. As the reporter from the *Hull Advertiser* said, "They rushed up ladders, broke windows and exhibited such great acts of daring which speedily won upon the crowd who cheered them lustily."

The situation deteriorated into complete confusion as the police took umbrage at this affront to their pride. Sailors got doused with water from the police hoses, the seaman claiming this was deliberate retaliation from the piqued policemen who, in turn claimed it was caused by the navy trying to take the hoses from them.

While the building continued to blaze furiously a disgraceful and full-scale fight broke out between the sailors and police. The noise was tremendous with the huge crowds by now ecstatically delighted by the spectacle, cheering the sailors and hooting the police, while swaying backwards and forwards in their excitement. In the mêlée one man was knocked down and died.

The navy were beginning to win the battle — one officer drew his sword and threatened to slit a startled constable's throat if he didn't hand over his hose. The response from the defiant policeman was to direct his hosepipe full in the officer's face. Eventually police were forced into a humiliating retreat with many being carried away by colleagues, their uniforms in tatters. The sailors began tackling the blaze afresh when, to their dismay, the water pressure failed. Eventually discovering the water had apparently been turned off suspicion immediately fell on some disgruntled policemen, who by now had started to return to the scene.

Eventually the fire was quelled but the heat it had generated was to remain in the situation for a long time afterwards. Local magistrates considered the matter but, according to their chairman the Mayor, they felt it did not require any action by them. This was soon followed by a statement from the watch committee which, while mildly supportive of police, adopted a fairly placatory tone. It said that after enquiry they felt police could have coped with the conflagration without assistance and the problems which had occurred were doubtless due to the great zeal and desire to help on the part of the men of HMS *Cornwallis*. In the event, the committee felt all had ended well and no ill-will existed between police and sailors. This masterpiece of understatement was sent to Captain Randolph for his information and the complacent committee found his reaction quite unexpected. They received a sharp note, delivered smartly by return from the worthy captain, complaining that no proper enquiry appeared to have been made and he strongly resented the inference his sailors had interfered. He maintained they had been asked to assist not only by the property owners but also by the Mayor. To the committee's consternation he also reported the matter to the Admiralty accusing the force of incompetence and claiming the fire had been subdued by his own men. As a result, the Home Office asked the Mayor to hold a proper enquiry.

The watch committee were by now determined to support their police against this troublesome sailor and instructed the Sheriff — Mr. Todd to act as advocate for the force.

Having little idea of the form the enquiry should take, the Mayor opened a very disorganised hearing in the Town Hall on 1st June. Captain Randolph gave evidence that McManus had been abusive and his general behaviour offensive both towards himself and his men. He felt the police Chief was also responsible for cutting the water supply to his sailors' hoses. He made a further complaint against Sergeant number 1 who, not only refused to direct him to any water supply but also, rather offensively, told him to "go and look for it yourself!" He had witnessed policemen striking sailors and turning hoses on them.

Still rather uncertain of the procedure to follow, the Mayor, hoping no doubt to gain time for reflection and cooling of tempers, asked McManus if having heard the Captain, he wanted the matter adjourned. To his dismay and consternation the forthright policeman pompously replied, "Let the case go on, I admit everything that has been said about myself by Captain Randolph". A bemused Mr. Ayre the Magistrates' Clerk asked hopefully, "You plead not guilty?" "No, I admit all!" McManus persisted. "Be quiet!" snapped Alderman Abbey, exasperated by the way the enquiry was proceeding and McManus, taken completely by surprise, sat down.

A lengthy discussion then took place on the way the hearing was developing and about the procedure to be adopted for the rest of the enquiry. To the great relief of the committee Captain Randolph suddenly interposed to say he did not wish to make any criminal charges against McManus, he merely wanted an apology and some reparation.

Having this clarified, the committee began to hear the complaints against Sergeant 1 Holdgate, particularly the allegation he had turned the water off. They were greatly assisted in this by the evidence of one — Councillor Thomas Wells. He claimed to have seen one of the pipes burst in the street with the consequent failure of the water supply. He had even heard one of the crowd comment "who would be a bobby now?"

It was decided Sergeant Holdgate was innocent of any malpractice but he was given a mild rebuke for his insolence. Captain Randolph appeared satisfied and the committee felt police had been generally cleared of blame as the evidence tended to support the account given by the Chief Constable.

To their chagrin a letter was subsequently received from the Secretary to the Admiralty in which the term 'disgraceful' was used in relation to the conduct of the Hull police at the fire. They felt they had no option but to put the 'true facts' before the Home Office and, a delegation including McManus and Mr. Todd, the Sheriff went to London taking a report which was strongly supportive of the police position. The Home Office accepted that the Hull force should be exonerated from the allegations against them and no more was heard from either the Admiralty or Captain Randolph.

Unfortunately violence on Hull's streets did not end with the *Cornwallis* affair. Whether involving servicemen, ordinary citizens or both, the explosive situation created by the two main problems of living conditions and strong drink, ensured that violent disorder was ever-ready to erupt for many years to come.

CHAPTER 4

THE YEARS 1860 TO 1914

GENERAL BACKGROUND

The second half of the nineteenth century saw continued and substantial increases in the size and population of Hull. The fishing industry, in particular, grew spectacularly with associated increases in population and the number of dwellings, particularly in the Hessle Road area.

The wealth and prestige of the town grew as well and in 1888 Hull became a county borough and, in 1897, was granted the status of a city. Despite this, a large part of the population remained very poor. Between 1884 and 1886 it was estimated over 1000 families were starving, many of them being immigrant Irish who had fled to England to escape the potato famines. On Sundays the squalor seemed, if anything, to be accentuated with young men lounging in streets looking for drink, gangs of ragged children running wild and fights taking place.

The other face of Hull was presented by the upper and middle classes together with the poor but clean and very law abiding section of the working class. Completely opposite to the wild and rough elements in the town, they had an almost puritanical outlook. They considered strong measures were necessary to try and save the so-called 'less fortunate' from their sinful way of life. A great number of societies and organisations existed for saving 'the fallen' and removing temptation, particularly drink. Despite their efforts, very heavy drinking and some taking of opium and laudanum did take place involving in some cases women and children.

Prostitution continued to flourish and although it was particularly associated with the apprentices in the burgeoning fishing industry, it was far more widespread than that. Houses of ill-fame were everywhere — one man was known to keep five places in one street! In many cases girls of very young age were involved and prostitutes were 'on their beats' in the town at all hours of the day. At nightime red lights and other encouraging signs were everywhere.

Many respected people in the town felt police were not doing enough to deal with the vexed problem of such blatant immorality and criticism of their efforts was particularly strong in the 1880s when it was openly being suggested in some quarters that the force was deliberately not dealing with vice. In 1885 the *Hull Critic* wrote:

> "Query for the Watch Committee! Can the police be said to be accomplices of the keepers of infamous dens in Hull because they are (r)aiding them at the present time?"

The same paper complained bitterly about lack of policemen on the streets of the town following an incident when its editor had tried to prevent an assault on a woman. "I went to look for a policeman. I walked up Lowgate, along Whitefriargate, up Savile Street, down Bond Street, and along Charles Street to Caroline Place and I never saw one! What capital police management there is. Not a policeman to be seen in all those streets at one o'clock on a Monday afternoon. It would be interesting to know what the Watch Committee does with all its policemen."

As the century was drawing to a close the newly created city saw a massive redevelopment of its centre with much of the squalid housing and courts giving way to fine electrically-lit streets with magnificent public buildings designed by Alfred Gelder to match the existing splendour of parts like George Street and Albion Street.

Unfortunately areas around the redevelopment remained poor with houses scarcely fit for human habitation. In 1899, out of 59,000 houses, 36,000 still only had one entrance. Night soil collectors, unable to gain access during the hours of darkness, were forced to visit at breakfast time and carry their stinking loads through the house to their carts. Conditions were particularly bad in parts of Sculcoates and around Savile and Chariot Streets.

The redevelopment proved a mixed blessing for police. While on the one hand they were forced to patrol in larger groups in the worst areas, because such areas had become smaller they had less ground to search for wanted criminals in the brothels and low class pubs!

It was about this time that a new problem was emerging for the constabulary — traffic. Great numbers of carts and wagons were in the streets, driving where and when they liked. Jams were frequent at notorious junctions such as Market Place with Silver Street, and Beverley Road with Spring Bank. Again police were blamed for not being around when congestion occurred. As early as 1886 a Hull newspaper suggested: "If our new chief wants to do something which will at once earn him the gratitude of the wayfarers in Hull — our traffic is in serious need of regulation and by compelling drivers to obey the rule of the road he would do away with the danger to life and limb which exists today to a serious extent."

Horse trams gave way to the first electric trams in 1899 and it wasn't long before the watch committee, ever mindful of the need to combat immorality, instructed police to keep watch on open spaces and unlit lanes on the city outskirts which were now accessible to boys and girls for a penny tram ride!

RECRUITING & STRENGTH, UNIFORM & TRAINING

As changes took place in the town, so they were reflected by changes in its police force. The larger area and bigger population required increases in strength and the watch committee quickly agreed with the Inspector of Constabulary that an extra 20 men were needed. By 1901 there were 362 men in the force and by 1890 the top management had been strengthened to include a Deputy-Chief Constable and two Superintendents. Public pressure in 1885 had resulted in the post of Deputy-Chief being established when, with Chief Constable Campbell's sudden departure, the force had been left with no recognised head for many weeks.

Despite the growing number of men available to them, Chief Constables of .

the period were not deterred from seeking support of other forces if they felt it was justified. On the occasion of a large agricultural show in Hull men were borrowed from Sheffield, Liverpool and Newcastle together with an Inspector and 23 men from the London force. Major public events with large crowds were thought to attract undesirable elements from other areas. By bringing in police from large cities it was hoped to identify trouble-makers from those places before they could cause problems.

Policing Hull was never a soft job, but potential recruits were always plentiful. Many still came from the town and surrounding county area but a growing number were ex-soldiers, encouraged by a succession of ex-military Chief Constables. Three testimonials or a certificate of good conduct from previous public service were required before any application to join could be considered.

The uniform changed in the 1860's. Out went the top hat and tail coat, to be replaced by the helmet and tunic which was to remain basic standard dress for the duration of the force. For office staff and Inspectors a forage cap with 'cheesecutter' peak was issued. Over the years the watch committee turned more and more to specialist suppliers from London for both uniform and other equipment and in the 1800s the cost of one tunic together with a pair of trousers could vary from £1 19s 9d to £3 4s 0d according to the type of cloth. Such costs resulted in economical ordering of uniform to such an extent that when Arthur Featherstone joined in 1909 he was asked to wear a pair of his own trousers with the helmet and tunic and he did this for his first week of service.

Some of the men were allowed to wear plain clothes for certain duties and while they originally received 3/- per week extra as a clothes allowance, this was stopped in 1881 by an ever cost-conscious committee. Their more illustrious colleagues, the detectives, not only continued to draw the valuable 3/- each week, they were also paid at Sergeant's rates although not promoted to that rank.

Training in the force had been non-existent until Chief Constable Campbell took the first steps in 1883 by issuing each man with a personal booklet containing regulations and advice how to go about his duties. In 1886, when Captain Gurney was appointed with no previous police experience, he immediately recruited an ex-soldier, constable Brewster who, he told the committee "had all the qualifications and, in addition, would be able to train the force in drill!" By 1901 training had been supplemented by a short course on court procedure, duties, first aid, ju-jitsu (a forerunner of judo) and the usual drill. Even so, a new constable was sent out to face the public with only the most rudimentary knowledge of his job. As the *Hull Arrow* pointed out at the time: "it was only the fatherly attention of the Sergeants that prevented serious errors occurring". After six months probation a constable was tested by his Inspector and, if satisfactory, was moved from the fourth or lowest class.

Superannuation now allowed a constable to retire after 26 years service or at 50 years of age on a pension of two-thirds of his average pay during his service. For higher ranks the retiring age was 52. In 1906 a further concession was made to allow retirement after 15 years on one quarter pay. Unfortunately women who were widowed during their husband's service were forced to rely on the generosity of the watch committee. One, whose husband had considerable

A 19th Century Hull police constable with helmet, guardsman type tunic and duty armband.

service and who died after a long illness, was granted a one-off gratuity equal to one year of her husband's pay.

THE POLICEMAN'S LOT

The actual job of the ordinary policeman had changed little since the force was formed and it remained a daunting prospect for any new constable when starting his duties. Three shifts were normally worked, a day shift starting at 9 am, a night shift from 10 pm and 'splits' covering both early morning and evening with a break in the middle. Duties were worked seven days a week with shift changes once per month. None of a man's far from generous seven days leave each year would be granted during the period October to March and, if absent due to sickness, 1/- was deducted from pay for each day's absence! Everyone was considered to be on duty 24 hours a day and liable for instant recall if not on shift.

In 1871 an effort to get the day's work reduced to a straight eight hours was refused because this would entail employing additional men, but at last it was agreed men need no longer wear their uniform unless they were on shift.

A man joining the Hull police would know that if he managed the not inconsiderable feat of surviving the first two years without getting into serious trouble, he would be upgraded to 2nd class constable and his wages increased by one shilling. A further trouble free 18 months and he could look to becoming 1st class but, it would take him a daunting eight years in all to reach 'service' class, the highest constable grade. He could aspire to winning merit stripes with their shilling a week extra if he showed particular ability and consistent good conduct.

By 1891 his new book of instruction would inform him of the work expected as routine when he was on the beat. On early shift all property was to be carefully checked and in lonely areas this was to be done twice! Evening patrols were to be especially alert for burglars, particularly on Sundays when many citizens would be in church. In fact Sundays required special attention to churches themselves to ensure congregations were not disturbed and that females, in particular, were not molested going to and from divine service.

All men on day duty were instructed to walk on the outside of pavements and flags.

Constables were to be particularly vigilant for instances of putting lucifers in pillar boxes, breaking insulators on telegraph wires with stones and were to strictly enforce the law banning the shaking of rugs and carpets in the streets before 8 am!

Our new recruit would invariably be put on the night shift at the outset of his duties. There would be no recognised break to rest from his patrol and take the refreshments which he would carry in a small blue bag. He had to consume them as and when he could. Senior officers could give permission for men to have refreshments and a smoke and were known to have indicated public toilets as suitable eating places. Our young man would soon learn the tricks his older colleagues had been forced to adopt to make their lives more bearable, especially if the weather was cold. He would learn how to keep his oil lamp lit beneath his cape to warm the hands and would discover that by shinning up the

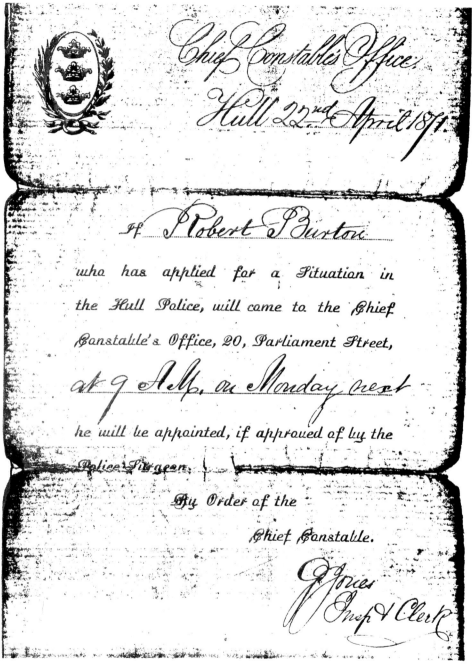

Chief Constable's Office,

Hull 22nd April 1871

If *Robert Burton*

who has applied for a Situation in the Hull Police, will come to the Chief Constable's Office, 20, Parliament Street,

at 9 A.M. on Monday next

he will be appointed, if approved of by the Police Surgeon.

By Order of the

Chief Constable.

Jones
Insp & Clerk

Notice summoning recruit to join force in 1871.

gas lamps it was possible to warm whatever beverage he had, over the mantle.

However uncomfortable his personal circumstances this could often be forgotten when he was dealing with some of the jobs he was called upon to tackle. Incidents ranged through cases of poor people dying in the street, women being found in labour, children requiring removal to the workhouse, to the mundane removal of paper blowing in the streets and calculated to frighten horses!

His greatest problem would be the ever-present threat of violence, often directed at himself. Serious assaults on police were an every day event and it was nothing exceptional for constables to be pitched bodily down the steps at the Old Alhambra in Porter Street, The Mechanics in

The venerable figure of 19th Century Hull policeman Robert Burton. Joined 1871.

Grimston Street, or at some disreputable house in town. A terrifying legend was always recounted to young recruits detailing how Waterhouse Lane was a particularly bad area for policemen to be jumped upon, have their legs broken and then be tossed into the dock!

An article in the *Hull Lady* in 1901 described the methods of attack so often faced by police as *"running kicks, foul play of any description with any kind of instrument calculated to inflict terrible injuries. The assailants are often desperate with whisky frenzy while he, (the constable) must act in cold blood. He is moreover alone, surrounded by a mob in which he sees no friendly face. If it is at night, so much the worse for him, as the darkness enables his assailants more readily to take him by surprise. He may have opportunity to blow his whistle or, it may have been snatched from him at an early stage, leaving him with nothing but his own resources to rely upon. Yet, whatever the odds, he may be trusted to do his duty to the last with bull dog courage, often clinging to his prisoner with clenched hands, long after consciousness has been kicked and battered out of him."*

Fortunately life in Hull's police force did also have its compensations. There was that indefinable something about being part of a body of uniformed men. Call it *esprit de corps*, comradeship, or what you will, most men felt a pride at belonging to a disciplined organisation.

Also, as soon as a constable was placed on the third class grade he was eligible, indeed encouraged, to join some of the many societies in the force. Some were entirely innocuous like the cricket club and Christian police association but, others like the Hull Police Temperance Society caused considerable controversy. As the name implies it was dedicated to the abolition of strong drink. Many found it quite incomprehensible that a police society of this nature should be necessary when so many similar groups already existed in the town. It also caused concern lest an officer imbued with the principles of such a society might find it difficult to carry out his duties in a fair and impartial manner when dealing with persons affected by drink.

It was an active organisation and actually ran a temporary home to shelter young persons who it was felt might be at risk. Appeals for funds were launched and an annual report was issued in which cases were described. In a year some 50 to 60 cases might be dealt with and were all briefly documented in the reports:

> S.E.L., 13 — Servant. Rescued from a Brothel.
> A situation was found for her.
>
> A.H., 18 — Grimsby. Found destitute on the Hessle Road by P.C. (200) Bird, was an incorrigible girl, had been in several homes and situations; was restored to her father.
>
> G.P., 17, Youth — Frodingham. Brought to the home by Mr. Wood of the South Street Mission. Was seeking work which was found for him at Alexandra Dock.

Police did much other charitable work in their spare time and considerable money was raised by a group who, dressed in the most outrageous fancy dress mostly lampooning police, would attend functions in the area and put on a comic show. They performed under the name — Hull Police Comic Concert Party.

Police swimming demonstrations were another popular way of raising money and regular exhibitions of police swimming in full uniform took place at Ferriby Sluice on the Humber. One particularly notable police swimmer at the turn of the century was constable, later Sergeant, Herbert Simpson. A keep fit fanatic and drill instructor in the force, he swam the Humber on three occasions. In 1912 the All-England police swimming championships were held with competitors from many forces tackling the treacherous waters from New Holland to Minerva Pier. Hull's champion, Simpson, was third to finish in 1 hour 32 minutes.

While speaking of champions mention must be made of constable Con O'Kelly or "Old Con" to his friends. A powerful sixteen-stone man with a lovely sense of humour, he joined Hull police in 1902 and six years later won the Olympic heavyweight wrestling title. On his arrival back in the city he was fêted by great crowds who gathered delightedly to see him paraded through the city on the force fire fly.

To everyone's disappointment he resigned from the force a year later to become a professional wrestler. The watch committee reluctantly accepted his resignation and commended him for the welcome advertising he had done for the city. He remained very well-known in the area and his son, also named Con, became a well-known and successful boxer.

In addition to sporting activities efforts were also made to ensure policemen and their families had social outings. For any such event permission was

Hull Police Charity Concert party at Newland Childrens' Homes – 1913.
(Courtesy ex Sgt. H. Simpson)

Champion police swimmer Sgt. H. Simpson and colleagues swimming in full uniform at a charity gala – location Ferriby Sluice, c.1910.
(Courtesy ex Sgt. H. Simpson).

required from the watch committee as on 9th July 1884 when Superintendent Trafford and his social committee submitted the following report:-

> Gentlemen,
>
> We, the undersigned officers of the Hull Police most respectfully beg that you will permit us to make arrangements for our 5th annual Pic-nic and Excursion to Mablethorpe for as many officers and constables of the force as can be spared with their wives, families and friends on Thursday 24th inst., so that we may enjoy a day together. We propose to issue tickets at 2/- each for adults and half price for children three to twelve years of age.
>
> We beg that you will permit as many members of the band who wish to go, to accompany us with their instruments.
>
> We also beg that you will allow us to publish Bills and Post and Distribute them.
>
> We are sir, Your obedient servants.

The carefully handwritten document was signed by the five men of the organising committee.

BUILDINGS

With the closing of living accommodation in stations when the Parliament Street rooms were condemned, Hull's policeman would have lived in rented accommodation. Whether or not arrangements were made on their behalf by the force or council is not clear. Certainly numbers of them often lived in houses close together as the 1851 census reveals. Numbers 6 to 9 New Village were occupied by the families of James Butler, Joseph Walton, Francis Asycough and John Kilburn, all policemen.

Some brief handwritten notes by constable, later to become Superintendent, Alfred Goodrum, give a good indication of the situation for an individual policeman in the later 1800s. He writes that he joined the force on 16th June 1886 and went to lodge at the house of James Greenslade at 19 Maple Street off Queens Road and took up duties at Norfolk Street station. Two years later, in October 1888, he was transferred to the Fire Station in Worship Street and moved his lodgings to 7 Silvester Street. He again moved lodgings, this time down the road to 17 Silvester Street some five months later and remained there until he got married in March 1892. He and his new wife 'took the house No. 17 King Street —rent 23 shillings per month clear. Landlady Mrs. Stone near Howden.'

The two police stations at Parliament Street and Jarratt Street continued to serve the force. To the whole population of Hull the name Parliament Street became synonymous with police and, even in later years when the force had moved headquarters, 'Parliament Street' still meant the main police station in town.

During the 1870s it became clear these two existing stations were becoming incapable of serving the rapidly expanding town. The Home Office was notified of the council's intention to relieve the problem by building four smaller district stations at Norfolk Street, Crowle Street, Gordon Street and

Constable O'Kelly Hull Police arriving to a tumultuous reception following his winning of World Wrestling Championship.

Wincolmlee. Norfolk Street was the first to open, the land having been purchased from a Mr. Bray for £1,350 and the station built by local builder, Mr. Frederick Blackburn for £1,535.

The new buildings enabled the city to be split into six areas with police stationed in each under the command of a Superintendent. But even this was insufficient to save the Parliament Street headquarters which, by the turn of the century, was becoming completely inadequate for its role. Pressure on space for administrative and detective functions in particular forced the watch committee to seek a new building.

On 25th March 1904 a brand new purpose-built, police headquarters was opened in Alfred Gelder Street. It had a grim and foreboding look from the outside with a heavy Victorian façade. Behind the facade was a rambling disjointed affair built in the form of a letter 'U' round existing privately owned office properties. The base of the 'U' consisted of a 35 yard corridor, the only purpose of which was to join the two ends. Apart from this peculiarity it was a fairly functional building with 24 cells, a third of which were for women. The Chief and Deputy-Chief Constables had offices on the first floor of the two storey front-end of the building.

DISCIPLINE IN THE FORCE

A disturbingly high rate of disciplinary problems in the force continued as the nineteenth century moved into its second half. As with society generally at the time, drunkenness and other problems associated with alcohol were still the major cause of trouble, but other offences covered a wide range. The

70

An F. S. Smith sketch of Section Station in Wincolmlee known variously as Church St. or York St. Station.

An F. S. Smith sketch of Section Station at Norfolk St. off Beverley Rd.

Central Police Station, Alfred Gelder St. 1904-57.

records of constables John Mumby and Michael Hester are good examples of the time:

John Mumby — joined 1877, pensioned 1906

Drinking on duty and being asleep on duty. Fined 2 day's pay and reprimanded by watch committee.

Neglecting to report door insecure before 4 am. Fined 1/6d by Chief Constable.

Being in watchman's box when on duty. Fined 1 day's pay by Chief Constable.

Neglecting to visit part of beat. Cautioned by Chief Constable.

Drunk on duty in Alexandra Spirit Tavern. Fined 1/6d and reprimanded by Chief Constable.

Breaking P.C. Miller's bedstead and failing to attend Chief Constable's office when ordered. Severe reprimand by watch committee and to pay cost of repairs.

Being in Webb's wine and spirit merchants. Reprimanded and cautioned by Chief Constable.

Making false statement about time he left court. Reprimanded and fined 1 day's pay by Chief Constable.

Michael Hester — joined 1866, pensioned 1892

Being in house of ill-fame at 12.05 am. Cautioned by Chief Constable.

Being absent from beat for 1 hour. Fined 1/6d by Chief Constable.

Being drunk on duty at 2.45 am. Fined 1 day's pay by Chief Constable.

Drunk on duty and assault on Sergeant Chapman. Fined 2 day's pay by watch committee.

Drunk and assaulting Charles Harrison. Fined 3 day's pay by watch committee.

In M.S. & L. booking office when on duty. Fined 1 day's pay by Chief Constable.

Drinking on duty and telling lies to watch committee. Fined 2 day's pay by watch committee.

Assaulting Mr. Newmarch. Fined 1 week's pay by watch committee.

Allowing absconder to escape from his custody. Severe reprimand and caution by Chief Constable.

The watch committee, the ultimate disciplinary authority in the force, showed inconsistency in dealing with individual cases and continued to lay themselves open to much criticism for their actions from both within and outside the force. They also had a tendency to deal with cases which, by their nature, would have been more appropriately heard in magistrates' courts. Yet in their defence, quite a number of persistent offenders, treated with surprisingly persistent leniency, did in fact finally seem to settle down and make the grade. Cynics might say this was misreading the situation and that the leniency the committee allowed in disciplinary matters taught men the fundamental lesson of how to avoid getting caught! Certainly there were many who failed to take advantage of any leniency or who caught the committee in a bad mood and were forced to leave their jobs.

The fact that the committee for no apparent reason, other than a fit of petulance, would dismiss a good man without the benefit of a proper hearing, together with a growing number of false complaints from the public, began to seriously undermine morale in the 1870s. So much so that accused men started to rebel against the treatment meted out to them.

The attitude of large sections of the public had in fact become aggravated with methods of policing over a number of years. This was exacerbated by the welter of legislation giving constables statutory instead of common law powers over an increasingly wide range of offences. The previous decade had seen the Larceny Act, Malicious Damage Act, Offences Against The Person Act, Poaching Prevention Act, and many others. These changes irritated large numbers of citizens, already anti-police, and they took every opportunity to make complaints. Matters first came to a head in Hull with an incident which became known as the Raywell Street riots. It also turned out to be the catalyst for a bitter battle which erupted in the town's council chamber between those who supported the police and the faction who denigrated them.

On 4th January 1870 at about 2 pm, constable Wright was on the beat in Raywell Street when he saw a man named Ritchie whom he knew to be an ex-constable who had been dismissed for drinking. Ritchie was, according to

Wright, drunk and causing a disturbance in the street. He claimed his presence apparently further provoked Ritchie who, despite being told to go away and be quiet, started shouting abuse and obscenities at him. Constable Harker arrived on the scene and Wright decided to arrest Ritchie. This proved easier said than done because as soon as Wright made his move Ritchie exploded in the most violent action and fell upon Wright, forcing him to the ground. The usual large crowd gathered rapidly and there was no doubt in which direction its sympathies lay.

Constable Harker, far from helping his colleague, stood apparently petrified by the turn of events. Some witnesses declared he just stood holding Wright's helmet, others that he in fact made off. In any event he failed to help and subsequently admitted being frightened and resigned from the force.

A number of off-duty policemen were living in Raywell Street and they soon became aware of what was happening and Inspector Morgan, who witnessed the fracas from his bedroom window, went to assist Wright. Before assistance could arrive the unfortunate constable Wright had taken a severe beating from a murderous Ritchie and near-frenzied mob. He became the focus of a full scale riot and was struck repeatedly with his own truncheon, kicked, stamped upon and punched. Eventually he was rescued, Ritchie arrested and the crowd dispersed.

Immediately claims and counter-claims began to circulate with the police evidence about the incident being strongly challenged. The main dispute centred around Ritchie's condition and many of the crowd claimed he had been sober and going home quietly when he was set upon and beaten by the police. They said it was P.C. Wright who had been drunk and both a special constable and a customs officer came forward, the latter claiming he had been struck by the aggressive constable, while the special constable alleged he had tried, unsuccessfully, to arrest the constable!

So political did the issue become the council was forced to set up a committee of enquiry and, as many allegations against the police surfaced, the terms of reference were widened to encompass all the conditions and methods of working of Hull police but, particularly as it related to the Raywell Street incident.

Much general evidence against the police and their activities was taken, varying from complaints of over-officiousness to allegations of wrongful and brutal arrests. It was claimed citizens were marched handcuffed through the streets and, at the end of it, those arrested were often exonerated by the courts. There was also a strong feeling police applied for too many remands in custody when bail could have been granted and it was claimed that some policemen, despite drawing their pension were still allowed to work and draw wages! Doubtless a lot of suppressed antagonism towards the police was released during the enquiry. Nevertheless the watch committee and police where shocked when the result was published in the *Hull News* of 5th March 1870:-

> "The report of the above committee was submitted which upheld allegations of brutality and accused Inspector Morgan and constable Wright of Perjury and Conspiracy."

The hue and cry was now on with a vengeance and newspaper headlines like

"Police Accused of Drunkenness" — "More Allegations of Violence Against Police" were common.

Such was the venom of a section of the public that even the following item in the *Hull News* did nothing to abate it:-

> "Constable Dickenson, whilst performing an act of heroism, was killed at a disastrous fire which destroyed the Theatre Royal in Humber St. last night."

On 12th March summonses were issued aganst Morgan and Wright but the magistrates dismissed the charges.

At a meeting on 19th March the watch committee tried desperately to stem the flood of vituperation against the force and "gave a vote of confidence to the Police and after discussion on the report of the Committee of Enquiry, resolved that in the opinion of this committee the conclusion come to by the enquiry committee is an unfair one as to Inspector Morgan and Constable Wright and we feel it is our duty to enter our protest at such decision believing that Inspector Morgan and Constable Wright are free from the charges made against them."

The matter soon degenerated into an intensely political fight between two parties with the unfortunate policemen the ammunition used by both sides. In August 1870 one of the groups was granted a warrant for the arrest of both the Inspector and the constable who then had the humiliation of appearing before York Assizes charged with conspiracy and perjury. Both were found not guilty and discharged.

Still the wave of anti-police feeling continued but in 1875 the men in the force had taken enough and two of them falsely accused of brutality hit back.

Unfortunately all the furore had done little to improve the watch committee's own handling of disciplinary matters. In fact, apparently unsettled by the Raywell Street outcry, they became if anything more inconsistent.

In April 1875 the case of constable Ballman came before them. Of previous good character, he was the subject of a complaint by one James Wilkins who claimed he had been arrested by Ballman on a false charge, the constable had been drunk at the time and had violently arrested him. The committee decided Ballman should be summarily dismissed.

The whole force was totally dismayed, the Chief Constable reported him to be an excellent officer and his fellows knew him to be not only a total abstainer but also a fair and just policeman. The general feeling was that yet another miscarriage of justice had occurred.

Ballman applied for reinstatement and claimed he had fresh and additional evidence to support his case. The committee agreed to re-open the matter and ordered the Clerk to examine the new evidence but at their next meeting they decided there was insufficient to justify reopening the matter.

By coincidence, at that same meeting they dealt with the case of constable Jennings. This young man, infuriated at being charged at all, had already tendered his resignation. Nevertheless the committee heard the case with allegations by a Mrs. Adie that Jennings had arrested her for no reason and in doing so had used unnecessary violence. When confronted by the officer at the hearing the lady retracted her allegations and eventually admitted it was all false.

In view of this turn of events the committee asked Jennings to withdraw his resignation. He refused and addressed the committee as follows:-

"We (the police) find it is beginning to be very difficult for us to discharge our duty in the streets. If we speak to the veriest roughs in the street we are threatened with the watch committee and it is now a common thing if they interfered with anybody to be told that they (the people interfered with) have friends in the council who would tear the uniforms from our backs. I have no other reason for resigning but, resign I do!"

Despite being pressed to remain in the force he declined to do so.

Whether as a result of this or not, a month later constable Ballman was allowed to bring his fresh evidence before the committee which cleared him. Those responsible for the original false complaint would not even attend the hearing and Ballman was reinstated.

The two exonerations and particularly the case of constable Jennings had a startling effect. An editorial in the *Hull and East Riding Herald* on the 6th May 1875, commenting on the two cases said:-

> *"Discontent in the police force must be guarded against and the cases referred to ought to receive most careful consideration, especially ought this to be so when we consider that men will be lax in discharging their duties if they conceive that obedience brings punishment and that the 'let be' mode of conduct is the road to safety and honour."*

The Chief Constable, sensing the force badly needed a 'morale booster', used the occasion of the forthcoming traditional anniversary parade to provide the much needed 'shot in the arm'.

Aware that the Stipendiary Magistrate, Mr. T. Travis, knew the difficulties under which police operated, he invited him to address the force. Although unwell at the time, the magistrate agreed and as expected he touched on the sore point of the men's treatment by their watch committee by saying that while he hoped no magistrate would ever 'whitewash' police, went on "... I defy any place in the kingdom to produce a body of men against whom fewer complaints could be made. The police have peculiar difficulties. You are brought into contact with not only the lowest criminals, not only the worst of characters, not only the most profligate but here and there with those who, socially might be superior but who, by their conduct, demeaned and demoralised themselves to a state below what I hope you will never reach. It is difficult to perform duties without fault, but your force do try. The rewards of correct attitudes and behaviour are ample, first, in your own consciences that you have done your duty and second, that you have the respect and moral support of every respectable man in Hull!"

While this may have had a heartening effect upon the men it was to be many years before the discipline records of members of the force became other than deplorable.

Neither should it be thought it was only the lower ranks who defaulted. Often senior officers of considerable service and experience fell by the wayside and were usually able to take advantage of the committee's extreme leniency on such occasions.

The cases of Superintendent Trafford, head of "A" division including the detectives and Inspector Graham who held the key-post of clerk at head-quarters, both occurred in 1884. Three of Trafford's men, constables Burton, Carroll and Piercey, had been responsible for apprehending a gang of poachers on Sir Christopher Sykes' estate. The grateful baronet had rewarded them and, the Chief Constable reported to the watch committee that, despite instructions to the contrary, Trafford had taken ten shillings of the reward from each man, for himself. When he came before the committee Trafford pleaded guilty. Following the tradition which usually worked he had penned a letter to the councillors.

> *"May I ask your goodness in reading one more word for me before any further decision of the watch committee on Wednesday – I have already admitted my offence and have not tried to keep anything back from the committee but the more I think of it the more I am convinced how wrong and foolish I was in taking anything from the officers – all I can say as to this is that I did not give sufficient thought to such a matter at the time especially as it had been done in other cases, and as to the rule it never struck me that as the amount had been allotted such a second division had to come before the committee again, but I now see I was wrong and I give the committee my solemn pledge that never again shall there be any breach of orders and after my very long services without a word against me for sixteen years, I hope and trust that they will not think necessary to reduce me which would be the greatest degredation and punishment –to anything short of this I must submit but I hope my word may be taken and that the lesson I have received will be a warning to me for life.*
>
> *I am Sir, Your humble and obedient servant...*

The committee took a long time to decide his fate. The first suggestion was for a strong line — he should be reduced forthwith to Sergeant, repay the money and receive a strong reprimand from the committee but other members who knew and liked the extrovert Superintendent felt this was much too drastic. A strong reprimand and refund of the money would be sufficient they felt. A compromise was agreed upon — he would receive a very strong reprimand, to be entered in the 'black book', ordered to refund the money and, be moved from "A" division to Norfolk Street — a very lucky man!

The case against Inspector Graham was more sinister than just taking a 'cut' from reward money. He was alleged to have made false entries in the gratuity book purporting to show that two men who had left the force had received two shillings each for services rendered at the Municipal Elections. He had forged their signatures and taken the money. He said it was to "square the petty cash!"

At the hearing, to the chagrin of the Press, the watch committee adjourned and reconvened as a sub committee so being able to exclude the public, including the Press.

As always, there was controversy between those who felt a strong line should be taken and others who favoured leniency. Quite a number of members felt Graham should simply be severely reprimanded for carelessness and irregularity! The chairman however would not agree. "This case," he said, "is surrounded by so many circumstances of such grave suspicion that it is not in the interests of the force or the public that Mr. Graham should remain in his present position. Instead he should be given the opportunity of applying for some other position in the force not so closely connected with the receipt of money." This was agreed and Graham technically lost his job, but was given the option of re-applying.

He wrote the usual letter,

Gentleman,

With reference to the resolution passed at the special committee on Saturday last 19th inst, respecting my position in the Hull Police Force.

I cannot refrain from taking this opportunity of expressing my very deep and sincere regret of the occurrence that you have had under consideration, and no language of mine can adequately express my sorrow for what has transpired, and although done innocently and thoughtlessly, yet I can now see the very grave and serious error committtted. With regard to your decision as to my leaving the office, I would respectfully beg to draw your attention to the fact that this in itself entails a loss of £35 per annum, in the least, to me, and therefore in your consideration of my future position to be held in the force, I hope you will kindly allow this fact to weigh with your deliberations.

I respectfully abstain from asking for any particular appointment, but leave the matter entirely in your hands, feeling sure that you will temper justice with mercy and appoint me to some office and grade in the force in which I trust I shall be able to redeem the past and regain your confidence."

The committee decided he should be appointed to an ordinary Inspector's duties at Church Street station.

Richard Cooke, well known for his criticism of the Council wrote the following scathing article in the *Hull Critic* after these cases.

"The moral defections of the Hull police are becoming a serious matter, and it is high time there was a sweeping of the Augean stable. Not long ago, the watch committee had occasion to punish the second officer in command for a grave breach of duty. Now they have had before them a case to which very serious terms have been applied by the committee themselves. Mr. Inspector Graham, a man occupying a position of importance and trust, has been accused of misappropriating money....... what seems most strange of all is that permission be given to him to apply for a situation in the force where he would have nothing to do with the receiving money. I should imagine that if the decision of the committee is based on reliable evidence, and if they have been justified in coming to the conclusion they did, then there is no position in the force he can fill, and it says little for the morale of the watch committee that they would still give employment to a man whom they declare to be of a sullied character. The committee should go further. If Graham has committed the offence for which he is cashiered, then he ought to be prosecuted; if not and he is innocent of any fraud, then his dismissal is wrong and the stigma on his character most unjust. Graham, it will be

remembered, is the officer who was employed in the recent betting raids and was connected with the Hull Police Mission Band. He is also a local preacher in the Methodist New Connexion. The force is the laughing stock of the town, so numerous are its shortcomings. It appears to me that the Chief Constable is wanting either in power or discipline or that the watch committee meddle with his department too much."

The article ended with the sentiment that "This process of whitewashing and compounding of felony which is going on in the watch committee just now does not speak well for the honour of the town."

PUBLIC DISORDER

As the decade of the 1870s dawned in England, Hull, in common with the rest of the country, was seething with argument about many controversial national topics. By 1872 gloom and despondency were everywhere — the weather was even more unusually awful, trouble had again erupted in Ireland and serious public protests were beginning to surface, by the wealthy about high rates of bank interest and by the remainder of the population about the proposed new licensing laws! As might be expected in a town with the second highest ratio of pubs to public at the time, it was the latter problem which caused the biggest outcry in Hull.

The trouble arose with the application of the new laws on November 1st which allowed local magistrates to impose shorter hours on public houses. At the time public houses opened at 6 am and closed at 11 pm. The new hours were to be from 8 am to 10.30 pm with early closing at 9 pm on Sunday. Public opinion was divided.

In September an 11,000 signature petition had been handed in from the Bill's supporters in Hull asking that the shortest possible drinking hours be adopted. In support of this it was claimed the working classes were asking to be relieved from temptation and statistics had proved that mortality among publicans was higher than in any other group. On the other side, the publicans and those who actually used licensed houses took the opposite view. There were three minor riots in the town during the first week of the new hours, the cry being, "Down with this petty tyranny — let's have none of it here!"

The following week it had been arranged that the town's two Members of Parliament, Messrs. Clay and Norwood, would address a meeting of their constituents at Artillery Barracks in Park Street. Demonstrators threatened to disrupt the meeting which was hastily cancelled by the organisers.

Despite this a mob gathered in Park Street at 7 pm on the appointed evening and, discovering they had been thwarted, set off for Mr. Norwood's house in Landsdowne Street. Here they were diverted by a group of policemen hastily deployed by cab and the crowd marched to Whitefriargate. By now over 1,000 strong, they knocked down hastily erected police barricades and moved to King William's statue where an impromptu meeting was held. When their leader was arrested they set off over the North Bridge towards Holderness House where Mr. Clay was staying.

Police had surrounded the house but the crowd did not reach it, turning back at Witham when they found the road was knee-deep in wet mud. They began breaking windows and gas lamps and stoning any policeman they saw. A strong detachment of police was despatched from Parliament Street and eventually order was restored. By 11 pm the streets were quiet.

Sporadic disturbances continued in the ensuing weeks, the main problem being at week ends when drinkers from the city would go to the surrounding country areas where licensing hours were more flexible and come home drunk and disorderly. Extra police had to be regularly drafted to the Anlaby Road area to contain trouble caused by the returning revellers.

The greatest cause of civil disorder at the time, however, came from labour disputes with virtually every type of trade or calling getting involved in some sort of industrial action in the decades leading up to the Great War. Fishermen, seamen, dockers, these were the groups involved in the most serious events and 1883 saw the first serious strike involving the town's fishermen.

There is little doubt the men withdrew their labour as a last resort in an effort to secure improvements in what were attrocious working conditions, but the justification or otherwise of their cause should have had no effect on the policing of the dispute. Yet owners complained bitterly, and with some justification, that the strike was only kept going because police refused to take action to prevent intimidation of those men willing to work. In the end they forced the Chief Constable to meet them and persuaded him to take some action.

As a result an Inspector and six constables attended the dock and escorted one non-striking man to his vessel. A large and threatening crowd gathered and, police later alleged, refused to disperse. Four strikers, including the fishermens' President, were arrested. After a two day trial before the Stipendiary Magistrate the men went free but with a warning from the magistrate who inferred they were lucky not to go to prison.

Exactly ten years later a much more serious situation arose when Hull's dockers came into conflict with the major ship owner in the town — C. H. Wilson, owner of the famous Wilson Line. Mr. Wilson found dockers were refusing to work one of his vessels because one crew member was not in a trades union. Bristling with rage at this impudence, he decided to face the men out and to import non-union labour from elsewhere.

On 5th April 250 strike-breaking 'free labourers' arrived by train in Hull and another 500 were reported on their way from London. The Chief Constable, Captain Gurney, and the watch committee, fearing the likely reaction of the dockers, could have had little idea of the violent disorder which was to erupt during the next three weeks.

Authority was given for an executive sub-committee consisting of the chairman of the watch committee together with the Chief and Deputy-Chief Constables to take any necessary steps to strengthen the force. Hundreds more strike-breakers arrived, initially to good natured hoots of derision from the local men. Their jovial mood soon changed when one of the visiting gangers decided to clear a way for his group by firing pistol shots in the air. Police were only just in time to prevent him being thrown in the dock by the enraged Hull men.

The Chief Constable quickly requested additional policemen from Leeds, Nottingham and the East Riding and sixty-four Leeds men arrived by train and were reported to have been "marched smartly through the town to the delight of

Helmet badge of Hull City Police
Pre 1933.
(Courtesy of Sgt. N. Woollons).

A detachment of officers parading for
night duty and presenting staves,
oil lamps and handcuffs for inspection,
c.1900.

Policemen on duty at Hull's annual fair October 1905.

a highly excited crowd.... Having been well fed by Mrs. Jenkinson at the central Police Station they were deployed immediately to the docks". In addition to the extra police 160 Royal Scots and a troop of Dragoons were called from York to assist.

The next few days saw a thick fog settle over the town, and being particularly thick around the dock area it enabled the imported workers to operate unhindered on the ships. This, however, turned out to be very much the calm before the storm. Violent confrontations began to occur between police and very large crowds, mostly of dockers, but joined by willing trouble-makers both local and from elsewhere. More police were requested as violence escalated and the Chief Constable asked the War Office to replace some of the infantry with more cavalry. The effect of mounted men on the crowds was much more dramatic!

Meanwhile the scene at the docks was chaotic as a vicious fusillade of stones met local Wilson Line clerks who volunteered to unload ships. A number of determined police baton charges rescued the clerks, but only after an estimated 2,000 dockers stoned the rescuers. Eventually the clerks were enabled to work the ships, but this further infuriated the strikers. At this stage Captain Gurney rather bravely expressed confidence that he had sufficient resources to cope, an assessment he was to revise in the next few days as violence increased further.

The Leeds police, whose reputation as strong men had preceded them, decided on swift action to sort out a conflict occurring at the Railway docks. They made a fierce baton charge, cracking heads as they moved in when, to their surprise, the crowd responded with such hostility and violence they soon found themselves in trouble and, to their great humiliation, had to be rescued by colleagues from Nottingham.

Two Hull detectives who arrested some lads at Prince's dock for pilfering found themselves quickly surrounded by an angry mob who released the prisoners and forced the detectives to seek refuge in a building. The crowd began to smash doors and windows to get at them and once again baton charges were necessary before they could be rescued.

The situation was deteriorating with police losing control and being unable to escort the 'free' labourers safely to work. At the Chief Constable's suggestion, arrangements were made to use a ship on the docks to house the workers, thus avoiding the difficult task of escorting them through the town. The Government agreed to retain the troops in Hull and the Admiralty arranged for two naval vessels to anchor in the Humber.

As ever in such situations a strong political element was present and required delicate handling by the watch committee. Shipowners wanted to force police to take sides in the dispute by calling on sufficient resources to reopen all docks to normal working. The watch committee refused to be drawn and, knowing the possible repercussions of enlarging the conflict, contented themselves with containing the existing situation. The correspondent of the *Times*, always against the strikers, wrote:

> *"The watch committee met this afternoon to consider the matter. A majority of one decided the fate of the resolution dealing with the matter, the arguments of the opponents of extra protection being that while work was proceeding but poorly at the other docks it was not right*

that work should be attempted at these two docks. What lies behind all this is a desire on the part of some of the watch committee to coerce the masters into compromise, and also a fear of the rate payer, for some day Hull will have a heavy bill to pay for this month of lawlessness!"

Acts of wilful vandalism and terrorism began to occur. On 23rd April a massive fire, strongly suspected of being deliberately started, wrecked the Citadel timber works. The smoke was so dense it could be seen over 20 miles away. Attempts were made to obstruct railway lines and, luckily, a plot was foiled to blow up one of the bridges on the Hull to Barnsley line.

The Chief Constable made yet more requests for urgent reinforcements but, to his dismay, these were not always sympathetically received by other watch committees. On one occasion, Nottingham City, having agreed to send 40 men, reversed that decision and refused to help. Nevertheless Captain Gurney succeeded in obtaining 75 extra men including 25 mounted police from London.

Still the violence and mayhem continued. A horse bus carrying 26 free labourers from Scarborough was attacked by a mob with stones. The windows were smashed and when the driver whipped up his horses the crowd chased the madly careering vehicle through the streets of the town. They caught it when it became stuck on Monument Bridge with police vainly trying to push it free. On its way once more, the crowd followed it with a hail of missiles along Whitefriargate and into Humber Street. Here, exasperated police were forced to draw their batons and make yet more charges before the crowd would disperse.

Another wagonette was heavily attacked in Osborne Street, women with aprons loaded with stones providing missiles for the angry strikers.

It was not until early May that the strike was settled and disorder continued to the very last day. At the height of the troubles Hull's police force, together with the police of the North East Railway Company, had the support of some extra 350 policemen from other forces.

The need for mutual aid, particularly in view of the difficulties raised by some forces, resulted in considerable discussion in police and Home Office circles. In 1910 a number of forces in the north, including Hull, made an agreement that they would respond to requests for help if received from a Chief Constable participating in the scheme. This came nicely in time for Hull's next major industrial dispute which occurred in 1911.

Discontent had been simmering in the city and elsewhere in the country during the first decade of the twentieth century. Unemployment, low pay, bad housing, and much poverty all contributed to increasing industrial strife. In 1910 fifteen hundred men staged a hunger march through the centre of Hull.

The year which was to see the Coronation of King George V opened with demands for improved conditions by the National Union of Seamen and Firemen. In February the Union began a national campaign in support of their demands and, as winter moved into spring, a strike began to look more and more likely.

George Morley had only been appointed in September 1910 as Hull's Chief Constable and his first major test was soon to arrive. Determined not to be caught unprepared the watch committee reconstituted the emergency sub-committee which had operated during the seamen's strike. The chairman, Chief and Deputy-Chief Constables were given authority to act on the committee's behalf on any matters connected with industrial action. On 14th June the Union declared a national strike which was marked in Hull by a massive meeting in Paragon Square when a rocket flare fired at 8.30 am signalled the start of the fight.

Much of the dock area was policed by the North East Railway Company police but the potential for trouble there was such that a joint operation with the stronger city force was inevitable.

The early days of June saw potential provocation arriving in the city in the form of black leg labour from as far away as Cardiff and it was known that unemployed cotton operatives in Lancashire were being offered 5 shillings a day plus food, to cross the picket lines.

As events moved into the third week of June, despite increasing reports of intimidation and attempts to fire bedding intended for the depot ships, the strike was generally peaceful and the men good humoured.

The first really serious incident occurred as strikers marched to Alexandra Dock to try and prevent a London vessel, the *Ladywood*, from putting to sea. With apparently no violent intentions, the seamen approached the vessel and, to their horror, were greeted with about eight revolver shots fired from the ship's bridge. One of the strikers, Joseph Walsh, was hit and rushed to hospital. The Chief Constable visited the scene and decided the man's condition was so grave that a 'dying deposition' should be taken from him. This was done by the Chief Constable in the presence of Dr. Holder J.P. and Mr. Shackles the magistrates' clerk. The *Ladywood* put to sea but the third officer responsible for the shots was arrested in Rotterdam.

The incident triggered a strike of Hull's dockers in sympathy with the seaman which, although only intended to be of one day's duration, continued after the Coronation on 22nd June.

The first days of the following week saw the strike still relatively calm with relations between police and strikers remaining quite good. The previous Friday had seen 600 strikers confronted by 20 policemen when they approached the Wilson ship SS *Novo* in Victoria Dock. The Chief Constable who was present, sensing that some discretion was necessary, arranged for the ship's master to receive a delegation of the strikers. This was greeted with loud applause from the crowd, who despite attempts to stop it by Union leaders, gave Mr. Morley three hearty cheers and rushed to shake his hand.

By this time, however, the leaders of the strike were fearful they would be unable to prevent violence. Many of the men whose families were suffering began suggesting more direct action to bring the matter to a quick conclusion. In the course of an address to a huge crowd in Paragon Square on the 26th June, Mr. Burn, the dockers' leader, attempting to keep his men calm, said he had received a message from the Chief Constable that in the course of his experience he had never yet seen a strike of that character carried on as orderly as this one. Burn said that he hoped the men would "Continue to the Chief Constable's opinion."

The next few days however were to see a worrying escalation of the dispute. Lightermen, dockgate men and local railwaymen came out on sympathy strikes

84

and other areas of the country began to settle, leaving Hull as *The Times* put it, "to be made the cockpit for the final settlement". The Mayor informed the Home Office of the deteriorating situation and the watch committee sent a request for 400 extra policemen. This latter move was heavily criticised by the Labour group on the council who said it was highly provocative.

Police were strengthened further by hastily recruited special constables and all men in the force were placed on 24 hour standby. They did not have long to wait. On 27th June, a mass of strikers attempted to storm the Finnish vessel SS *Titania* as it was being unloaded by women stewards and cooks under the protection of police.

The women were rolling barrels of butter from the ship into railway wagons to the accompaniment of loud jeers from the crowd when a picket approached Mr. Morley and asked to go aboard and explain the position. The Chief Constable felt unable to give authority as he was only acting in support of the N.E.R. police and, as the crowd got angrier, police requested the unloading be suspended. Numbers of strikers boarded lighters in the dock and cut them adrift. One approached the ship unobserved by police and men started to scramble up the side. A posse of police hurriedly scrambled on board and cut the lighter adrift.

Police reinforcements marched to the scene and, forcing their way through the jeering mob, they moved to a standby position under one of the dock sheds. In no time at all they were called into action when as the *Daily Mail* reported:

> *"There was an ugly rush at the entrance of the fault shed towards the stern of the **Titania**. The police emerged from the struggle without any injury although a number of the men fell to the ground. Some stones were thrown at the police and as they came away their clothes were covered with dust and dirt. The remarkable scene continued for some little time. Strikers had taken possession of the keels and let them drift wherever they would. A bridge was formed by dragging a number of keels into a line and along this the intruders moved at their own sweet will with the police powerless.*

The following day as the strikers tried to escalate the unrest by enlisting support from other workers trouble broke out at Reckitts. Initially the workers here refused to stop work and fighting broke out. Thirty Birmingham policemen who were guarding the factory were forced into baton charges to restore order and many bystanders were swept unwillingly into the conflict as the police came by. Order was finally restored when Mr. Morley arrived in his car soon to be followed by a strong force of 200 policemen.

The men from Birmingham already had something of a reputation in the town, one letter writer to a local paper accusing them of unmanliness in the way they had charged one crowd. It appears they were all volunteers and well known by colleagues back in the Midlands for their ability to consume intoxicating liquor. When they had initially arrived in Hull they had been taken straight to the docks and locked into their home — the SS *Marengo*. Due to oversight or by design they found they were consigned to an area where no bar was open! Bitter complaints were made to senior officers, police authorities and the Press in Hull

James Reckitt gold medal awarded annually to best constable in
Hull Police. This one awarded to ex Insp. Barker.
Medals were discontinued c.1925.
(Courtesy of ex-Sgt. Barker — son of holder).

and Birmingham. So loud were their protests that eventually a Birmingham brewery made a special delivery of beer to the thirsty men and this was gratefully received!

At the time of the Reckitt's incident many workplaces in the city were being guarded against disorder breaking out and tradesmen, who had reported being harassed by strikers, were given police escorts.

Winston Churchill, the Home Secretary, telegraphed the Mayor and reminded him of his duty to maintain order and to take adequate measures to secure the landing of cargoes but, despite their best efforts, it was found impossible to adequately police all the dock. Arrangements were therefore made to confine work to one dock only and to billet police on that dock.

Police in plain clothes were being used to infiltrate the strikers in an effort to gain intelligence about their intentions as the violence continued to escalate.

There was a great concern among the Union officials about the way in which the dispute had developed. In a telephone call to the Home Office, the Chief Constable said, "A split has now developed between the men and their leaders and the committee of dockers are thoroughly frightened!"

The 29th June saw eight hours of riotous behaviour in the city. A pitched battle between police and strikers took place on the approaches to Albert Dock with many casualties on both sides. The Chief Constable personally led 100 police reinforcements from the Central Police Station and they were soon in action against a crowd in Castle Street. The conflict moved into Myton Street where all the street lamps were smashed and the crowd even removed tombstones from children's graves in a cemetery and smashed them in their frenzy.

It was 11 o'clock in the evening when the Chief Constable decided to clear the packed Myton Street. The *Hull Daily Mail* reporter described what followed:-

> *Two columns of police were drawn up..... as the advancing rank came level with Castle Street and Myton Street a shower of projectiles fell in their midst. The Chief Constable who was marching on the extreme right of the file was struck with an ugly looking missile on the knee and almost felled to the ground while the constable next to him was struck on the chest and on the back of the head with two stones. The almost cynical coolness of Mr. Morley steadied the men whose temper was rising under such treatment.... One would almost have believed at times that police were enjoying their position as targets..... In infinitely shorter time than it takes to write it, the Chief Constable had ordered a right flank movement and Myton Street was cleared in an instant.*

Trouble continued in all parts of the town with Sheffield police charging crowds in Commercial Road and a solitary policeman, attacked by a crowd in Dagger Lane and being rescued by a fierce charge of mounted men.

The day had also marked the arrival of 500 policemen from London. Sent at the suggestion of a perturbed Home Secretary, who at the same time ordered two battalions of troops to stand by at York, they arrived at 9 am and were marched, with their bedding to Albert Dock. In a later report to his superiors, the officer in charge Superintendent West, rather smugly related that:

> *"Our men, it is asserted by many of the best people, made such an impression on the dockers and others when they marched from the Railway Station....that it has had the effect of keeping them quiet and we are treated with respect."*

Historians might conclude it was not so much the appearance of the London men as the fact that the strike was almost coming to an end.

Two days later a settlement of the dispute was achieved, but, to make sure there was no further trouble, the police reinforcements did not leave the city until a further two weeks had elapsed. The exception was the Metropolitan contingent who returned to London on the day the strike ended.

The authorities, still recovering from the dreadful scenes in June, began to make immediate preparations for any new outbreak of disorder and decided to put themselves in a strong position.

A contingent of Hull officers destined for Liverpool to assist police there was held back and, although Union officials took every step to keep control of their men, the Chief Constable requested military assistance. He felt the dockers would soon be involved and told the Home Office, "their ranks contain many of the worst characters in Northern England and with no military help it would be impossible.... to preserve order in Hull."

Two battalions of the 6th Infantry Brigade were sent to the City for guard duty and they worked with fixed bayonets and 200 rounds of ball cartridge in each soldier's possession. The cruiser HMS *Attentive* and fisheries protection vessel HMS *Skipjack* both arrived in the Humber and efforts were made to strengthen police by recruiting special constables, but with little success.

Most surprising of all 37 army engineers arrived in Hull with a Maxim gun mounted on a truck. The Chief Constable is alleged to have specifically requested this weapon for possible use during the limited movement of trains.

There was strong condemnation of the steps taken, particularly the bringing in of the military, which was considered by the local Press to be highly provocative. However, the 24th August saw the resolution of the dispute and the military left Hull the next day. There was no violence, and maybe that was because of the show of strength!

MAJOR CRIME 1860 — 1914

With violence an everyday occurrence murder was no stranger to the town and the detectives in the force dealt with many notable cases.

Being a busy sea port also ensured a great number and variety of criminals visited the place and two of the most notorious cases involved Osmond Otto Brand and Frederick Bailey Deeming.

Brand was a 27 year old Hull man, skipper and proprietor of the *Rising Sun* fishing smack operating from the port. Among the crew was a 14 year old lad —William Papper. Also from Hull, he was described as a cheerful boy and obedient shipmate.

The boat left Hull for the North Sea fishing grounds on a bitterly cold 16th December 1881 with Brand, two seamen and three boys. The youngest was Papper and he was deputed to be cook. As they sailed it appears Papper passed by Brand and, innocently remarked that his sister knew the skipper. For some reason this apparently innocuous remark caused Brand to react with a campaign of unbelievable ferocity against the youngster. During the course of the voyage the skipper, and all the crew, except for the youngest apprentice, subjected Papper to the most savage treatment.

When the vessel reached Sunk Island, Brand began beating him with a ratline the end of which was weighted with pieces of iron. To justify this, Brand accused him of badly arranging the trawl nets so making the previous cast a failure. This succeeded in arousing the wrath of the rest of the crew who believed it would reduce their earnings.

Each day that passed was marked by fresh outbreaks of savagery, Brand apparently relishing the inventing of new tortures for the lad. He was continually starved, kept on deck night and day in the coldest weather, regularly drenched with sea water and was both beaten and jumped upon. When Brand himself tired of this enjoyment it seemed the rest of the crew were only too willing to take their turn in adding to the boy's misery.

On 29th December the culminating act of cruelty occurred. Papper was thrown into "the dill" and rendered unconscious. He was then dangled overboard in the hope the sea water would revive him for further maltreatment. The lad never recovered and when the ship docked the matter became known to

*Deeming, the Infamous
Hull Murderer.*

*William Pepper,
a young murder victim*
(Courtesy of Christopher Ketchell,
Local History Archives Unit, Hull
College of Further Education).

Hull Police. Brand was arrested and his case committed by the local magistrates to Leeds Assizes. On Tuesday 23rd May 1882 he was hanged at Armley Gaol for as cruel a case as can ever have been dealt with by Hull police.

Another notorious character with whom Hull's detectives were involved was Frederick Bailey Deeming. Not a native of the town, his first appearance in the area was when an apparently wealthy man named Lawson appeared in the Hull and Beverley areas. Said to be recently returned from Australia he let it be known he was a sheep and cattle rancher in that country. Not particularly good-looking he nevertheless dressed very well, spent a lot of money with Hull and Beverley traders and, stayed in the best hotels.

Before long he struck up an acquaintanceship with a young single lady —Nellie Matheson who lived with her widowed mother and sister in their house at New Walk, Beverley. In no time Mr. Lawson became a lodger in the Matheson house and, in the new year of 1890, was married to Nellie by the Reverend Canon Quirke at St. Mary's Church.

Prior to the marriage some local people had already become suspicious of Mr. Lawson and their suspicions increased when they learned he made secret journeys to Market Weighton to collect his mail! Unfortunately these apprehensions did not reach the Matheson household and the newly wedded Nellie arrived at Hull's Royal Station Hotel for her honeymoon. On their arrival Mr. Lawson left her in the bedroom and never returned.

In fact the man had become aware that police making enquiries concerning certain of his dealings in Hull were closing in on him. He had purchased considerable amounts of jewellery from Reynoldson of Whitefriargate and, the cheque he had issued had been found to be worthless. He travelled directly to Southampton and, it was later discovered, left the country on SS *Coleridge* bound for South America.

The distraught Nellie, on realising she had been deserted, returned home to Beverley where another, even greater, shock awaited her. A woman arrived who said she was a Mrs. Frederick Deeming from Birkenhead and that it was her husband who had purported to be Lawson and gone through a form of marriage with poor Nellie. They had a family and had recently moved to Birkenhead. She knew what had happened because her husband had told her! He had telephoned and asked her to deny being married to him if police arrived and asked questions. Outraged, she had immediately travelled to Beverley.

Detective sergeant Grassby, who was dealing with the case in Hull, made urgent enquiries and sent messages for the *Coleridge* to be intercepted at the first possible port. This transpired to be Montevideo in South America. Lawson was arrested there and, because no extradition treaty existed with Uruguay for bigamy the Hull fraud charges were used.

Sergeant Grassby travelled to Montevideo and spent a long trip escorting his prisoner home. During this time he found him to be an exceptionally difficult and vicious man to deal with.

Lawson, alias Deeming, received a sentence of nine months imprisonment for the Hull offence and was released from Hedon Road prison in July 1891.

Sometime later a major enquiry began in Liverpool when a woman and four children were found murdered at Dinham Villa, Rainhill. The house had been

A group of policemen 1910.

recently rented for the family by a man giving the name Albert Oliver Williams. It transpired Williams had been seen at the house one day when the mother had taken the baby out. Startled neighbours heard shrieks of terror which were apparently made when the three elder children were being viciously murdered. On the mother's return Williams felled her with a stick and slashed the tiny baby's throat while still in its mother's arms.

A great hue and cry was raised and it was discovered Williams had sailed from Hull to Antwerp in SS *Zebra*. It was thought he may have gone to Australia but enquiries were difficult to pursue satisfactorily at such a distance.

Then a number of coincidences took place. A Hull skipper went to have his photograph taken in Antwerp and saw a photograph of a man who had previously been a passenger on his ship to Belgium and who had called himself Lord Dunne. He had claimed to be a very wealthy self-made man from Australia, but most passengers were very suspicious of him. The skipper, intrigued by the circumstances, bought a copy of the photograph.

Deeming, alias Lawson, ever vain, had also had a photograph taken by Mr. Barry of Park Street, Hull to whom he introduced himself as an M.P. So suspicious was Mr. Barry he insisted on a deposit before taking the photo!

Eventually the photographs and the man using the names Williams and Lawson were tied up as one and the same person, but little progress was made in locating him until the most amazing coincidence of all occurred.

Harry Webster, the Governor of Hull Prison, retired. His doctors recommended it would be beneficial to his health if he moved to Australia to live. When in Melbourne he was reading about a murder in that city and was struck by the description of the man in custody. He also thought the

91

circumstances of the murder were very similar to the Rainhill case which had been heavily publicised prior to his leaving England. After some debate with himself he went to see the Chief Constable of Melbourne and subsequently identified the man in custody as Lawson who had been in prison in Hull for nine months.

Deeming, alias Lawson, alias Williams, alias Lord Dunne, was hanged at Melbourne for the murder of his Australian wife and admitted the Rainhill murders. It subsequently transpired that, at the time, yet another girl was on her way to Australia to marry him and he had already dug her grave under the kitchen hearthstone in Melbourne! Nellie Matheson of Beverley had been a very lucky young lady!

Surprisingly quite a few long voyages were undertaken by Hull policemen to extradite fugitives and return them to the city for trial. A bankrupt was brought back from Spain by Inspector Graham, but longest trip of all — Inspector Trafford travelled to Fiji to collect Octavius Ward for defrauding a High Street firm of a large sum of money by forged instruments. Ward was sentenced to twenty years hard labour.

CHAPTER 5

FROM 1914 to 1939

The Great War 1914-18

On 4th August 1914 Inspector Alfred Goodrum entered in his neat and concise daily journal:-

> *"I attended Police Court re Walker, Oxford Street, allowing offensive matter to run from their premises – fined 40/- including costs. Mr. Pym prosecuted. Proceedings taken under Town Police Clauses Act. Mr. Harker said a heavier penalty could have been inflicted under the Public Health Act.*
> *All reservists called out this date.*
> *War declared against Germany!"*

This last laconic line for the day marked the final end of an era not only for the country but for its police forces. It saw the start of a period of increasing work and great changes brought about by the development of technology in transport and other fields.

The wave of patriotic fervour which immediately swept the country did not leave Hull's police force unscathed and many of the younger men volunteered for the army. To replace them older men were recruited where possible, recently retired officers were recalled and a large number of special constables were sworn in. Little leave was given or expected and two years after the outbreak, a memorandum was issued declaring that any man who had recived no leave by June 30th 1916 would be allowed to take one day's special leave before the end of that year!

An extra duty that fell to police with the onset of war was the checking and general control of aliens in the city. As a port Hull not only had a sizeable resident population of foreigners but a constant number of ships visiting with foreign crews. Fear of spies and subversives operating in the area to steal secrets and undermine morale was ever present.

In an effort to stop rumours spreading, sometimes by persons who should have known better, plain-clothes police were ordered to travel on trams to listen in on casual conversations. They would also "occasionally be allowed to enter and remain in licensed premises. When doing so they should only drink non-intoxicating liquor!"

So obsessed did the authorities become about public morale that a memorandum issued by the Chief Constable to the force in 1917 directed that:-

> *"Police must control newsboys from shouting exaggerated descriptions of news. For example the loss of a mercantile cruiser was shouted as British Naval Disaster! In another case a boy shouted 'Revoulution in German Army' with no reason at all. If this is suspected by officers off*

The first motor car in Hull police force 1914.

Zeppelin air-raid damage in Hull, 1914-18 War.

*duty and in plain clothes they should buy a paper and take the boy's
name. The cost of the paper will be refunded."*

Another effect of the war was the sudden importance and spread of motor
vehicles. When war broke out police checked on all known owners of these still
quite rare contraptions in the Hull area, to ascertain if they would be available
for commandeering in case of invasion. As motor fuel became scarcer a regular
function for police became the mounting of road checks to enforce the 'Motor
Spirit Regulations'.

Both food and other materials began to be in increasingly short supply and
policemen were encouraged to be careful with cleaning and writing materials,
particularly ink! As an incentive to grow more food, in 1917 the watch
committee generously agreed that, "men who have allotments could have their
annual leave in not more than 2 days at a time for the purpose of cultivating
same".

Also, because they were working a constant seven-day week and, as an
exceptional concession, the period granted for refreshments was increased
from twenty to thirty minutes per shift. Superintendents directed the places
where the food could be taken and night men could only rest at a place where
there was a 'phone.

One completely revolutionary change came in 1917 when Miss Sandilands
became the first woman appointed to the force as a Woman Police Assistant.
Although only part-time, the force was encouraged to use her for statement
taking and if she was required when off duty, arrangements had been made for
her neighbour, Mr. Parker, who had a telephone, to take messages for her.

Another sign of things to come was the order that men would be granted
1/- extra per month if they provided themselves with an electric lamp in place of
the existing issue of oil lamps. They were responsible for ensuring it was fully
charged before each shift.

The most traumatic moments of the First World War both for the
population and police of Hull were the rather sporadic but quite frightening
attacks by Zeppelin airships between 1915 and 1917. Usually the city was
attacked either in error or because the craft was unable to reach its designated
target. Although few air-raid precautions or defences were in place, Tom
Arksey working at the central police station, was one of the officers to have
'buzzers' fitted to his home. These were to warn of impending attacks and recall
men to the station. His daughter still recalls the neighbours in De La Pole
Avenue congregating anxiously outside their house waiting to hear 'if the
buzzers had gone'.

Attacks in June 1915 caused quite a number of deaths and injuries as well as
considerable damage. People were terrified and one witness saw two prostitutes
on their knees in King Edward Street praying for deliverance. Infuriatingly
there appeared to be a complete lack of opposition to the airships which could
be clearly seen by the citizens below. They hovered brazenly overhead and
when a light showed in the craft people below knew the bomb doors had
opened and death and destruction was on its way.

So violent was the reaction that mobs took to the streets attacking anything
they knew, or thought, to be German. Shops such as Kress and Wagner were

*Chief Superintendent Tom Arksey
Hull Police. c.1900.*
(Courtesy of Phyllis Pybus).

*H.M. Queen Mary visiting
Newland School 1917.*
(Courtesy Hull Daily Mail).

attacked simply on the basis of their names. Police had considerable difficulty in controlling these disturbances and on one occasion military support had to be enlisted.

The air attacks stopped in 1917 and, eventually the war was ended and those police who survived returned to their jobs, some of them heroes. One particular hero, John Cunningham, who won the Victoria Cross for his valour on the western front actually joined Hull police on demobilisation for a short time.

Beginning of Change

Attempts to form a national police union in association with other trades unions of the time, were started well before 1914 and men were forbidden to join it. Mainly centred on London it gradually attracted more and more men in the provinces as grievances grew about pay and conditions of work. Pay scales were not standard nationally and many police families were virtually on the bread line and living on wages equivalent to the labouring classes. Matters came to a head in London in 1918, at the height of the war, when police went on strike. It was ended after a hurried and muddled agreement by the Government who however remained adamant that they would not officially recognise a police union. They were particularly concerned lest such a move should cause unrest among the troops at the front.

Discontent continued to simmer in 1919 and in Hull the authorities tacitly acknowledged the existence of the Union, which by now had members in the city, when in January they allowed publication of union notices in the force. This may have been the reason no trouble erupted there, when elsewhere in the country a total of 2,364 men from seven forces responded to a new strike call. The strikers were summarily dismissed and never reinstated.

Another reason why Hull and the bulk of the country's police failed to support the strike was the existence of a Royal Commission known later as 'The Desborough Committee'. Hastily established by the Government in March 1919 it was to review pay and conditions of police nationally. At the time of the strike the Government had already announced its acceptance of the Committee's hurried first recommendation that police pay should be standardised nationally with a constable's wage being raised immediately to £3. 10s per week. In Hull this meant a rise of almost 200% and took police from a position near the bottom of the pay league to the level of lower middle classes.

More was to come with the final report of the committee which recommended among other things that there should be standardisation of pay, allowances, leave, hours of duty and other conditions of service. Rent-free accommodation or an allowance in lieu was also proposed. It meant a constable would progress to £4. 10s per week at maximum with two further long-service increments available to encourage the mature man to stay in the service. The constable had been moved in one giant step into the category of the semi-professional man.

A national Police Federation was established with a branch in each force, half the cost of each force's total expenditure was to be met by the Exchequer, not just half the cost of pay and clothing as previously and, importantly for Hull, power of appointment, promotion, and discipline was transferred from the watch committee to Chief Constables. In practice this did little to affect the influence the committee still wielded in such matters in the city, dependent on the relationship between them and their Chief Constable at any given time.

While all these dramatic changes had an effect on policemen's personal lives they did little to change the very mundane and often boring job of being on the beat. The gradual increase in police transport and the growth of wireless communications affected the individual's role but little.

One thing that did improve was training. Everyone now had three months rudimentary instruction by a part-time instructor at the Central Police Station supplemented by periods at Londesborough Barracks for drill and Beverley Road swimming baths for life saving, before being sent on the beat. During the 1920s a long-serving force training instructor was the tough ex-swimming champion, Sergeant Herbert Simpson.

By the 1930s training had progressed further with new entrants being recruited in groups of fifteen at a time so forming a class for 12 weeks under a permanent instructor. Personal assessments were made by weekly examinations set and marked by the Chief Constable!

One effect of the war had been to force police to take motor vehicles seriously as a form of transport. Although it had made an appearance as the 'horseless carriage' in the last decade of the nineteenth century, vehicles generally only moved at the pace of a walking horse at its slowest and a trotting horse at its fastest. There had been no great need for fast transport for police as a constable riding one of the "new fangled safety bicycles" was able to keep pace with, or even exceed, the speed of the majority of vehicles. The criminal classes had not yet turned to the motor car and, as far as Hull police were concerned, they were merely a nuisance which caused horses to bolt!

On the other hand, a constable who arrested a prisoner still had to walk him, how ever violent he was, to the nearest Station. This often meant a hazardous journey of up to two miles. If the prisoner was drunk and incapable of walking the constable was permitted to borrow a two-wheeled handcart from a builder and wheel the arrested man to the station. There were no ambulances, but at each station and at a few other places there were light two-wheeled carts with stretchers attached. If anyone was injured in the city, a constable would set off with his cart and eventually the patient would arrive at hospital!

In 1915 it was finally decided a more rapid form of transport was required for police and the watch committee purchased a motor car. This first vehicle, a Wolseley tourer with a 'Surrey' type canopy, was a great novelty but not put to any meaningful use. Senior officers were the main users and on ceremonial occasions it would be turned out dressed overall!

The heightened interest in motor vehicles after 1918 resulted in Hull police replacing the 1915 model for a slightly more up-to-date machine. In a general order issued to the force in September 1925 the Chief Constable refers to "the car",

"A motor car (KH1525) has recently been purchased for use exclusively by police and will be available for police purposes other than the conveyance of prisoners and street accidents. It will be garaged at the Fire Station. Superintendents will please see that no

*Inspector Gall,
Hull City c.1920*
(Courtesy Mr. Gall,
son of above).

Hull Police Charity 'Bigaphone Band' used to raise money for good causes. 1913.

H.M. Inspector of Constabulary visits the mounted branch of Hull City Police, c.1930.

The first motor road patrol, 1931.

unnecessary use of the car is made. A green light showing to the front will be fitted in the centre of the car and will be shown only when the duty on which it is employed is urgent"

Meanwhile the handcart ambulances were still in use until a motor ambulance was presented to the force by a local philanthropist in 1923.

Two additional cars and three motor cycles were purchased in following years but, it was an irresistable bait for the Hull Authority when, in 1931 the Home Office offered to fund the whole cost of establishing road patrols. The force purchased three extra Brough Superior motor cycle combinations. The machines, with powerful 800 cc engines first made their appearance on the city streets in 1931 and were known in police circles as 'R.F.G. patrols' as they were maintained from the road fund grant.

It was not until the Road Traffic Act was passed in 1933 that the force really entered the motorised age with the formation of the force Mechanical Transport Department. In no time the new unit was staffed by an Inspector and 30 constables with four cars, two vans, two ambulances and three motor cycles.

The next major step forward was when radio became available in 1942 so allowing much improved control and deployment of the vehicles. In the first years some criminals assumed they had been very unlucky to have been stumbled upon by police when in fact they had been directed to the scene by the new 'wireless'.

As the department grew it began to take on other duties associated with traffic, one such role being the registration and licensing of taxi-cabs operating in the city.

However, despite the increasing mechanisation and romance for the few who were transferred to the traffic department, the work of the ordinary patrolman was virtually unchanged. Many worked the same beats for years and became familiar, perhaps sometimes too familiar, with everyone in their area. Shifts remained the same with the regular monthly stint of night duty. Even with the introduction of the new police box system, which will be described later, the life of the beatman remained somewhat humdrum.

City shops remained open daily until 9 pm and Saturday evenings were particuarly busy for policemen. There were crowds of shoppers to keep an eye on, twenty or thirty unofficial handcart salesmen in the Market Place area to keep on the move and, plenty of drunks, which all made the late shift an interesting one. Pubs turned out at 10 pm and three pairs of constables would always be present to clear the Square after 11 pm when the last tram had left.

Shopbreakers were numerous and often caught on premises by patrolling night-duty constables. Whistles were seldom, if ever, used to summon assistance. If help was required a few taps on the kerb with one's truncheon brought rapid response to surround a building. P.C. Henry Llewellyn Bateman recalls in his diary how he once discovered two men in a Whitefriargate shop, armed with a sawn off shotgun and how the truncheon tapping brought rapid reinforcements to his aid.

Day shifts could be full of unexpected incidents but the routine jobs were always there. Relieving the pointsman on one of the many traffic points in the

Constable Henry Llewellyn Bateman on point duty at Jameson St. corner after a May snowstorm – pre 1934.
(Courtesy Mr. Bateman of Beverley).

Point duty at Victoria Square, Hull, c.1950.

102

city, escorting children across roads at particularly busy spots, and, as always, having to deal with the regular cases of violent behaviour.

One such case, coincidentally involving the same P.C. Henry Llewellyn Bateman was reported in the *Hull Daily Mail* of 8th January 1938.

> *"This is the fourth assault on police in seven days, all in the same locality with three actually in the same street, Adelaide Street", said Inspector Huxley at Hull police court, when Harry Butcher, 28 years, of Frederick Terrace, Strickland Street, was sent to prison for thirty days.*

The report went on to describe the violent scenes when Butcher attacked the officer who was trying to take a woman into custody. So savage and persistent was the attack the officer had been forced to resort to his truncheon to defend himself.

Some policemen managed to escape from the beat by being transferred to the plain-clothes department. By day their function was to investigate cases of missing persons and execute warrants. On the evening and early night shifts they concentrated on the sleazy problems of vice, with the ever-present prostitutes and brothels.

By the time the centenary of Hull's new police had arrived in 1936, four hundred and thirty four policemen were working in the city, using a new police box system, getting well paid and being allowed three weeks annual leave a year as well as one rest day every week. The force had increased five fold in numbers and the town had become a city with its population trebled, its geographical area quadrupled and, the length of streets to be patrolled increased out of all recognition.

Presentation by Chief Supt. and Deputy-Chief Constable Crack to Det. Sgt. Howgate on his retirement in 1933. Taken in the recreation room of Alfred Gelder St. Police Station. D/Supt. James Smith (later Assistant Chief Constable) in centre.

Centenary 1936.

104

The centenary was marked by a massive parade. A photograph of the whole force and a small centenary booklet outlining the force's history were published.

The General Strike 1926

When in 1926 the country was being threatened with a general strike, it became obvious the fairly recent Desborough awards would prevent any possibility of the police service being involved.

In Hull, where the Chief Constable, Captain Woods, was too ill to take charge of arrangements, Deputy-Chief Constable Howden advised the watch committee that history suggested the city could well become one of the national flash points in the dispute and, as a precaution, messages were sent to neighbouring forces to arrange for reinforcements if necessary. Trouble was expected to centre on the docks, but on this occasion transport and public utilities were also likely to be involved.

On 3rd May, Mr. Howden announced the first police reserve had been mobilised and given some hastily arranged extra training and that motor coaches were being requisitioned, one for each police station, to provide transport for police. In answer to queries he indicated that military assistance would only be enlisted as a last resort.

When the stike started the next day the centre of the city was crowded with people volunteering their services to the Voluntary Services Committee in the city hall. Extra police began to arrive and the cruiser, HMS *Enterprise* berthed in King George dock.

In the event, the first few days passed peacefully with volunteers cheerfully supporting the city's services where necessary. However it proved to be the calm before the storm and as the week-end approached trouble began to break out.

On Friday, 'rowdy youths', as they were dubbed by the Press, began to jeer and taunt people queueing to volunteer at the city hall and trouble soon broke out. A policeman was assaulted and a number of fierce baton charges were made by both foot and mounted policemen. Some forty people, including one policeman, were later treated at the Infirmary for injuries. Crowds reassembled in the city square during the evening and missiles began to fly. Shop windows were smashed and looting occurred. More police baton charges were necessary to clear the streets.

The disturbances continued on the Saturday, involving according to the *Hull Daily Mail*, "foolish hooligans, chiefly irresponsible youths in their teens or early twenties". Gangs went on the rampage, smashing windows and looting in the Wincolmlee district and again police were forced to resort to baton charges. A large crowd of men armed with pit-props and other weapons faced police in Dock Street and Grimston Street. Fortunately a resolute baton charge quickly removed their stomach for a fight and once more the streets were cleared. Trouble was widespread throughout the day with window smashing and looting reported in Midland Street, Porter Street and Anlaby Road. The courts acted swiftly and firmly with perpetrators being given, by and large, salutory sentences of hard labour.

On the Sunday it appeared the worst was over, calm returned to the streets and buses ran once more, albeit with wire netting covering the windows. The strike itself was beginning to fizzle out and early the following week a settlement was reached. It had been a violent few days which police had coped with well by firm and resolute action. No doubt because of its short duration, the National Strike, although dramatic in its way, had caused fewer problems for Hull police force than some of the similar situations faced in earlier years.

Other industrial disputes in 1926 did not directly affect Hull itself and this was the case with the coal strike in October. Police in the coal-producing areas became hard pressed to maintain law and order and the Chief Constable of the county of Durham, Sir George Morley, who had been Chief Constable of Hull during the 1911 troubles, now asked his old force for assistance under the 'Mutual Aid Agreement'.

The collieries in Durham were, for the most part, situated in village areas away from large centres of population and in normal times were sparsely policed. Serious pockets of unrest and civil disobedience were now centred on these colliery 'villages'.

It was alleged at the time that members of the local forces who lived alongside the miners and knew the dreadful conditions in which they worked were, to a considerable extent, in sympathy with them and therefore somewhat lax in the application of the law.

Two contingents of 28 men each were despatched from Hull on 27th October. One party under Inspector Fanthorpe went to Chopwell, the other under Superintendent Dewen, to Consett. On arrival they were billeted in huts and private houses and established a headquarters in suitable public buildings. The Chopwell contingent, rather provocatively, used the Miners' Executive Club.

Chopwell was a large village popularly known as 'Little Moscow' because of the large number of communist sympathisers there and the main task facing the Hull policemen when they arrived was to restore law and order and escort non-striking miners to work. For the latter task large canvas topped lorries, soon to become known as 'covered wagons', were used.

The policemen chosen to go from Hull were the tallest, fittest and youngest men the Chief Constable could muster and the villagers soon spread the rumour that they were in fact Guardsmen 'dressed as polis', sent especially by the Government to break the strike. The Hull uniform lent credence to this theory with the 'Lancer' pattern greatcoats with a double row of gleaming buttons and helmets with polished chinstraps, plates and apex. This contrasted particularly with the local constabulary's flat caps and black buttons. The local village policemen were temporarily transferred elsewhere.

Initially, as was to be expected, the local population were hostile towards the newcomers and a few skirmishes, with police baton charges, took place before control was secured. Usually, when police moved in the cry went up in broad Geordie, "Ay up mon, 'ere's yon big polis wi' ye knobs".

Once control was established things settled down and the locals seemed to realise that the policemen, while determined to enforce the law, were impartial and friendly. Before long genuine friendships were being formed without

Hull police helmets – dress helmet on right with metal chin strap and ornate top piece.

Hull police band c.1937.

familiarity and with mutual respect on both sides. Such was the confidence that sprang up between them several constables became regular visitors to miners' homes. Some also took the opportunity, in off duty-time, to visit and descend the pits.

In 1966, ex- Inspector Duncan McRae, recalling his stay at Chopwell forty years previously as a constable, said,

> *"I found the Durham miners on the whole to be kindly, honest, hardworking people with a great sense of humour. When we marched out of the village at the end of our six week stay, we were cheered. We had made many friends. During the time we were there, I had served up to me, some of the finest meals I have ever had!"*

Stations & Police Boxes

As the 1920s drew to a close, Thomas Howden, the Chief Constable, realised policing arrangements for the city required a major re-appraisal. The city was continuing to expand into outlying areas, stations were becoming old and in need of modernisation and traffic was increasing and required more men for point-duty. In addition to suggesting extra traffic lights should be installed, he also looked at developments taking place elsewhere which were leading the way in the more efficient use of resources. Having studied in particular the methods being used in Sheffield, a leader in new policing methods, in February 1930 he submitted proposals to the watch committee, which not only set out his plans but also gave a very clear picture of policing methods and attitudes in the city of Hull in the early 1930s. An edited version of his report is now reproduced:

"Chief Constable's Office,
Hull, February, 1930.

To the Chairman and Members of the Watch Committee,
"Gentlemen,

I wish to place before you recommendations with a view to a change being made in the existing police organisation of this city, and to offer as an alternative a redistribution of the strength based on the Police Box System."

The report continued by explaining that beat patrolling methods had remained unchanged for years. Policemen reported for duty to their stations and walked to their beats. Half hour refreshment breaks had been granted some ten years ago, these refreshments being taken back at the stations. In the case of the beats farthest away, it could take an officer half an hour to get to and from his beat and time lost in this manner, at the beginning and end of shifts and at refreshment time, could result in the beat being unmanned for 15% of the day.

To ensure an officer could be contacted in an emergency he had to conform to well established patrol patterns. Not only could criminals use their knowledge of a beatman's route to avoid capture, it was still necessary for a messenger to be sent to contact an officer if he was wanted. The report went on,

"It has often been said a policeman is never available when he is most urgently needed. The reason is not difficult to find. Some beats are so large it takes a constable fully two hours to walk round them, consequently when a member of the public, who naturally does not know the method of working beats, wishes to call a policeman to the scene of some disturbance or accident, he had a fairly hopeless task in finding him..... How much more quickly a policeman could be brought to the scene by simply telephoning to Headquarters from a neighbouring police box, the position of which would naturally be known to all residents in the neighbourhood."

Public telephones said the Chief Constable were not only few and far between in the city but, more importantly, when members of the force needed to contact Headquarters and speak on police business it was imperative they should not be overheard by the public. Criminals were moving about more quickly than in the past, they were even sometimes using motor vehicles and it was imperative a system of rapid passing of messages was available in the force.

Then there was the problem of conveying prisoners to the station. "....during the year 1929, there were 118 prisoners conveyed to the police station in public vehicles at a cost of £14 3s 6d. During that period, however, there were no fewer than 1,367 persons arrested. Had they all be conveyed in a similar manner the cost would have been approximately £165."

The Chief Constable then went on to set out his proposals for a new arrangement to overcome the deficiencies he had outlined. The new scheme was known as the Police Box System. "It has been adopted by many cities through the country with complete success. This system consists of a box or boxes being placed on each beat in the city. Every box will be fitted with a telephone connected to Headquarters or branch stations."

The boxes would act as an operational centre for each beat with officers reporting on and off duty there, taking refreshments in them and using them as administrative and information centres. All recent circulars on crime, criminals and other matters of importance would be available in the boxes. Most important of all would be the communications link for both beatman and the public to contact the local station. If the officer was wanted the telephone would operate a blue lamp on top of the box until the policeman answered it.

Public would not only have access to a telephone fitted in the outside wall of the box but also to first aid supplies. In addition to calling police, any other emergency service was available by phoning from the box.

Turning to the strength of the force Mr. Howden reported that the authorised strength was "...at present 472, but for reasons of economy we have only recruited up to 466 of which 33 form the fire brigade, leaving only 433 for police duty. Owing to the increased amount of work which has been thrown on police in recent years, this number is inadequate. In September 1929 there were 11,500 motor vehicles licensed in this city as against 2,389 in September 1919, or nearly five times as many. The number of inhabited houses in 1919 was 66,110 compared with 72,410 in 1928. The population was 277,991 in 1911 and 287,150 in 1921."

The report continued by referring to a further anticipated increase in the size of the city which would necessitate an additional 16 constables at an annual cost of £3,384 16s whereas if the police box system was introduced bigger beats could be devised and no increase would be necessary in police strength.

Referring to the existing police stations at Alfred Gelder Street, Gordon

Street, Crowle Street, Wincolmlee and Norfolk Street, the Chief Constable said the two last-named were completely out of date and should be abandoned. By slightly enlarging the accommodation at Gordon and Crowle Streets, those two stations, together with the central station, would be sufficient for the city with the new boxes.

The estimated costs of all the recommendations, including provision of some extra motor vehicles to service the new boxes was as follows:

		£	s	d
Cost of Installation	. . . .	1783	1	6
Total annual charges of system	. . . .	916	15	0
Purchase of motor vehicles	. . . .	1200	0	0
Total annual charges of motor vehicles	. . . .	373	17	6
Alterations to police stations	. . . .	5200	0	0

A total of 48 locations where police boxes should be sited throughout the city were recommended and having heard the report with considerable interest Alderman Mell proposed it be adopted forthwith. He was seconded by Councillor Wheeldon and the motion was carried and the report forwarded to the Home Office for approval. No objections were anticipated from Government.

Over the next few years the new boxes were built throughout the city, and at a stroke both the efficiency and working conditions of the police improved immeasurably. The small branch stations at Wincolmlee and Norfolk Street were abandoned, the latter being reactivated in 1939 but, only for use as an air-raid precautions centre.

A proper place to take refreshments on the beat, with a sink, running water and kettle available made a dramatic change in the life of a beatman, but such privileges were still begrudged by some senior policemen of the old school. Refreshment time was still quite a short break and many a Sergeant or Inspector was to be found idling outside a box to catch anyone taking a minute extra!

In conjunction with the expansion of the city and the building of police boxes, in 1936 pedal-cycle beats were instituted on the city outskirts.

At the time of the outbreak of war in 1939 there were 60 boxes and 6 police pillars in the city. Unfortunately when the air-raids began the boxes were found to be particularly susceptible to damage, so much so the committee had to take action. In 1941 urgent instructions were issued to replace thirty boxes with brick buildings, six of which were to be large, the others of slightly smaller size.

Meanwhile, the proliferation of police boxes and the improvements in Crowle and Gordon Street stations allowed thoughts to turn to the headquarters in Alfred Gelder Street, or "Parliament Street" as the building was still widely known. Unfortunately while reasonably laid out, as so often happened, it had been planned only with the needs of the day it was built in mind. By 1930 overcrowding was becoming unbearable and departments were being moved to premises elsewhere in the city. The 'Mechanical Transport Department' was moved into a former banana warehouse on the side of the former Queen's Dock. By 1937 plans had been drawn up for a new central headquarters and the go-ahead was given later that year for building to commence, a mere 30 years after opening Alfred Gelder Street!

Even before work started on the new site at Queens Gardens the old premises were sold to Littlewoods stores with a proviso they would obtain possession when the new building was completed, but in any case not later than 1940. The outbreak of war saw the compulsory cessation of all new building work when the new headquarters was a tangle of barest steel girders. It was agreed police could stay in the old building as tenants at a 'peppercorn' rent. No-one could foresee that this situation was to last for eighteen years!

During one wartime air-raid the civil defence control centre in the city was badly damaged by a parachute mine. It was impossible to repair and new premises were an urgent requirement. The girders of the abandoned new police headquarters site stood over an excavation intended for a basement and sub-basement for the new building. It was requisitioned and in no time had been heavily fortified to form a new civil defence control. Meanwhile the city's police force, expanding to meet the calls of the emergency, overflowed into every conceivable type of building throughout the city.

Hull Eastern Division Tug of War team 1937. A. Smith, G. Tyson, H. W. Roughton (Sec.) F. Allerston, C. F. Piggott, J. S. Christopher, A. Widdas, Supt. J. A. Armitage, A. Bean.

Members of Western Division (Gordon St.) c.1940.

CHAPTER 6

THE FINAL DECADES

The 1939-45 War

The outbreak of the Second World War, while not exactly unexpected, seemed to catch Hull City Police somewhat unprepared judging by the description of ex-Sergeant Lawrie Harvey. Not having been involved with those officers who had previously been on twelve hour shifts assisting with the evacuation of children, he had simply been told, in the event of war being declared, everyone should report immediately to central police station, in full uniform.

Asleep after his night-duty, he was awakened by his landlady on 3rd September with the news of Neville Chamberlain's announcement and he staggered sleepily down to Alfred Gelder Street. The whole force was there amid a scene of complete confusion! It was obvious no-one had the slightest idea what should be done next. Men were lined up and checked and rechecked by busy Inspectors. There was considerable noise and speculation was rife until, frustration visibly increasing, the day ended in anti-climax when at 5 pm everyone was dismissed and told to resume normal duties.

A very tired young policeman returned to his night duty only to be faced with a considerable dilemma when the air raid warning sounded. Vaguely recalling his instructions he commenced running through the streets of his beat blowing vigorously on his whistle until, virtually out of breath, he met the constable on the next beat. Veteran of World War 1, Chalky White said calmly, "Steady, steady lad — don't panic!" Taken aback by this placid figure the gasping young Harvey panted, "But what are we supposed to do?" "Just let me think a while," Chalky replied, scratching his chin reflectively. After musing for a moment or two he said, "Look, we'll go down the side of that bank and put our backs against the strongest wall in the building — the one with the night safe —and we'll have one of *your* fags!!" In fact no raid took place — they were to come later with a vengeance.

All police recruiting stopped at the outbreak of war and, by the end of 1940, all men under thirty years of age in the force had been drafted into the Armed Forces. Initially they were replaced by the First Police Reserve, a body of men half way between special and regular constables who, unlike the specials, were paid to be on the Reserve. Retired policemen were encouraged to rejoin and, as demands grew, a new force of people over conscription age became the Police War Reserve. Despite receiving extremely rudimentary training they did much valiant work and suffered casualties during the worst of the war. By 1943 Hull had over 800 regular and reserve police working in the city.

Invasion was a very real threat, particularly for East Coast areas, in the early years of the war and the problems of maintaining communications in such an eventuality resulted in an unusual operation being mounted by police in Hull.

With the authority of the counter-intelligence service (M.I.5) a carrier pigeon service was set up between Hull, Beverley, Goole and Leeds. Tom Fowles, a well-known Hull pigeon fancier, from Gillshill Road was recruited as a War Reserve policeman to run the enterprise.

Birds were loaned to the force by local fanciers and initially operating from their owners' homes they were eventually kept in a specially made loft in a room in the force aliens' office on the corner of Quay Street near Hull Guildhall.

The existence of the unit remained a closely-guarded secret until well after the war although the enterprise only remained in existence for the first three or four years of the war.

At the outset all stations had been sandbagged and made centres for air-raid precaution work. Men were put on 12 hour shifts with no rest days and, in addition, were required to turn out at any hour, even if off duty, when an alert sounded. After the first six months it became obvious they were not going to cope with such a strenuous routine and the arrangements were modified except during the period of heaviest raids.

The major air attacks on the city were in 1941 and police spotters plotted bomb bursts from a number of observation points in the city. The points were fitted with compasses and telephone and by calcuiating the bearings from the different posts the approximate location of explosions could be decided.

One such point was on top of a tower at the University where, initially, the unfortunate police spotter was required to stand in a highly exposed position with death and destruction falling all round him. After many complaints protection was provided on the tower.

The major function of policemen was to act as incident officers at each bomb site and when an explosion or fire was reported they would attend, mark the scene with a blue paraffin lamp and decide what services were required that were not already in attendance. They also kept a log of comings and goings at the scene, recovery of dead and injured and any other relevant details of the incident.

In 1941 the B.B.C. news constantly reported air raids on a 'north each coast town' as some of the heaviest raids experienced in the war were directed at Hull. Police worked night and day to maintain a service for the city and this was not without tragic losses. Constable Craven was driving the Assistant-Chief Constable, James Smith, to duty after one alert when their car was hit by shrapnel. Badly wounded himself, Craven saw his passenger was also seriously hit and struggled to drive to hospital. On arrival it was found Mr. Smith had died.

Constable 'Jock' Bell was sent to one incident in Farraday Street and full of apprehension he hurried to the scene, only to find his worst fears confirmed. It was his own house that had been hit and his wife killed.

There were very many lucky escapes. Constable Bucken was at North Bridge when his tin hat was completely flattened like a pancake by a vicious explosion. He survived but his face remained heavily pockmarked for the rest of his life.

Raids would continue for hours and one officer recalls what he considers to have been the worst night of his life. It was in 1941 and the alert went early as he was on duty at Gordon Street. Requested to go to the city centre to help the hard

First meeting of Hull Police Choir at Alfred Gelder St. formed at the height of the War c.1941.

Police continue their work after the Blitz in 1941
(Courtesy Hull Daily Mail).

pressed men there, he had to walk through the streets as bombs were falling all around. Finally assigned to help in King Edward Street, he found hoses everywhere as fires burned on all sides. Suddenly a heavy explosion indicated a very close hit and it was discovered the Prudential Building had been set on fire. Screams could be heard coming from the basement where, it was discovered, a large number of young girls from the Women's Royal Naval Service had been sleeping. Frantic efforts to reach them were driven back by the intense heat from the oil bomb involved. Everyone in the building perished and so serious was the incident considered that an Inspector took over as incident officer.

Many were the acts of bravery by Hull's policemen during the terrible ordeal, most of them unreported and unrecorded. An example of some of those which were remembered appear in the book about Hull's ordeal. *A North East Coast Town.*

> *"Once a constable burrowed on his stomach for four hours, making a tunnel through which the rescue of a woman was effected. On another occasion a Sergeant, seeking missing people, found eight children sheltering in a gas cupboard in their night attire. Their ages ran from three months to 16 years. He retrieved their clothing, dressed them and handed them over to others for safe keeping while he went on with another job. A young constable, having extinguished some incendiary bombs, was resuming his normal patrol when a stick of explosive fell nearby. He was knocked unconscious, had both his jaws broken, was blinded for three weeks, had three fingers and a wrist fractured and when in hospital, had a hundred stitches in his face and body. Yet he was on duty again in six months!*
>
> *A regular constable, with the assistance of a special constable, rescued five people from some vaults, though the roof was continually sagging and debris had to be scraped away. It took them four hours working in confined space with only a torch for light. They were in great danger of being buried but they made the rescue!"*

Yet, despite everything and, perhaps in order to save their sanity, there was often humour, even in the midst of tragedy. It caused much hilarity when War Reserve constable Simpson reported back in the police car having been to an incident in a very heavy air-raid. The car had been damaged by shrapnel on the way back but Simpson, delighted to be in one piece, reported the damage to his Chief Inspector. That worthy's reaction was a laconic, "Just try and be more careful in future, Simpson!"

Many police forces were working under great pressure during the air-raids and in recalling the stresses involved, Home Office Under-Secretary, Tom Critchley, in his *History of the Police in England and Wales* says,

> *"A single example must suffice to recall its magnitude: the city of Hull suffered 73 attacks in which over 1000 people were killed and 100,000 rendered homeless. Here and everywhere the police behaved superbly. Their staunch defiance of danger and unfailing good humour steadied, stiffened and finally rallied public morale during these critical months."*

Inspection of force at end of Second World War – August 1945 with new Chief Constable Sidney Lawrence.

In February 1942, Winston Churchill broadcast a tribute to the civil defence services and said,

> *"If I mention only one of them tonight, namely the police – it is because many tributes have been paid already to the others. But the police have been in it everywhere, all the time. And, as a working woman wrote to me in a letter, 'what gentlemen they are!'"*

The end of the war saw men returning to the force and many resigned soon afterwards, not being able to readjust to another life of discipline and conflict so soon.

The following members failed to return:

Assistant Chief Constable J. Smith — killed in air raid.
Constable 382 Davies — killed in air raid 1941.
Fireman 576 Richardson — killed in air raid 1941.
Fireman 506 Hewitt — killed in air raid 1941.
Constable 127 Garton — killed in air raid 1941.
Constable 81 Needley — killed in air raid 1941.
Fireman 587 Best — killed in air raid 1941.
Constable 128 Robinson — killed in air raid 1941.
Tel. Op. Robinson — killed in air raid 1941.
Constable 108 Stapley — killed on active service 1942.
Constable 390 Lister — killed on active service 1943.
Constable 397 Stothard — killed on active service 1944.
Constable 7 Owen — killed on naval operations 1944.
Constable 281 Hewitt — killed on active service.

Tel. Op. Croom — killed on active service 1944.
Constable 405 Dixon — killed on active service 1945.
Constable 211 Lockey — killed on active service 1945.
Tel. Op. Bateman — killed on active service 1945.
Tel. Op. Frank — killed on active service 1944.
War Reserve Hembrough — killed on active service 1943.
War Reserve Worley — killed on active service 1944.

After the 1939-45 War

The last thirty years of Hull's own police force were as eventful in their way as the McManus years at the beginning. They started in an atmosphere of great uncertainty, the war had just ended, ideas and aspirations of members of the force had changed, and there were the problems associated with Thomas Wells the Chief Constable. There was also an unpleasant and lingering whiff of corruption in the city generally and the police force in particular. All this had an adverse effect on morale in the force and was further exacerbated by the level of police pay which, once again, had fallen below other groups. Many men returning from comparatively senior ranks in the armed services were not content to accept things as they were.

It was also the beginning of a period of great change for police and for the city which was beginning to rebuild. Modern technology was about to make its impact on the service and officers needed adequate training to cope with the vastly increasing complexity of their work.

In 1946 basic recruit training was removed from the force and all new entrants were sent to a district training centre for their first twelve weeks. Those from Hull joined colleagues from the East and North Ridings of Yorkshire, Durham and Northumberland and all cities and towns therein, at the Newby Wiske training centre near Northallerton. Recruits returned to the centre for further fourteen day refresher training after twelve and twenty-four months service. The Home Office also authorised the appointment of a training Inspector in the force to be responsible for educating the staff in local requirements.

By now it was not only men who were going for recruit training! Not exactly in the forefront of using females in the force, Hull had dragged its feet while many other areas were using women. From its inception in 1836 when policemen's wives had been used to search female prisoners and, with the one exception during the 1914-18 War, the authorities seemed content to merely employ police 'matrons' to care for the interests of female prisoners.

The Second World War had seen the introduction, albeit for the duration of hostilities only, of the Women's Auxiliary Police Corps (WAPC). Their male colleagues discovered that these women, recruited to be drivers, clerks and telephonists, were very useful in matters involving women and children and vice cases. Their only shortcoming was that as WAPCs they were not properly attested in law and therefore had no proper authority for their actions.

Their usefulness could not be ignored by the authorities and in 1945, eight of the ladies were sworn in as fully-fledged constables. A policewoman Sergeant was sought and Jean Lyon Stewart from Manchester was appointed. Miss

*Supt. James Ferrier
HQ Admin. in post war
senior officer's uniform.
c.1967.*

*Force Headquarters and
Central Divisional station at
Queen's Gardens, Hull.*

Stewart was eventually to retire from Lancashire after a distinguished career.

The policewomen's section grew to total 35 officers during the following three decades and formed a specialised unit which not only provided an important service for the force and the community but also a career structure for its members. The unique section was to vanish with the force when the 1973 Equal Opportunities legislation decreed it was no longer possible to have units staffed by women only. While this may have resulted in a modest increase in the women's pay it unfortunately also destroyed uniquely useful units in the police service.

Housing police officers after the war became a major headache. Much of Hull's accommodation had been destroyed and there was a great demand for the limited amount of housing to rent. Police were forced into the market to purchase properties for officers who were entitled to free housing or a rent allowance in lieu. By 1964 the police authority owned fifty houses and two flats in the city. At the same time, the Council had agreed to allocate 2% of the corporation housing built as part of their slum clearance schemes, to police. By 1965 police had 107 such dwellings available to them.

A sophisticated communications and operations room had been introduced in the force in 1946 and provided comprehensive facilities between stations, boxes and vehicles in the area. It was the proud boast in Hull that any 999 call would be attended in two minutes, and any failure in this standard resulted in a major inquest in Chief Constable Sidney Lawrence's day. When the day came to move headquarters it was most important that the force communications system and control was out of action for the shortest possible time. In the event, everything was transferred to the new building with a loss of contact with the public amounting to ..... two minutes!

A primary function of the operations room was controlling force radio-equipped vehicles and it therefore came under the aegis of the transport department, later to be renamed the Traffic Department, an area of the force which grew vigorously after the war.

The late 1940s and the decade of the fifties saw acute manpower problems throughout the police service, and Hull was no exception. Not only were there difficulties in attracting recruits the problem of training them once in was almost unsurmountable. Disenchanted with the conditions of work and pay caused massive wastage from the force, particularly of young people still in their probationary period or in the first five years of service. It became obvious to Sidney Lawrence that one of the few alternatives available to maintain some sort of adequate police cover was to increase the mobility of the men who remained. It was decided to purchase 34 light-weight and extremely silent Velocette motor cycles and equip them with radio. They were to be used on the larger surburban beats. To offset their lack of any load-carrying capacity a number of vans were also purchased and fitted with emergency equipment.

By 1966 a transport department which had started with 31 men in 1930 had grown to a total of 112 including 18 civilians and with over 70 vehicles in the fleet. The number of cars was soon to be increased even further and at Central Government's expense.

In 1967 Roy Jenkins, the Home Secretary, promised to provide each force

Parade of Hull's motor patrol of Wolesley cars in 1948.

*Hull police motor/cyclists in 1960 including quiet running Velocette machines
for beat patrol.*

with a substantial number of small patrol vehicles, 'Panda cars', if they adopted the revolutionary new unit beat policing system. Whether or not this worked will be for history to decide. It was certainly modified in many respects in the years that followed but certain aspects of it remained intact when amalgamation overtook the force.

Perhaps its greatest impact was on the role of the ordinary constable. Except in the very heart of the city, tramping traditional beats became a thing of the past and perhaps the most far-reaching change of all, every man was issued with a personal radio and was, for the first time, in constant touch with his station. At a stroke he could throw away his whistle and become completely flexible in his movements.

The system was designed to provide a neighbourhood policeman for a local area or beat and he would work that area at his discretion. To assist him and to cover for his absences, a twenty-four hour patrol by one officer in a Panda car covered up to four beat areas. Detectives were to be assigned to particular areas, but this feature was not implemented in Hull although a collator was established in each sub-division to receive and disseminate intelligence. Many more officers had to be trained to drive and in general police found the system much preferable to the previous tedious foot and cycle beat work. The public reaction tended to become less and less favourable as they perceived what they thought was a transfer of policemen from foot beats into motor vehicles.

Over the years and particularly in the last decades of its history, Hull police force had become a much larger, better trained, very mobile and well equipped organisation to deal with an ever-growing population and workload. It was a far cry from McManus and his little band. In fact the only thing which over the years had, fortunately, decreased was the number of officers dealt with for disciplinary offences.

Nature of Crime	1969	1970	1971	1972	1973	1938
Murder	1	1	1	2	1	2
Attempted murder	3	3	3	6	3	—
Threats to Murder	—	—	2	—	—	—
Deaths by Dangerous Driving	—	—	4	4	2	—
Maliciously Administer Poison	—	—	4	—	—	—
Assaults and Woundings	455	550	638	682	864	23
Possess Firearm	—	—	1	1	5	—
Procure Abortion	1	2	—	—	—	1
Conceal Birth	—	2	—	—	—	—
Allow permises to be used for U.S.I.	—	—	1	—	2	—
Buggery	2	8	3	5	12	—
Gross Indecency	6	3	7	8	6	—
Indecent Assault-Male	26	40	25	27	31	3
Indecent Assault-Female	110	154	159	105	157	15
Unlawful Sexual Intercourse	52	45	54	51	59	6
Rape	7	2	71	3	7	1
Incest	4	9	2	5	2	—
Bigamy	1	2	1	—	2	3
Procuration	—	—	2	—	—	—

Nature of Crime	1969	1970	1971	1972	1973	1938
Burglary House	2004	2691	3507	3126	2937	386
Burglary Shop, etc.	2083	2323	2021	2227	2065	505
Going equipped to steal	10	19	34	22	17	5
Robbery	35	41	50	75	56	1
Blackmail	3	69	3	2	11	—
Theft employee	729	603	642	509	340	14
Theft from person	43	73	67	63	66	12
Theft from dwelling house	143	146	217	303	246	15
Theft from postal packets	15	69	1	2	13	1
Theft cycles	1387	1403	1505	1392	1259	897
Theft from shop	899	1213	1742	1528	1232	188
Theft from unattended vehicles	1266	1329	1005	1268	1067	161
Theft motor vehicle and take conveyance	789	778	790	907	1002	10
Theft meter	886	1046	951	873	679	365
Theft simple	3204	3444	3195	2891	2858	708
Fraud, etc.	617	494	507	449	386	57
Dishonest handling	246	414	355	380	365	33
Arson	17	32	49	84	104	1
Criminal Damage	14	11	14	303	428	2
Forgery	63	208	132	174	138	—
Other offences	107	85	83	147	71	34
TOTALS:	15228	17312	17848	17624	16493	3449

A higher quality and better-educated recruit, better training and a growth of the general acceptance among police officers of the need for discipline, particularly self-discipline in the service — all played a part. As late as 1890 the Chief Constable had reported some 83 men, almost a quarter of the force, had been dealt with for disciplinary offences. Seventy years later, the then Chief Constable said in his annual report:

> "During the year 11 men and 1 woman appeared before me and 1 man appeared before the watch committee, on charges alleging breaches of discipline. This is 8 fewer than in the previous year."

This was in a force which had approximately doubled in size in the intervening years.

Crime had certainly not shown any decrease and in 1973, the last year of Hull police force, although the figures showed a slight decline compared with the two previous years, indictable offences still totalled 16,493. A comparison of crimes by category for the last 5 years of the force's history, together with the figures for 1938, is reproduced above.

The End of the Road

Since earliest times, police forces in England and Wales have been subjected, from time to time, to reorganisations and amalgamations. Initially,

123

Police horse "Wilberforce" gets his new shoes from farrier Mr. Albert Binns at Lambwath.

The Chief Constable Mr. R. Walton leads Hull City Police in their final parade before amalgamating 1974.

Hull City Police Commemorative Plaque in Hull Parish Church (Holy Trinity).

virtually every borough in the land has its own police force, sometimes only one or two men.

Amalgamations quickened after 1945 with scores of tiny borough forces vanishing into surrounding counties in 1947, but the proud larger forces always put up strong resistance to any suggested changes which might alter their identities.

Hull found itself included in the major amalgamation programme announced by the then Home Secretary, Roy Jenkins in 1966/7. Together with other similar forces, particularly Bradford, Cardiff and Coventry, Hull put up a spirited fight against the plans. The proposal was that Hull should be joined in a single force with neighbouring East Riding and York. Secretly anticipating that change was probably inevitable, the force began planning, with the others, for the new force. It caused great surprise when news was received that this particular amalgamation scheme had been abandoned.

James Callaghan had become Home Secretary and was also one of the M.Ps for Cardiff. There is no doubt it was pressure from his constituency which forced him to allow the Welsh capital to escape from its scheme and once he had done so there was no case for continuing with the other three. For some perverse reason, only Coventry failed to escape despite a full public enquiry.

The reprieve was short-lived, however, and in 1974 the Home Secretary, following new Boundary Commission proposals, decided that the city of Hull, together with its police force, should become part of the new county of Humberside.

In his final annual report as Chief Constable of the city force Robert Walton said, "It is not without a tinge of sadness that I conclude this final report on the Kingston upon Hull City Police Force. If the police service has a reputation second to none, then I can say without fear of contradiction that this force has been one of the finest in existence."

An independent assessment of the force's record since its inception in 1836 would no doubt demur from such fulsome praise. Few, if any, of England's police forces can claim to have had an unblemished history and the Hull force, in common with the others, had a few blots on its escutcheon. It could, however, be claimed with some justification that by 1973 the force in Hull could fairly stand comparison with any other in the country.

On 31st March 1974, the last day of the force's existence as a separate identity, a church parade was held at Holy Trinity in the old town. The police, headed by their Chief Constable, marched proudly through the city they had served in peace and war, with heads held high.

THE END.

APPENDIX 1

Hull's Fire Fighters

Fire has been a menace ever since primitive man first learned to produce it, but for centuries the problem of fire prevention and extinction received little attention. It was probably the disastrous fire of London in 1666 that first awoke interest in the need for some degree of organisation to deal with outbreaks of fire and in 1680 the bench books of Hull Corporation record that the following persons:-

> *"were required to keep in their houses, leathern buckets:- Aldermen –4 buckets; those having served as Sheriff – 6 buckets; those having served as Chamberlain – 4 buckets"*

and

> *"....at the charge of the town, there was to be provided, 5 ladders, thirty feet long; 5 ladders twenty feet long and 60 leathern buckets."*

In spite of this activity, more attention was paid to re-couping losses than to any direct action for combatting fire. It seemed better to have strong insurance companies than strong fire brigades.

In an attempt to reduce their own losses, insurance companies began to establish their own private fire brigades in the late 17th century when it became apparent the cost of fires could be substantially offset if they were tackled promptly. The companies employed fire fighters in each town on a part-time basis and, when a building was insured by a particular insurance firm, its unique fire sign was fixed to the wall to assist in identification. Each company's men would only deal with fires at premises bearing their sign and then, only when it had been confirmed the premium had been paid!

In Hull the Corporation purchased its first machine 'for casting water' in 1673, and by 1831 there were about twelve 'engines' in various parts of the town, mostly owned by insurance companies.

With the formation of the new police in 1836 the force undertook certain fire fighting duties in addition to the normal policing work. At each of the police stations and at the four fire boxes in the town, ladders and hose were stored. On receipt of a report of fire, the reserve constable on duty at the nearest station or box, ran with ladders and hose to the scene whilst other constables on nearby beats were rounded up and sent to assist. Although the men were untrained in the art of fire fighting, the city was fortunate to have an excellent supply of water. The council had laid water to every part of the town in wooden water mains and high pressure was available.

Sheahan's 'History of Hull' records that in 1860:

> *"One of the functions of the police force of Hull is the extinction of fires and it may be said that few towns in the Kingdom have so excellent a*

Old Sculcoates Hall, Police and Fire Brigade station 1900.

A fire-tender 1900. Used to transport the main body of the police fire-brigade.

fire brigade. They have no fire engines but, on the first alarm of fire, they attach lengths of hose to the fire mains, which are always under sufficiently high pressure to throw water over the tallest house. The result is that since the system has been in existence, no fire has ever extended beyond the building in which it originated. And this most effective protection of the property of the people of Hull costs them nothing."

About the same time, the *Morning Star*, commenting on the costs of fires and fire brigades in the country, said on 23rd August 1862:

"...but at Hull the organisation is still more admirable and the arrangement is perhaps the nearest possible approach to absolute perfection!"

Against this background of super-efficiency the watch committee purchased a Merryweather fire engine capable of pumping 600 gallons of water per minute in 1884. Oddly enough they failed to purchase any horses to pull it. When it was required, a constable from the town yard would run into the streets and do his best to commandeer sufficient horses. This state of affairs continued for two years before six horses were finally purchased for the purpose.

At the end of 1886 the committee had established a sub-committee to organise and run a full-time, professional brigade as a department of the city police force and several items of equipment were purchased. A second engine, a fire fly which was a light horse-drawn gig for transporting as few officers and men rapidly to the scene to make an assessment of the situation; and, a fire tender which was a heavier vehicle for transporting the bulk of the brigade.

An Inspector and nine constables formed the brigade and they all lived near to the fire station and were on 24 hour stand-by. It was estimated the total annual costs of the brigade would be £426 1s 4d per annum, exclusive of wages.

Coincidentally, just prior to the sub committee's formation a volunteer brigade had been started in Hull. They were initially in temporary premises but moved to a specially built building in Hall Street a few years later. They were equipped with a manual fire engine, hose and ladders and turned out to assist the regular brigade until 1891 when, for some obscure financial consideration, they were disbanded.

Unusually, the Hall Street premises had keystones on its archways bearing the sculptured likenesses of the Captains of the brigade during the period the volunteers operated.

The brigade's strength was increased to 34 in 1896 and an agreement was reached in the same year to protect the nearby village of Sutton on Hull from fire, for an annual retainer of £10.

In 1900 a 'chemical' engine was purchased from America but the real mechanisation started during the First World War with the purchase of two motor fire engines with wheeled escapes. From this time on the brigade progressed to new stations, equipment and much-improved training for staff.

The fire-fly 1900 used to transport officers to the scene of a fire.

After 1918 it was realised that many men who did not meet the stringent entry qualifications for the police force could, nevertheless, render extremely useful service in the brigade and it was decided to split the staff into two groups. Firstly, police firemen who, in addition to being firemen were also police constables in the Hull force and secondly, professional firemen, often time-served tradesmen recruited to the brigade because of their technical knowledge of buildings and building construction.

The policemen provided the supervisory grades and professional firemen could only be promoted to 'waterman', roughly the equivalent of a police Sergeant. The 'waterman' was tested on his knowledge of hydrant locations and sources of water and, always travelled beside the driver of the engine to guide him to the nearest water supply to the fire.

In 1936 a Leyland/Metz 150 foot turntable ladder was acquired and until 1962 was thought to be the longest escape in Europe.

The coming of the Second World War saw the end of police involvement in the fire brigade. In 1938 the Auxiliary Fire Service was formed and became part of the city's defences. The National Fire Service was later formed and, as its name implied, operated throughout the war under national control. After the war the fire service returned to local control, but was by now a highly specialised organisation under control of its own officers. In Hull, as elsewhere however, there was always a close affinity between the two services who have continued to work in harmony with each other in a variety of situations.

APPENDIX 2: HULL POLICE MEMBERS 1836 to 1974

Author's Note

Every person joining Hull police swore an oath or declaration of allegiance before one or more Justices of the Peace. At the same time they signed their name in the "Police Constables Statutory Declaration Book". The Magistrate countersigned the entry and the policeman's number in the force was indicated. The number remained with the new recruit until either he was promoted to the rank of Inspector or left the force. The number would then be reallocated to another recruit. The details in the book are reproduced in this appendix.

The repeated and rapid appearance of some names and numbers, particularly in the early years, indicates the rapid turnover of manpower and the fact that some men joined, left and rejoined, sometimes on two or three occasions.

While every care has been taken with the transcription of details, a few signatures in the books are difficult to decipher because of the age and quality of the writing. Any errors are entirely my responsibility.

"I do solemnly and sincerely declare that I will well and truly serve our Sovereign Lady the Queen in the office of constable for the town or borough of Kingston-upon-Hull and county of the same town or borough until I be therefrom discharged by due course of law, according to the best of my skill and knowledge."

When Sworn	Signature of Constable Sworn		When Sworn	Signature of Constable Sworn	
1836			May 2	William Richardson	48
May 2	Patrick Coulehan	1		William Maughan	49
	Henry Kirkwood	2		William Dickenson	50
	Abraham S. Cudworth	3		John Woodward	51
	John H. Simpson	4		William Hardy	52
	Henry Smith	5		Thomas Hunt	53
	Matthew Spencer	6		John Davison Shotton	54
	David Vickerman	7		John Anfield	55
	James Bashforth	8		George Teneson	56
	William Postill	9		John Giles Pinder	57
	Brayshag Baines	10		George Green	59
	Charles Witty	11		Joseph Bower	60
	Thomas Bainton	12		Henry Farrow	61
	Isaac Boynton	13		John William Tacey	62
	Stephen Giles	14		William White	63
	George Tuppen	15		Thomas Wilkinson	64
	Thomas Codd	16		William Barron	65
	William Butler	17		Thomas Pattinson	66
	James Dring	18		William Frenneaw	67
	Thomas Leams	19		Thomas Butler	68
	William Druffill	20		Richard Cooper	69
	John Bulmer	21		Thomas Foster	70
	Henry Meek	22		Thomas Higgins	71
	Charles Ross	23		William Wilson	72
	James Wallis	24		Ins. Leggott	73
	Thomas Stephenson	25		William Milner	74
	Charles Worsdale	26		John Shields	75
	Nathaniel Lucas	27		William Easton	76
	Anthony Thundercliffe	28		Richardson Hobson	77
	John Edgcombe	29		John Dodsworth	78
	John Lyth	30		George Audas	79
	John Watkinson	31		James Stephenson	80
	John Blatherwick	32		Abraham Batty	81
	George Stephenson	33		John Darby Jnr	82
	John Robinson	34		James Halestone	83
	James Smith	35		William Whitaker	84
	William Drummond	36	May 2	George Clark	85
	Samuel Johnson	37		Fisher Loten	86
	George Gardhouse	38		A. McManus	Supt
	Robert Bricklehank	39		Charles Christopher Stephenson	Insp
	William Padget	40		Robert Craven	Insp
	William Baker	41		Richard Pobon	Insp
	William Drake	42		William Lang	Insp
	Edward Stourton	43		George Freeman	Clrk
	Samuel Walton	44	May 9	George Newton	79
	Joseph Akester	45	10	Edward O'Hara	
	Henry Dorsey	46	12	John Ockleton	48
	John Osbourne	47			

When Sworn	Signature of Constable Sworn		When Sworn	Signature of Constable Sworn	
May 12	George Haddon	21	Nov 11	John Fell	44
13	George Beaumont Taylor		Dec 5	Richard Nicholson	51
17	Thomas Bolstrood	58		William Dunn	73
20	Joseph Cockin	68	8	Edward Robinson	20
21	Thomas Collinson		12	James Allin Siddons	59
Jun 4	William Cleaver			William Harper	32
9	Thomas Whincup		17	Robert Arnold	69
24	John Hewerdine	10	21	George Luert	19
	Charles Dodds	16	**1837**		
	William Shepherd	25	Jan 4	Thomas Stephenson	31
	James Burroughs	35	11	Thomas Page	39
	George Ferguson	47	17	George Thwaites	25
	Hugh Colgar	59	31	Anthony Smith	36
28	George Cottison	38	Feb 7	John Witty	83
July 6	William Tenison	59	9	H.S. Latcoss	73
	George Collingwood	72	14	Robert Wilson	83
	Philip Doran	60	17	Roberto Taylor	45
7	James Smith (Re-appoint)	67	27	Witham Abbott	64
	William Henry Cross	49		John North	47
8	William Henry Cobb	32	28	William Gibson	26
11	Isaac Warcup		Mar 6	Thomas Birch	80
13	John Clayton	22	10	Robert Ryley	44
	Francis Smith	82	11	George Morgan	56
20	Charles Latlin	12	17	William Nicholson	24
29	William Mulligan	12	20	Richard Roberts	49
Aug 5	Robert Longman	13	21	Samuel Hastings	65
	John Halestone	37	Apr 18	Samuel Foreman	77
10	David Bell	54		Henry Penrose	75
20	William Jenkinson	37	21	William Smith	78
22	Samuel Johnson		25	Charles McHugh	66
	(Re-appoint)	31	May 8	George Harvey	15
23	Edward Allison	50	12	George Boynton	69
	Samuel Stathen	74	Jun 16	William Bennison	43
29	Robert Craven		24	Thomas Halgate	66
	(Re-appoint)	73	28	Robert Delanoy	83
Sep 8	Thomas Newton	53	July 6	John Millson	65
12	Ins. Leggot (Re-appoint)	62	18	John Cox	85
17	John Danson	39	20	George Seaton	47
19	Jonathan Furin	23	28	Joseph Yates	83
	John Hewitt	82	Aug 3	Joseph Robinson	47
21	John Wreggit	33		William Whitaker	45
23	John Franks	82		Thomas Pattinson	25
29	Johnson Hunter	10	5	George Cross	64
30	William Rudston	44	11	Patrick Farrell	69
	William Loft	13		Robert Clark	24
Oct 5	Thomas Bainton	53	28	Robert Morgan	86
7	Richard Niass	57	Sept 2	William Ellis	82
Nov 10	John Midgley	85	11	John Wilson	60

133

When Sworn	Signature of Constable Sworn		When Sworn	Signature of Constable Sworn	
Oct 23	George Weatherill		Aug 17	George Clarke	63
	Crowther	57	31	Thomas Gedner	42
27	Joseph Charlton	65		Joseph Waudby	56
	Peter Bolton	55	Sep 13	Henry Reed	29
Nov 1	Timothy Barmly	79		James Dawson	63
17	Joseph Potts	56	14	William Wakelin	41
	George White	48	Oct 4	William Beavan	53
Dec 8	George Bushby	72	8	James Burgess	41
22	William Blackburn	57	11	David Spittlehouse	77
30	William Whitehead	50	16	Thomas Waldie	33
1838			23	Joseph East	58
Jan 3	William Brewster	46	26	James Butler	59
4	John Butler	14	Nov 2	James Brown	79
10	William Wilkinson	25	6	John Stott	37
	Alexander Marrisa	64	9	Jonathan Smales	71
	Mathew Faulding	48		John Smales	29
12	John Crow	25	15	James Langston Doulton	37
17	John Beard	79	21	Charles Lindale	49
22	George Smith	80	24	John Ashbridge	50
26	James West	72	Dec 21	James Pinder	77
Feb 24	Henry Graver	82	**1839**		
Mar 27	John Mennell	55	Jan 15	George Yates	55
30	James Collinson	73	17	William Charlesworth	46
Apr 3	Richard Stephenson	63	23	Levi Jessop	76
18	William Richardson	51	25	William Anderson	47
19	William Tillson	64	Feb 12	Francis Jackson	74
20	Thomas Hines	60	13	George Bradford Harper	40
May 1	Robert Clark		14	Richard Batley	37
4	John Jones		23	James Bailey	52
12	Wilberforce Herdsman	18	Mar 2	Ridge Swannack	71
	Matthew Greenwood	35	4	Henry Walker Bird	41
14	Freeman Cook	41	5	Jonathan Hatfield	64
17	Ins. George Pinder	60		George Lazenby	58
18	John Thorpe	47	9	William Harrison	33
19	James Stephenson	63	23	John Rippin	50
June 1	William Woods	72	Apr 4	Henry Cook	37
20	John Watkinson	47	8	James Yates	—
26	Jonathan Wright		9	Robert Clarke	71
	Marshall	15		Leavens Kay	69
July 13	K. Nicholson	22	13	J. Ogglesby	37
23	William Seaton	64	25	Isaac Jackson	23
	George Needham	50	May 17	Charles Hatfield	56
	William Darby	26	18	John Glew	48
Aug 1	John Jackson	15	24	John Coates	29
7	John Sanderson	18	June 11	George Ranshaw	—
	Thomas Jackson	42		Martin Burn	—
17	William Robinson	23	22	John Pollard	—
	William Winter	25	26	Charles Hotham	31

When Sworn	Signature of Constable Sworn		When Sworn	Signature of Constable Sworn	
July 5	James Little	31	June 30	James Baxter	24
9	Robert Smith	18	July 10	Philip Colbert	18
17	Robert Holton	58	27	Thomas Parker	74
18	Francis Naylor	77	Aug 7	Thomas Moore Blanshard	67
25	John Alan Pearson	—		Richard Stamp	71
31	Mo Germas Lee	—	25	Henry Pearson	74
Aug 6	Richard Moss	52		William Billerby	49
21	Johgn Alcock	80	27	George Addey	42
Sep 2	Richard Nicholson	44	Sept 1	James Smithson	49
	Thomas Ward	48		Joseph Gardiner	51
	William Sleights	55	7	Robert Handley	24
12	Matthew Wright	53	Oct 1	James Mayman	24
14	John Fairburn	22	19	Francis Richardson	22
20	Robert Nicholson	66	20	Edmund Page	74
Oct 25	John Overton	—	23	John Howard	80
28	John Naylor	56	26	William Fields	34
Nov 7	Charles Dade Blanshard	39	31	Robert Sowerby	69
22	John Cox (re-appoint)	37		William Smales	74
Dec 9	George Holmes	68	Nov 2	William Nudy	46
12	George Cracknell	19	17	Thomas Bennett	52
	Christopher Pickering	46	19	Thomas Wilson	51
17	Isaac Wilson	53	Dec 2	William Thompson Taylor	18
1840			**1841**		
Jan 13	William Johnson	77	Jan 6	John Killygan	33
19	Robert Follitt	29	9	William Love	32
Mar 4	William Shephard	13	21	John Smith	49
5	Isaac Anson	77	Feb 24	Milner Bowser	65
17	Thomas Allison	17	Mar 13	George Botsey	65
19	Thomas Moverley	17	Apr 19	John Jones	78
21	Edward Golland	73	May 1	Stephen Townend	34
24	Henry Sunley	29	14	George Slight	16
Apr 1	Henry Babington	13	27	William Nixon	74
6	Thomas Wilson	17	June 1	William Cooper	54
13	William Harper	13	4	Stephen Barker	41
14	Thomas Lea	39	10	John Carlton	57
May 6	Stephen Barker	19	July 10	Henry Toomey	73
11	John Fawcett	45	22	John Taylor	41
May 19	Thomas Levitt	45	29	George Mooney	62
25	George Richardson	80	Aug 2	Robert Wilkinson	57
	John White	33	21	Robert Potts	29
June 5	Joshua Bentley	60	23	John Taylor	16
12	Patrick Gerraughty	49		Christopher Pickering	78
15	James Robinson	57	Nov 6	William Kean	41
18	James Hamilton Thompson	47	20	John Campion	85
29	William Brien	73	Dec 2	Joseph Morritt	24
	Thomas Wood	62	3	John Coulon	74
30	George Neal	85		John Marsh	54

When Sworn	Signature of Constable Sworn		When Sworn	Signature of Constable Sworn	
1842			Mar 28	William Sigsworth	62
Feb 26	George Lockwood	56	30	Robert Robinson	15
Mar 1	Robert Anthony	39	Apr 6	J. MacCleary	50
2	William Noble	—	10	George Barker	55
4	Thomas Marr	34	22	William Pearson	38
31	Charles Elliot	54	May 11	John Daniels	75
Apr 14	William Smith	16	20	David Smith	71
28	William Harman	17	Jun 16	William Smith	22
May 4	R.P. Smithson	73	July 4	William Jefferson	11
24	Thomas Roberts	85	11	Robert Adamson	43
30	George Parker	76	24	Samuel Woodbridge	89
Jun 3	William Gamwell	80	Aug 19	John Grey	96
10	James Grasby	56	26	George Coggon	45
17	John Downs	81	28	Daniel Butterwick	20
30	Joseph Faulkner	66	29	George Fewster	75
July 20	William Bingley	66	Sep 22	John Whitfield	45
Aug 1	Samuel Brown	87	Oct 10	John Dewick	88
	Thomas Croshaw	88	13	Thomas Hanby	17
	David Simpson	91	30	Henry Stephenson	42
	Thomas Marshall	89	Nov 7	William Horsfield	23
	John Bell	90	15	Augustin John Emerson	87
	James Cole	92	17	James Elliott	85
	James Norwood	93	21	Abraham Ellis	52
	George Freeston	94	Dec 11	Edward Haxley	67
	William Jackson	95	12	John Simpson	47
	William Gill	96	21	Thomas Cook	47
11	Edmund Blacker	94	27	Edward Coffey	96
Sept 3	Brittain Hunter	42	29	Frances D. Morley	74
	Raspin Cherry	—	**1844**		
9	Henry Forbes Barker	73	Jan 4	Bartholomew Gould	65
16	Edward Connor	44	8	Jonathan Trent	25
23	James Willoughby	15	Feb 1	Robert Garton	41
26	David Howarth	66	17	John Wood	32
	James Hilton	89	20	William Pearson	34
Oct 28	George Gordoe	46	Mar 16	William Houlton	66
Nov 14	Otty Brown	48	Apr 6	Thomas Southwick	—
17	Walker Cherry	76	25	Stephen Barren	81
Dec 9	Robert Bartlett Jackson	42	May 18	Robert Raby	81
20	Thomas Clark	12	23	John Horne	17
22	George Clement Johnson	—	June 17	William Andrew	96
1843			20	Henry westerdale	84
Jan 5	George Gilliard	69	July 4	John Smith	74
9	John Longbones	87	27	Abraham Marsh	83
12	William Sharp	71	Aug 30	Joseph Shester	62
27	Daniel Dalmahoy	22	Sept 30	John Wallis	97
Feb 13	Edmund Hoe	48		Robert Foster	98
17	Robert Ellekers	18		John Fitzgibbon	99
18	George Hall	78		Robert White	100

When Sworn	Signature of Constable Sworn		When Sworn	Signature of Constable Sworn	
Sept 30	Mathew Ranson	101	Sept 18	Samuel Grundy	29
	Emlyn Buswell	102	22	Anthony Lineham	20
	Thomas Lickiss	103	Oct 24	William Usher	41
	John H. Owen	104	Nov 26	Thomas Gibson	86
	George Lamphugh	105	Dec 24	George Revell	109
	James Wright	107	26	George Lynch	110
	Wilson Martindale	108	**1846**		
	John Belbewby	55	Jan 8	William Fishwick	88
	Henry Hayes	16		William Page	92
Oct 1	Charles Sanderson	106	14	Thomas Ruxton	102
3	John Thompson	84	Feb 26	John Belton	103
4	William Kitching	42	Mar 11	George Fowler	51
Nov 15	Isaac McKee	105	18	William Mentham	—
22	Zahariah Wood	65		Thomas Brown	—
28	John Runson	17		Thomas Moss	—
Dec 19	John G. Pinder			William Nicholson	—
	(Re-appoint)	101		Samuel Quinton	—
1845				Charles Edmonds	—
Jan 6	Robert Rounding	103		Thomas Ashforth	—
24	Jabez Mason	36		James Everett	—
Feb 1	William Wilson	96		John Graham	—
11	William Goodman	90		Aaron Weatherill	—
13	John Colley	81	Apr 9	William Thompson	56
15	Enoch Atkinson	20	13	Moses Gray	45
Mar 21	Thomas Bentley	81	16	George Ritchie	77
29	Headley Ostler	103	17	George Ellerker	42
31	John Horsfield	108	18	Robert Greaves	106
Apr 3	James Penrose	96	20	Thomas Rickets	12
4	John Driffill	104	21	William Medd	32
7	George Albert Robinson	96	27	James Dann	41
	George Hankin	79		Robert Richardson	96
8	James Lucas	49	May 5	James Bell	32
11	Henry Kirby	108	7	John H. Owen	12
25	William Suddaby	83		John Hutchcroft	32
29	Robert Squire	97		William Jakeman	94
May 7	Joseph Wright	15		James Thompson	105
9	John Roberts	11	8	Thomas Myers	25
13	John Johnson	96	14	Henry Hayes	16
May 17	John Fillingham	—	18	James Noble	20
19	Michael Weald	92	June 23	Robert Watson	45
22	George Morgan	78	July 2	William Ashby	12
	John Longhorn	79	10	Robert Mason	105
Jun 11	John Atkinson	100	16	John Scott	12
12	Peter Coghlan	107		Robert Shaw Murgatroyd	96
July 28	William Bradley	98	18	Edward Thompson	78
Aug 6	David King	61		Joseph Rushby	86
30	John Boynton	43	27	William Smallwood	83
Sept 11	John Leggott	101	29	Thomas Brown	43

When Sworn	Signature of Constable Sworn		When Sworn	Signature of Constable Sworn	
Aug 6	John Kitching	40	Apr 28	Richard Gillett	18
7	James Storr	78	May 6	George Flint	91
20	Michael Thropsel	81	9	William Huggins	18
25	John Pickard	84	17	Francis Johnson	44
	Thomas Hornby	61		Watson Bingley	99
26	Edward Orry	85	20	George Dixon	117
29	George Eccles	11	24	Robert Lid---y	39
Sept 1	Charles Hart	83	27	Edwin Sandan	15
30	John Fowler	86	June 5	William Dresser	72
Oct 1	William Ingham	104	9	John Munckman	29
5	Charles Pickard	13	July 10	Thomas Dunderdale	97
8	Francis Ayscough	77	15	George Wombwell	17
9	George Hancock Cawkell	93	16	Thomas Needham	18
	William Howard	—	17	William Walker Burkett	104
20	John Naylor	43	31	Miles Davis	105
	Joseph Young	71	Aug 3	William Pycatt	48
29	William Stather	20	9	William Coulson	97
Nov 11	Ralph Burton	43		William Needley	83
12	Robert Squires	78	23	John Greaves	85
13	John Page	84	Sep 8	John Durnbrough	104
	Philip Marshall	81	10	George Smith	48
14	George Sunderland	68	11	T. Pittaway	108
18	Joseph Clark	98	17	Charles Firth	21
19	Richard Spink	108	23	James Robinson	76
	James Brown	48	Oct 5	William Mason	24
21	John Edward Benson	81	18	Joseph Walton	—
25	Wilberforce Taylor	79		John Redfearn	102
26	John Lamb	93	22	Michael Clarke	97
Dec 4	Walton Bristow	102	25	Joseph Mather	80
10	John Watson	78	Nov 2	Joseph Green	107
12	Horiner Coulson	11	8	John Daneon	83
	Thomas Robinson	54	12	William Connel	25
16	James Robinson	84	30	Thomas Foster	51
1847			Dec 2	Joseph Cooper	76
Jan 4	James Winter	49	9	Robert Shout	84
19	Thomas Coulson	32	13	Aaron Lawson	110
20	Elisha Routledge	25		Francis Marshall	111
Feb 6	William Killick	52	14	Walter Walker	112
Feb 11	Hansel Greenhagh	—	24	Charles Tipton	83
16	Hiram Wright	101	28	Joseph Saunderson	113
Mar 2	Christopher Hammond	52	**1848**		
	William Fallan	55	Jan 6	Robert Harrison	16
20	George Parkin	40	26	John Chappel	110
Apr 12	William Little	38	Feb 1	Joseph Best	104
20	Charles Howard	103	18	Thomas Best	85
23	James Tickelpenny	53	21	William Galloway	88
24	Edwin Crowther	79	Mar 14	William Kay	86
	Robert Prounding	25	30	William Chapman	86

When Sworn	Signature of Constable Sworn	
Mar 30	Joseph Underwood	68
Apr 4	George Pashly	48
22	Thomas Ferrand	85
29	Freeman Cook (Re-appointed)	17
May 31	Anthony Mulligan	51
June 3	Robert Bingley	71
20	Thomas Smith	46
25	John Foster	38
July 6	Walter Couldrey	99
	Arthur Murphy	60
18	John Smith	95
	Patrick John Clarke	104
Sept 20	Eli Fletcher	31
Oct 2	Thomas Sanderson	36
9	John Jakeman	53
16	John Crosby Grindrods	40
1849		
Jan 15	John Thompson	97
18	James Nair	35
23	Richard Martin	40
Mar 3	Henry Wilby	83
16	Benjamin Wheater	85
30	Thomas Carson	85
Apr 16	Thomas Peacock	83
May 2	Richard Tuckman	53
7	George Eccles	85
8	Wellington McTeanby	40
23	Edmond Vanse	21
July 3	John Rutherford	63
7	Frederick Jacobs	114
	John Moorhouse	115
	William Bristow	116
	John Featherstone	117
	Peter Alfonso	118
	James Tresser	119
	Alfred Melsom	120
	James Sheenan	121
	John Northend	122
	Thomas Antcliff	123
	James Dawson	97
30	John Hodgson	116
Aug 13	Thomas Smith	116
16	Thomas Wilson	105
18	Arthur Biglin	115
27	George Gibson	69
Sept 1	John Moorhouse	60
	Edward Wood	19

When Sworn	Signature of Constable Sworn	
Sept 10	William Beech	120
11	William Bland	17
21	Nelson Bell	51
24	Theophilus Nicholson	55
25	Thomas Hope	40
28	Warcup Robinson	92
Oct 13	John Witlam	27
16	John Ruddforth	123
18	William Price	57
Nov 9	Samuel Stephenson	114
	John Leggott	54
21	Thomas Briskham	100
Dec 1	George Greaves	55
3	Henry Fielder	69
10	Joseph Lumley	71
26	Thomas Freer	40
	Robert Sullivan	—
1850		
Jan 12	George Waumsley	16
Feb 18	George Wallace	19
Mar 7	William Thornhill	57
Apr 9	William Smith	91
May 7	George Atkinson	110
9	Nicholas Storey	69
July 17	Peter Jackson	—
24	William Clark	83
30	Henry Thompson	114
Aug 16	John Allan	90
17	Thomas Palethorpe	115
20	Thomas Binnington	96
26	Patrick Meahey	16
Sept 2	George Branton	16
11	Thomas Nicholson	114
28	Thomas Lumley	123
Nov 2	John Bowes	16
	Joseph Renton	29
Dec 5	Robert Harrison	42
14	William Kemp	79
16	George Martin	90
27	Thomas Foster	90
1851		
Mar 6	William Young	66
10	Charles Alcock	28
	James Robinson	30
11	Joseph Thompson	124
	William Wigglesworth	125
	Rueben Todd	126
	William Jackson	127

When Sworn	Signature of Constable Sworn		When Sworn	Signature of Constable Sworn	
Apr 24	John Lyth	117	Mar 28	John Scott	87
May 1	William Moody	38		David Jackson	110
3	George Whitlam	116	Apr 2	Walker Cherry	98
June 5	William Weatherill	117	9	Emerson Atkinson	92
Aug 27	Joseph Premingham	35	Mar 2	Leonard Henry Smales	95
29	Alexander Marshall	100	3	George Kirk	79
Sept 8	John Leayland	21	6	John Dalton	96
	George Willison	27	19	William Thorley	83
10	Robert Morris	94		John Maudsley	30
11	Joseph Swaby	53	May 31	Charles Read	47
	Thomas Rumby	101	June 23	William Wilson	66
16	Thomas Sanderson	35	July 4	Edwin Thistleton	21
27	William Houlton	63	8	John Roll	66
Oct 1	Robert Marshall	37	16	William Ruston	71
Nov 28	Thomas Colley	37	25	James Stuart	94
Dec 1	Thomas Burroughs	116		William Chapman	86
24	William Mason	24		Thomas Lumley	63
29	John Menton	122		William Weatherill	117
31	Joseph H. Smith	70	29	Joseph Mather	—
1852				William Dresser	—
Feb 21	Charles Walker	37		Thomas Palethorpe	—
Mar 5	George East	40		Henry Forbes Barker	—
11	Daniel Morris	47		John Redfearn	—
Apr 1	Joseph Fenton	126		John Bowes	—
5	John Nicholson	48		Joseph H. Smith	—
17	James Fenton	48		James Wright	—
May 3	William Grace	94		George East	—
14	John Wilkinson	30		Thomas Meeson	—
July 1	James Wright	114		William Grace	35
13	Robert Ward	27	Sept 10	Thornton Johnson	47
Aug 14	Thomas Sleesom	38	Oct 15	Jonathan Reader	57
27	Thornton Johnson	48	24	William Coates	12
Sept 17	Henry Smith	99	Dec 31	Thomas Adamson	90
18	Edward Skerrow	89	**1854**		
Oct 4	Jonathan Jarvis Reader	120	Jan 9	William Coverdale	90
9	Samuel Walker	59	30	George Kirk	48
11	George Billney	112	May 13	James Dresser	72
Nov 8	Thomas Fletcher	126	15	Leonard Henry Smales	42
Dec 16	George Duckworth	103	June 3	William Smith	78
1853			July 13	James Sheeran	12
Jan 1	William Coates	63	22	James Palethorpe	17
19	Joseph Hullak	89	Aug 5	Francis Galbraith	81
25	Henry Holmes	78	Sept 12	John Hemingbrough	56
Feb 3	Thomas Adamson	89	Oct 17	George Boss	24
Mar 9	Benjamin Doughty	98	19	William Dawson	31
10	William Richard Coverdale	103		John Roll	45
19	Solomon Reed	87	Nov 28	Thomas Freer	45
			Dec 5	John Walsh	27

When Sworn	Signature of Constable Sworn		When Sworn	Signature of Constable Sworn	
Dec 7	Bilton Whisker	93	Feb 19	John Thompson	31
19	Williams Croft	56	21	Edmund Phillingham	16
1855				John Marshall	96
Jan 1	Harrod William Gilbert	49		George Wheare	97
11	Joseph Fletcher	49		Harvey Warner Hill	98
17	James Brown	72		Michael O'Hara	99
Feb 9	Johnson Parkin	42		John Suter Smith	100
Mar 20	Joshua Whitehead	38		Henry Smith Osborne	101
22	Allis Brown	48		William Anderson	102
27	William Maw	48		George Tomlinson	103
Apr 9	James Chamberlain	38		John Stout	104
27	George Barnard	49		John Mulligan	105
May 16	John Doherty	94	Mar 11	Alfred Dickinson	105
22	Hiram Wright	55	31	Jonathan Hatfield	66
Aug 7	David Crowther	57	Apr 2	Philip Graves	64
13	William Storr	72	3	John Rose	106
20	John Varey	42	11	Thomas Hyme	103
23	William Cain	42	16	William Hepton	24
Sept 11	Thomas Conlon	45	21	Rowland Patchett	55
27	Francis Martin Hyett	12	22	John Thompson Dickinson	16
Oct 29	Thomas Crowshaw	21	24	Samuel Edwin Webster	89
Nov 23	Thomas Rawson	42	27	John Hime	20
30	James Rippin	88	30	George Clay	16
Dec 12	Peter Witty	43	May 25	Henry Wilkinson	55
1856			June 1	Turner Devlin	59
Jan 4	William Fenton	17	8	George Scott	31
17	Peter Henegan	50	23	John Goodman	77
Feb 4	George Clark	66	25	John Cahill	93
11	William Wentworth Ounsworth	59	July 17	George Pauson	106
Mar 4	Henry Macklin	50	20	Johnson Parkin	107
14	William Hardy	50		John Gooday	110
17	Michael Gilmartin	47		Robert Jackson	111
Mar 26	John Sealing	17		George Monkman	112
Apr 17	Timothy Scrivener	57		Robert Pickering Dunn	113
30	William Cawood	30		Robert Crake	114
May 22	James Sheeran	12		James Makey	115
June 26	Lewis Wright	76		Benjamin Eyre	116
Aug 7	Thomas Monkman	31	30	Edward Scott	108
Oct 14	Thomas Heeson	23		William Clarvis	109
Nov 4	Richard Horan	57	Aug 6	John Scales	100
Dec 10	John Stennett	82		Edward O'Brien	109
1857				Joseph Kavanagh	55
Jan 14	Richard Ahearn	48	13	Joseph Walsh	50
20	William Winter	24		Thomas Healy	36
Feb 13	Henry Graves	48	27	William Storr	72
16	Edwin Barley	64	Sept 1	Henry McDonald	50
	George Southwick	55	10	Charles Ward	23

When Sworn	Signature of Constable Sworn		When Sworn	Signature of Constable Sworn	
Sept 11	William Smithers	62	Nov 5	Edmond Wright	26
	George Allison	111	18	Isaac Gray	108
17	William Arram	112	19	Thomas Nicholson	114
24	George Hobson	77	22	George Clark	97
	Joseph Murphy	111	Dec 3	James McCounick	96
25	William Broomhead	114	22	Luke Morgan	114
Oct 1	Thomas Kirk	24	28	Francis Ruston	73
8	William Smith	100	**1859**		
	Stephen Allan	109	Jan 10	William Stark	59
15	Joshua Adkins	50		Robert Hotson	38
22	John Hallam	58	Jan 14	William Carr	75
	Charles Milner	105	15	George Wright	28
29	William Watson	—	Mar 23	Thomas Charles	103
	Henry Musgrove	—	26	William Walsh	75
Nov 5	Alexander McDonald	28	Apr 5	William McGilroy	45
6	James Jackson	14	8	Thomas Dixon	75
12	John Thomas Kirkman	14	23	Richard Lister	23
17	Beaumont Newsome	36	28	Henry Lacey	93
27	John Charles Smelt	101	May 5	Charles Burton	85
	William Whitelam	100	17	Elijah Goodhand	56
Dec 3	John Marner	64	June 22	Robert Wilson	74
19	George Stringfellow	62	July 7	George Kirton Pell	28
28	Thomas Hepworth	11		Joseph Tarporly	23
1858			14	John Brackenbury Whiting	106
Jan 1	John Thomas	23		Robert Scott	109
5	Matthew Oldroyd	104	Aug 11	Charles Kyme	38
26	Patrick Bermingham	55	Sept 2	George Tindle	109
Feb 16	Anthony Rogers	85	15	Robert Foster	102
Mar 12	Samuel Masser	104	Oct 4	William Lazenby	100
Apr 22	William Hutty	42	Nov 28	Robert Osborne	85
May 17	George Cockin	89	Dec 17	Thomas Flintoff	58
20	Thomas Bartlitt	56		Benjamin Smith	20
26	Thomas Walker	39	**1860**		
June 16	John Brownbridge	106	Jan 18	Thomas Allen	55
19	James Leonard	48	26	Brian Lazenby	82
25	Thomas Revill	36	Feb 4	Adam Thompson	107
	George Stark	31	16	Isaac Harrison	36
July 17	Eneas McFall	38	21	Leonard Dodsworth	47
24	George Kirton Bell	114	24	Thomas Smith	53
July 26	Ellis Head	73	28	Charles Collinson	115
Aug 6	Thomas Conlon	33	Mar 8	Thomas Chapman	56
11	Charles Kyme	—	16	John Davis	82
Sept 1	Charles Bricklebank	56	Apr 10	George Clark	62
29	Henry Naylor	115	12	Robert Crossland	93
	Thomas Mulrenan	36	May 10	George Jones	62
Oct 4	John Wrixan	31	31	David Stone	27
18	Charles Plant	112	June 7	William Squires	56
	Moses Stephenson	106			

When Sworn	Signature of Constable Sworn		When Sworn	Signature of Constable Sworn	
June 22	Thomas Leavens Tindale	103	May 30	Francis Grainger	70
	John Henry Giles	26	31	James Sanger	58
28	William Green	114	June 7	Henry Killick	95
July 12	George Roberts	106	14	James Smith	29
27	William Hesk	24	July 17	Greenhead Smith	118
Aug 3	Cornelius Curran	27		William Bean	119
	Michael Reilly	36		Mark Robinson	120
	Martin Keane	38		William Fernison Hall	121
9	Charles Scanlon	77		John Short	122
16	George Whare	113		William Huntsman	123
	William Harker	114		John William Briggs	124
20	John Shipinson	49		Charles Elvin	125
23	Benjamin Rusholme	107		Francis Robinson	126
	Charles Warrour	85		John Dixey	128
Sept 6	David B. Gainsley	28		Michael Mahon	129
	John Walkington	53		John Fisher	130
27	William C. Taylor	26		Samuel Hare	131
	Isaac Matthews	102		John Haldenby	132
Oct 26	John Franks	107		William James	133
Nov 8	Henry Verlin	117		John C. Dillon	134
9	George Alexander	92		George Jolley Sanders	135
Dec 18	John Crane	115		John Wilson Laing	136
19	Jeremiah Browne	99		Thomas Monkman	137
22	Benjamin Neave	56	20	Charles Moore	127
1861			24	Robert Suddaby	
Jan 14	George Bird	48		Kilvington	87
21	Abraham Harland	55	26	John Ray	113
Feb 7	John Andrews	70	27	George Blades	113
14	Charles T. West	65	Aug 1	Thomas Linch	126
21	William Proctor	55	9	Anthony Duffy	58
Mar 2	Joseph Bolton	85	10	Patrick John Clarke	87
14	Joseph Regard	23	17	George Porte	137
15	William Robinson	56	30	Richard Greenwood	57
28	Charles Smalley	103	31	John Jackeman	52
30	Johnson Atkinson	82	Sept 6	William Shire	35
Apr 1	John England	104	17	John Hall	66
6	John Cawood	32	19	John Byrne	31
8	Henry Fuller	114	21	Martin Dillon	119
12	George Suffill	58		Michael Caveney	65
Apr 18	Thomas Allen	31	28	Preston Chessings	120
	William Clean	111	Oct 8	Henry Jaques	35
	Robert Kinder	26	26	William Rhodes	
	Tom Fox	74		Warrender	124
25	Cubitt Florey	113	Nov 11	John Beevers	36
May 2	John Wilkinson	31	14	William Knaggs	98
4	William Martins	115	19	William Sherwood	52
9	Thomas Gooday	66	29	John Wilkinson	66
21	Durvel Gates	66	Dec 10	John Negginton	52

When Sworn	Signature of Constable Sworn		When Sworn	Signature of Constable Sworn	
Dec 30	John Hardbattle	111	May 11	James Hornsey	129
1862			22	Charles Tutty	105
Jan 4	William Weyman	58	June 5	Thomas Martin Page	129
10	Mark Devlin	136	6	Richard Filey	105
Feb 21	Thomas Brodigan.	60	12	Thomas Brears	94
Mar 7	Jesse Harman	115		Henry Proctor	24
19	Elam Sizer	126		John Cullingworth	19
28	J. Dillon	89	July 2	Hugh Henry Crossby	77
Apr 19	John Stephenson	33		Thomas Overfield	79
26	Robert Atkinson	33	Aug 18	Mark Hunter	34
May 9	Thomas Jefferson	115	25	Samuel Blackburn	35
15	Robert Eyre	77	29	Charles Creasy Wray	119
June 30	Michael Lawson	117	Sept 18	William Wride	126
July 1	Samuel Marshall	112	30	Edward Burns	35
Aug 4	Edmund Wilson		Oct 2	George Russell	71
	Middleton	58	Nov 2	Thomas Reilly	57
21	Thomas Brown	65	18	John Hall	79
30	Thomas Alingwell		20	William Graham	19
	Robinson	32	Dec 8	Charles Parker	22
Sept 3	Samuel Connelly	52	15	Charles McDonagh	23
	John Andrews	103	**1864**		
12	Edmond Cauroy	89	Jan 5	Alfred Brough	38
30	Jeremiah Sweeney	126	22	George Bean	19
	James Cooney	95	26	Arthur Robinson	25
Oct 17	Joseph Tarpy	34	Feb 6	George Floater	25
	Patrick McNaulty	103	Mar 5	Thomas Horsfield	71
28	Samuel Jackson	35	23	George Stones	35
29	George Dixon	79	29	Thomas Alingell	
Nov 4	Matthew Raleigh	79		Robinson	122
18	Charles Plant	89	30	Charles Tutty	71
25	Thomas Fitzstephen	79	31	Richard P. Lonsdale	135
Dec 30	William England	130	Apr 11	John Anson Hogg	82
1863			29	William Gibson	93
Jan 3	Robert S. Kilvington	92	May 16	John Henry Bray	129
8	John Chevin	130	June 11	Edward Burns	71
20	Charles Garbutt	60	17	Rabest Wade	32
Feb 4	James Gray	104	18	William Munsley	36
17	William Murdoch	124	July 12	William Martin	107
20	William Stones	32	18	John Hall	79
27	Joseph Seth Midglow	60	Aug 15	Daniel Nutchill	117
Mar 17	George Alexander	35	23	Edward Trafford	79
Apr 1	Thomas Wilson	34	Sept 14	James Henry Brooksbank	113
2	Thomas Atkinson		Nov 5	George Teal Thompson	24
	Stevenson	33	25	Dunham Bird	107
7	Matthew Longhorn	116	Dec 7	William Kilvington	134
10	Thomas Levett	129	9	Joseph Liney	104
24	William Thompson	56	21	James Brocklesby	36
May 9	William Atkinson	24	23	William Townend	52

144

When Sworn	Signature of Constable Sworn		When Sworn	Signature of Constable Sworn	
1865			Jan 4	T. Hooker	74
Jan 2	Charles Scott	24	Feb 8	Michael Tiplady	137
4	Robert Proctor	19	12	John Stainfield	25
Feb 14	John Tiplady	32	15	Patrick Phillips	87
16	John Towle	133	23	John Pinder	93
20	James Ritchie	126	Mar 2	Daniel Mitchell	117
24	Robert Salmon	65	9	Sykes Vickers	71
25	William Acey	113		Walter Burton	26
Mar 14	Robert Smithson	63	10	George Kitchen	146
16	Charles Waller	133	23	Samuel Jackson	19
Apr 15	Robert Garbutt	111		George Bell	63
19	Thomas Grasby	82	31	Edward Cherry	26
29	Richard Sweeting	77		James Mulrinan	95
May 4	John Mulrenan	95		Michael Hestor	134
6	Patrick Feeney	105		Charles Hick Blackburn	137
12	William E. King	68	Apr 6	Robert Waller	25
15	John Hornby	129		John Dillon	139
May 19	E. John McConnell	115		Theophilus Kinsey	74
June 10	Thomas Pearcy	113	9	Christopher Michael	109
29	Thurmeon Smithson	136	16	George Scott	74
Aug 4	D. Bicken	130	27	John Henry Bray	19
8	William Robinson	56	May 1	Charles Brown	77
Sept 8	Thomas Sweeting	87	11	Robert Linton	52
9	William Hancock	113		John Mulrenan	137
23	Charles Alden	36	18	George Dannatt	57
29	W. Pallister	26	19	John Pearson	92
Oct 3	W. Harman	107	25	Joseph Sharp	18
4	Marlin Dunne	136	June 1	James Balderson	23
9	William Higgins	25		John Hogarth	109
20	George Backhouse	90		George Tidd	126
27	John Bryan	109	2	Robert Riggall	142
Nov 1	Mark Denton	137	29	Edward Hall	63
	Septimus Grant	138	July 6	Anthony Haran	146
	William Harker	139	13	John Deyes	122
	Pattinson Clapham	141	27	John Beverly	18
	John Don	142	Aug 7	James Clayton	139
	William Hare	143	8	Jonathan Hart	105
	Arthur Bramley	144	9	Robert Denney	115
	George Bell	146	11	Thomas Collingwood	48
3	Joseph Dobson	145	13	Robert Young	29
8	James Ellerington	140	14	John Tregise	109
Nov 10	Luke Owston Warters	138	17	Tom Goodwin	138
11	John Nettleton	146		Charles Hunter	77
18	Robert Walker	117	18	Seth Lipton	36
Dec 9	John Kelly	34	24	William Wildridge	144
21	James Parrott	113		Tom Rothwell	92
1866			Sept 1	Robert Sentney	48
Jan 1	William H. Tate	91	7	John Richard Brown	111

When Sworn	Signature of Constable Sworn		When Sworn	Signature of Constable Sworn	
Sept 8	William Malton	46	Nov 14	Thomas Dawson	150
18	Enoch Ducker	115		Joseph Stockdale	156
28	William Arnold	115		Samuel Holiday	154
Dec 13	A. C. Hewitt	117		Robert Canty	155
21	William Brown	117		J. Stephenson	152
1867				William Powell	151
Jan 2	George Hargrave	91		Benjamin Wilson	149
22	Richard Sweeting	18		James Veitch	153
Feb 4	George Belton	81		Septimus Grant	135
12	George Chapman	95		Richard Warrener	145
22	Moses William Bell	34		James Faulkner	63
Mar 5	Joseph Mather	67	**1868**		
8	William John McIntyre	46	Mar 28	Thomas A. Hale	63
22	John Gray	71	Apr 6	Mark Shaw	137
Apr 8	George Blades	146	18	William Burgess	156
11	William Scott	145		William Staveley Wilson	149
12	George Butters	115	June 9	Joseph Thomas	135
20	Thomas Pickering	125	10	George Dean	145
22	William Elliott	139	22	Brigham Ward	90
	Walter Spurr Palmer	146	July 6	Henry Hill	93
	William Poster	46		John Smith	52
	Thomas Wharram	24		John Franks	43
May 3	William Longstaff	41	8	William Henry Deyes	50
	Benjamin Ducker	138	10	Patrick Robinson	147
9	John Masterman	138		William Bainton	83
22	Charles Brown	137	17	George Pickering	111
June 1	James Maquire	29	Aug 11	John Burkhill	90
26	Richard William Gibson	131		William Bean	138
July 16	Joseph Hewitt	63	19	John Curtis Hunter	62
29	John Carroll	26	21	George Farnell Wiles	150
Aug 2	Johnson Parkin	139	26	James Elston	101
	Henry Wright	40	Sept 4	William Cox	133
10	Rowland Bradley	18	Oct 9	Thomas Batty	29
15	William Cowper	131	15	Edward Thompson	116
16	John Pearson	90	27	John Tullock	69
Sept 9	Charles Parkins	29	Nov 11	Thomas Stennett	29
18	Patrick Barrett	50	Dec 1	Robinson Gray	150
21	Robert Barton Blyth	131	**1869**		
24	William Allitt	111	Jan 4	William Milner Gossy	52
28	John Thompson Lyth	144	28	William Elliott	119
Oct 31	John Hogarth	81	Feb 2	James Wray	20
Nov 7	Frederick William Briggs	73	5	Jonathan Hogarth	63
Nov 12	Robert Searby	69	16	William Hartley	156
13	James Casper Bough	122	26	Stephen Kirkwood	145
14	Henry Dawson	93		Samuel Hare	52
	Charles Rousseau	90	Mar 19	A. G. Reid	25
	Edwin Wood	147	27	John Sanderson	27
	Samuel Leighton	148	Apr 8	William Rowberry	133

When Sworn	Signature of Constable Sworn		When Sworn	Signature of Constable Sworn	
Apr 12	William Acklam	25	July 14	Charles Richardson	67
28	George Harness	156	18	George Pilgrim	98
May 8	Joseph James Sapcote	86	Aug 1	James Dawson	84
14	John Powell	150	15	Robert Blackburn	145
15	Peter Harkin	23	26	James Veitch	123
	John Callaghan	107	Sept 22	David Jackson	71
17	Mark Durkin	61	28	Charles Pratt	136
26	John George Smith	149	Oct 11	Robert Dyas	136
31	James Good	81	20	Alfred Beales	72
July 17	Isaac Nurse	54	24	Willows Tharratt	88
28	John Hall	23		John Slack	139
30	Thomas Parker	54	Nov 1	Edmond Mullins	132
31	James Charles Elliott	86	4	George Cabon	72
Sept 18	Alfred Shaw	107	9	Henry Smith	117
24	Anthony Jackson	153	15	John Straker	85
27	John Hemshall	54	25	William Mumby	117
Oct 16	Arthur James Booth	52	Dec 2	Henry Deeds	90
29	Thomas Edmund Wood	139	26	Simeon Suddaby	137
Nov 19	Alfred Smith	145	29	Charles Rouseaux	72
20	Thomas Lloyd	81	**1871**		
1870			Jan 25	David Gillis	63
Jan 4	Michael Pickering	116	Feb 3	George Cabon	157
8	Jonathan Haigh	163	18	William Lambert	137
	William Grainger	166	27	George Smith	108
	George Ellis	159	Apr 12	William Batley	111
	Thomas William Hakes	162	26	Robert Burton	34
9	John Stanfield	165	May 1	James Campbell	49
	William Frost	157	12	Joseph Kemp	64
	Albert Heald Gower	158	15	George Ringer	—
	William Banks	160	19	John Carew	47
	Thomas Gamble	161		Thomas Ward	145
	Edwin W. Brown	164	July 20	William Belshaw	63
Feb 2	John Pett	86	Sept 5	John Clark	30
Mar 15	William G. Thompson	153	Oct 3	Bilton Clark	157
17	William Robinson	149	23	William Hill	71
25	Henry Underhill	151	Nov 20	George Brown	98
Apr 5	William Cuthbert	63	25	Robert Squire	86
9	George Alcock	84		Georgeson Thompson	126
18	Joseph Sharp	30	Dec 2	Edward Simons	88
27	Charles Dowd	98		James Thornham	148
May 18	Samuel Garnet	158	8	John Smith	153
23	Tom Goodwin	139	10	Thomas Lonsdale	162
May 23	William Stacey	27	13	Henry Hillaby	59
28	Thomas Smith	90	15	Charles Dannatt	153
June 13	John Keary	84	22	Henry Slater	131
21	William Jenkins	132		William Hoult	73
July 1	John Greenwood Holnes	34	**1872**		
2	William Robinson	98	Jan 2	William Hulland	86

When Sworn	Signature of Constable Sworn		When Sworn	Signature of Constable Sworn	
Jan 12	Charles Grasby	37	Mar 21	William Johnson	132
Feb 13	Thomas Emerson	85	Apr 25	John Crighton	151
22	Leonard Jennings	110	May 3	Thomas Chestnut	102
Mar 1	William Staveley Wilson	117	6	Willows Tharratt	145
	John Horsley	161	8	Richard Lonsdale	167
	Richard Laking	159		Harrison Hookham	158
13	John Billam	21	9	William Metcalf	168
16	James Potter	153	14	Charles H. Bailey	169
22	George Pickering	126		Reuben Suddaby	171
Apr 17	Tom Turfleet	59	15	Frederick Elgey	170
19	Joseph Thompson	21	17	John Clarke Howes	173
May 3	Joseph Foster	49	19	Edward Robinson	174
28	Robert Sigsworth	159	22	William Barman Sparrow	172
June 15	Thomas Smith	74	June 9	Andrew Ballman	175
22	John W. Breeze	48		Robert Watson	63
	John Frankish	102		George Turner	176
July 17	Joshua Hunter	24	21	George Plaxton	153
18	Nathaniel Wilson	111	27	Thomas Morgan	30
19	William McDonald	164	July 5	Alfred Shaw	174
Aug 1	Robert Fiary	30	17	Keighley Robert Keighley	49
5	Arthur Bramley	132	26	John Gillings	169
30	Edwin Smith	74	31	David Gardiner	30
Oct 12	George Egerton	47	Aug 30	George Maw	170
	James Crashley	48		William Smith	171
17	John Tate	139	Sept 25	John George Smith	83
28	Thomas Clare	30	Oct 31	Frederick Gott	102
	John Enwright	74	Nov 4	George Willingham	63
Nov 2	William Cook	59	17	John Atkinson	95
	Francis McKee	77	Dec 11	James Clarke	136
8	James Dougherty	98		Ishmail Flavell	161
	William Turner	73	20	Frankish Kirby	49
15	Bernard McDonough	161	**1874**		
	Patrick Horkan	158	Jan 17	William Brady	54
16	George Ringer	146	Feb 16	George Woods	131
22	William Robinson	149	25	John Barmby	146
23	Simpson Coult	102		William Bishop	164
29	Edwin Smith	107	Apr 23	David McAdam	147
30	Edward Twidale	80	30	James Scurrell	30
Dec 5	John Harper	139	May 4	George Smith	95
13	Thomas Fairweather	88		Francis Waudby	86
27	James H. Pennock	135	22	Frederick Smith	111
1873			June 3	Giles Mitchell	171
Jan 20	John James Wright	48	4	Aaron Gilbery	153
Feb 1	William Bates	35		John Davies	161
20	George Lefley	153	17	Robert S. Kilvington	74
24	Thomas Osborne	158	July 2	William Boynton	54
25	Richard Leedham	81	9	Edwin Gossip	129
Mar 14	Edwin Burton	54	30	Samuel Gerrard	126

When Sworn	Signature of Constable Sworn		When Sworn	Signature of Constable Sworn	
July 30	Thomas Oakes	150	Aug 23	Herbert Jones	146
Sept 9	Nathaniel Wilson	109	Sept 4	Robert Blackburn	95
24	Francis Garnett	123	6	William Barry	79
24	Robert William Rogers	154	11	William Worall	147
29	John Twiddle	111	15	Jabez Barker	187
Oct 7	George Dibuly	157	24	William Brown	188
	John William Atkinson	158	Oct 2	William Gardham	79
8	Anthony Steinman	47	15	William Wilson	189
16	Hiran Canan Hare	74	22	Robert Watson	136
18	Edward Charles Gardner	71		Nathan Wright	191
24	George Enderby	146		James Bishop	192
Nov 2	Joseph William Boyd	135		Robert Woodhouse	193
12	William Mawhinnk	78		Samuel Gerrard	190
20	William Foster	126	29	William Pullman	96
Dec 1	Thomas Gedney	102	Nov 3	John Wilkinson	194
8	Thomas Thacker	74		George Crofts	195
31	John Wood	30	8	John Blackburn	185
1875			11	William Matchan	186
Jan 4	Thomas Costello	135	26	Charles Joseph Jones	183
8	Joseph Hornby	157	Dec 30	George Jackson	74
13	John Humble	151	**1876**		
Feb 3	Charles Williams	25	Jan 27	Thomas Milner	141
20	Robert Garbutt	135	29	Moses Clayton	25
Mar 11	Amos D. Knapp	129	Feb 9	George Gunson	94
31	Samuel Goodhill Battle	122	14	John William Lazenby	146
Apr 12	Robert Andrews	158	19	Thomas Pearcy	84
	Thomas Walker	35	28	Leonard Jennings	143
13	William Allen	175	Mar 6	Edwin Yabsbey	194
May 15	Andrew Ballman	157	13	Dominic McNally	141
24	Bernard Burns	110	14	S. Elkins	63
28	George Straw	177	22	Thomas Moss	189
29	John Neville Drury	35	Apr 1	Bilton Clark	194
June 1	William Burgess	176	10	Charles Watkin	19
10	Thomas Johnson	178		Robert Medforth	123
	Edward Blythe	179	May 8	John Buck	144
	Samuel Newlove	180	15	Mark Steel	100
	Thomas Hunt	181	22	Frederick Gott	113
11	John Donlan	182	June 1	Thomas Bannister	51
19	Asher Brocksom	183	5	George Scott	41
28	Henry Kingston Wray	184	17	William Boyce	74
July 8	Amos Keal	186	19	William Rhimes	100
9	John Evaghorn	185	July 11	Thomas Peter Gowing	112
13	William Kettlewell	62		Thomas Marshall Wray	185
31	Joseph Wilton	122	Aug 7	Albert Schofield	141
Aug 9	John Auckinleck	84		Robert Staveley	102
14	John William Lawson	100	14	Thomas Kirkby	113
	David Jardine	25		Frederick Snowden	172
21	Robert Fordyce	172	21	John Mitchell	181

When Sworn	Signature of Constable Sworn		When Sworn	Signature of Constable Sworn	
Sept 5	Joseph Hornby	194	Jan 28	Mark Dawson	143
18	James Scott	157	30	Frederick T. Webb	36
Oct 9	Joseph Harland	153		Charles Blashill	189
24	Frederick T. Webb	45	Feb 6	Harrison Dunn	77
30	Aaron Kemp	184	Mar 15	Daniel Gardiner	77
Nov 4	James Clarke	71		Francis M. Williams	124
8	Thomas Waldron	72	25	Francis Hardouin	39
11	Charles Frederick Bailey	144	Apr 8	Edwin Holbrook	197
Dec 4	Thomas Johnson	44	9	John Walsh	196
11	Helen Reed	138	20	Charles Baldwin	179
1877			May 1	Randall Curling	193
Jan 3	Edward Douglass	157	23	James Welburn	188
11	John E. Lee	22	29	James Greenslade	45
30	William Booth	16	June 5	James Grubb	114
Mar 6	Henry Sperage	172	13	Richard Nathanial	
	Frederick Wilson	126		Coupland	22
25	Frederick Fisher	63	19	William Alvy	196
	Frederick John Calvert	119	Aug 12	Christopher Crow	80
Apr 2	John Mumby	30	Sept 12	George Henry Chapman	193
4	Henry Robinson	141	13	Lawrence J. Jenren	124
5	William Wilson	190	Oct 11	Marr Dale	152
27	Joseph Wright	77	Nov 21	Thomas Thacker	73
May 22	John Shaw	153		Ralph King	188
31	James Greenwood	155	23	Henry Bird	161
	John Price	122	Dec 26	William H. Ashford	170
June 15	George H. Coulthard	72	**1879**		
July 11	Charles Stamp	100	Feb 8	Robert Humphrey	22
	George Goff	185		Frederick Giles	183
25	John Smith	119	10	Isaac Page Mair	20
Aug 3	William Humphrey	45		Thomas Dowman	201
6	John Hynes	168		James Wilson	14
7	James W. Fruborough	141	11	John Ness	6
13	William Tindall	193		John Noble	11
Sept 28	Joseph Randall	41		Francis O'Connor	17
Oct 11	Martin Hallman	51		Thomas Tighe	18
15	David Dye	128	13	Thomas Robinson	19
29	Robert Woodhouse	99		James Johnson	202
Nov 14	Charles Sanderson	117	17	William Hunter	203
20	William Butler	188		Abel Murray	204
Dec 5	Aaron Waines	62	Mar 17	James Booth	166
12	Joseph Henry Mawes	195	21	Joseph Thompson	163
1878			24	Edwin Burton	181
Jan 11	Edmund Mullins	198		Thompson Wrightson	121
	William Wilson	199	31	James Rennison	149
Jan 11	William Bramble	196	Apr 22	William Ford	111
	David Hardy	197	May 22	Patrick Regan	171
14	George William Bird	200	June 9	Robert Hart	98
28	William Elliott	126	12	Christopher Lamb	181

When Sworn	Signature of Constable Sworn		When Sworn	Signature of Constable Sworn	
June 26	Robert Gray	165	Jan 17	Joseph Wilkinson	138
Aug 8	Walter James Woods	202	Mar 1	William Cocks	138
18	Valentine George	122	9	William John Marks	105
26	John Doughty	137	Apr 3	Fred Johnson	95
Oct 17	Tom Wilkinson	97	5	George Robert Coulthard	87
	William Phillips	108	May 1	D. W. Hopper	189
Nov 4	William Coates	47	30	James Catton Cook	145
Dec 9	James Bird	107	June 27	Edward Mackey	182
1880			July 4	William Appleby	96
Jan 7	Eli Booth	188	28	George Salvidge	145
17	Joseph Attwood	113	Sept 6	George Orford	89
	Michael Tighe	137		Francis Walker	161
Mar 9	William Wright	169	Oct 13	George Henry Harpham	207
15	William Phillips	201		Charles Bourne	111
May 13	Benjamin Barnicoat	114	23	Thomas Walker	208
June 3	James Smedley	165	31	William Gray	137
5	Michael Mannion	141	Nov 21	James Cox	87
17	Thomas Mackay	177	23	Henry Bird	188
Sept 23	James Campbell	—	Dec 11	James M. Grubb	145
28	George Dale	119	26	Charles Blashill	205
Oct 1	William Ball	183	**1883**		
12	Robert George Rippon	64	Feb 22	George William Bailey	206
Nov 5	George Girling	90		James Clarke	141
17	Henry Maltby	77	Mar 14	John Miller	209
	Robert Suddaby	119		Thomas Whileyman	214
24	John Rutherford	124		Arthur Harrison	—
27	George Anderson	89		John F. Johnson	221
1881				James Plowman	217
Jan 1	Reuben Suddaby	77		Robert F. Boynton	210
10	Edwin Humphrey	89		Joseph Hargrave	220
11	James Adamson	176		James William Wright	215
	John William Crosby	188		Samuel Rylett	218
14	Lewis Hemingway	53		Leonard Nicholson	212
May 27	James Henry Grant	74		Charles Burton	219
	George Caleb	177		William Wallis	216
31	George Sinderson	107		George Thomas Bowers	211
	John W. Wardall	171		Henry Boddy	213
Aug 5	Welburn Royston	89		Robert Hodgson	222
Sept 5	Reuben Milner	206		William Loconstew	—
Oct 4	Harry Hardy	182	29	Joseph Porter	225
6	Edwin Arthur Cook	96		Herbert Suddaby	154
	Charles McAnliffe	138		Frank Scrimshaw	227
10	Thomas Alvin	129		James Parker	223
24	Frederick Ashton	—		William Hester	184
Nov 18	Charles Panitzke	53		George Watson	228
Dec 9	George Stockdale	54		John C. Southwick	158
	William Kirk	68		Errington W. Arkley	226
1882				William Atkinson	229

When Sworn	Signature of Constable Sworn		When Sworn	Signature of Constable Sworn	
Mar 29	Joseph Coverdale	230	Dec 24	George H. Dawson	63
	George Nettleton	231	**1885**		
	James Blanshard	244	Jan 1	Bartley William Felstead	260
	Richard William Leighton	232		Thomas Sawdon	258
May 8	George Chambers	226		Gibson Knox	249
June 23	John Almond	145		John Cherry	266
	George Dawson	150		William Rawling	265
July 2	James Lavin	125		William J. Fussey	264
Aug 20	Thomas William			William Foreman	263
	Atkinson	212		George Edwin Jackson	261
	George Thomas Douglass	213		James Fawcett	259
Sept 25	John Magnus	147		John William Simpson	257
Oct 13	Richard Keal	141		Fred Horseman	255
Nov 21	John Charles Neale	94		Edward Davison	254
Dec 8	William Hairsine	143		Thomas Appleby	253
10	Robert Sanderson	69		Charles Byron Harper	252
24	George Robson	227		Henry Augustine Doran	251
1884				William Bristow	250
June 2	Wilkinson Sharp	78		Robert Hill Mace	256
Feb 29	George F. Wilson	147		Thomas Marshall	262
Apr 29	Arthur Ferrand	145	19	John William Sowersby	54
	Anthony Savage	117		William Spicer	55
May 16	James Wharton	210		F. Gooderham	167
June 24	Levi Scott	161	Mar 5	Edward Hotham	125
Aug 9	Charles Dickinson	145	20	Wrightson Smithson	54
Sept 6	William Ruddiforth	50	Aug 8	William Cowp	249
Oct 7	Henry Hind Amos	38	Sept 3	John George Hoyes	156
	John Conley	130		Thomas Mennell	123
30	James Skelton	125	7	Joseph Crisp	193
Nov 4	James William Dalton	201	Oct 24	George Dukes	50
Dec 23	William Watson	127	**1886**		
	Edward Savill	156	Jan 30	Walter Edward Gilbert	
24	Henry Dickinson	233		Major Chief Const.	—
	William Geave	234	Feb 4	J. Thirsk	63
	James Edward Hill	236	22	James Wood Dunaghan	257
	George Hairsine	247	26	West Hoggard	209
	Thomas Tuton Rogerson	244	Mar 4	Francis Platen Denovan	224
	Henry T. Dukes	240	11	Charles William Brewster	267
	Charles W. Smith	248	Apr 1	Joseph Walker	56
	Thomas Veal	241	9	Thomas James Coulthard	256
	Arthur Credland	238		Edwin Sanderson	70
	Charles Sewell	239		Charles Onions	138
	G. Watson	242	May 10	A. Murray	261
	Danvers Hart	246		James Greig	260
Dec 24	Henry Beckett	243	June 9	John William	
	R. Harrison	237		Wigglesworth	50
	T. Hewson	245	19	Alfred Goodrum	149
	T. Knight	235		John Hudson	76

When Sworn	Signature of Constable Sworn		When Sworn	Signature of Constable Sworn	
July 1	William Griffiths	169	Nov 13	William Holmes	206
Aug 12	Fred Mathews	169	Dec 21	Thomas Barker	264
Sept 23	Thomas Sawyer	208	**1890**		
Oct 1	William W. Wright	266	Jan 1	Robert Burton	128
7	Harry Lound	226	25	Robert Shooter	111
Nov 1	F. R. Gurney		Feb 14	James Proctor	46
	Capt. Ch. Constable	—	Mar 24	John North	44
18	George Mulcare	139		Eric Frederick Spencer	252
1887			Apr 9	George Pickering	127
Jan 13	John Tamplin	150		Walter Gant	50
Feb 3	John Matthews	211	May 16	Henry George Ward	95
10	James Henry Nicholson	128	July 4	Harry Naylor	240
Mar 8	John Prince	237	10	Harry Playfoot	186
24	Edward Thompson	127	28	John I. G. Dilley	259
May 5	John Weldon	224	Aug 1	Adam George Barker	264
July 23	John Thomas Carter	184	8	James Ramedin	122
Sept 13	John Cherry	89	Sept 10	George Ellis	209
Nov 17	George Benson	138	25	Samuel Tolson	93
1888			Oct 3	John W. Marshall	249
Jan 4	George William Marshall	267	Nov 11	Frederick Onions	253
12	Arthur Edward Anderson	63	13	George William Mitton	234
Feb 2	James William Burton	145	27	Edwin Bailey	60
9	Abraham Thomas		Dec 2	John W. Wardell	146
	Leonard	111	3	John William Hunter	267
May 3	Thomas Blackburn	216	**1891**		
24	John Cooper	257	Jan 12	Tom Barrett	—
June 7	Thomas Bratton	41	20	John Brewer	95
22	George Spriggs	99	Feb 4	J. A. Burroughs	93
July 3	William Stephenson	193	7	Richard Kitchen	—
18	William Ambrose Hall	73		George William Asher	95
	A. Haigh	267	14	John William Barton	—
	A. Maple	250	Mar 7	Thomas Hoyes	113
Sept 20	Charles Jones	184		Edwin James Field	158
1889			12	George H. Winduss	146
Jan 10	John William Wardell	249	Apr 2	George W. Carter	127
	J. V. Morris	113	15	Joseph Henry Howlett	224
Mar 28	Walter Pike	111	18	William Harrison	130
May 9	George Bean	41		John W. Baker	90
July 5	Alfred Bromley	207	25	George Hardy	224
11	Job Strange	51	May 14	Robert Jefferys	235
Aug 19	T. E. Holmes	209	June 1	William Catley	10
	George W. Ellerington	51		George Holtby	106
	Thomas Walkington	206		John Barker	118
28	Charles Smith	113		G. T. Harrison	3
Aug 30	George Nawton	127		Timothy Barmby	254
Sept 10	T. Baker	95		George Kilvington	7
Oct 8	James Grindall	226		Sam Taylor	94
11	James Stephenson	87		D. Sleight	82

When Sworn	Signature of Constable Sworn		When Sworn	Signature of Constable Sworn	
June 1	Robert Danby	120	Mar 1	Frederick Smith	261
8	Charles Richardson	67	14	Henry Ayers	259
9	Willie Rhodes	268	Apr 27	Horson Jackson	174
July 14	William Cherry	130	June 6	William Thompson	253
21	Herbert Fallgate	61	9	John Peasson	—
Sept 3	Amos E. Young	183	29	William Hunt	167
22	Benjamin Grainger	62	July 12	Albert Edward Fisher	216
Oct 8	James Henry Nicholson	—	21	John Graham Mann	142
Nov 4	Francis J. Wilson	117	Aug 29	Samuel Day	78
9	David Owens	206	Sept 11	Henry Turner	140
12	William Witty	216	Oct 28	Arthur Moore	142
14	William Tiplady	150	Nov 13	William John Burke	90
	Robert Bray Maplethorpe	168	22	Charles Ivens	91
Dec 17	Charles Marsh	90	**1894**		
1892			Jan 9	George Henry Williamson	140
Jan 8	Simpson Clarke	—		Ernest Hammond	166
19	William North	43	10	George Parsons	106
	James W. Stark	50	12	Robert Saxton	167
Feb 19	Thomas Briggs	—	Feb 13	Edward Palmer	206
Mar 1	Thomas Whelan	—	15	George William Butters	35
	Thomas Flanagan	—	Mar 7	Willie McTavish	44
5	Thomas Williams	63	8	J. West	85
Apr 20	Wilton Curwen	257	Apr 10	William George	
26	John William Robson	84		Thompson	128
	Arthur Santon	56	18	William Eastoe	159
May 5	John E. Dobson	57	May 4	Thomas Cornwell	115
6	Donald Dunbar	216	June 4	Harvey Bateman	206
June 20	Arthur George Bland	—	22	Walter W. Leah	100
Aug 12	John Pinkney	134	27	W. H. Parker	140
	Frank Potts	51	July 26	W. H. Lyons	213
13	Mark Richard Chapman	—	Aug 1	R. C. Rule	115
23	William Wilkinson	—	13	Edward Albert Clifford	
Sept 7	Robert Wright	252		Gowings	—
	William Henry Taylor	16	Sept 17	John William Cross	—
19	John Bell	188	Oct 10	Joseph Hudson	173
Oct 5	George Cook	—	Nov 29	John Robert Rangecroft	—
10	Vincent W. Brooks	—	Dec 7	William Ashton	253
17	Thomas Edward Brunton	90	12	William J. Hunt	101
24	John Pillinger	92	17	David McGregor	213
Dec 14	Samuel Harness	146	21	Jackson Maplethorpe	190
15	William Durham	167	**1895**		
17	James Tiplady	188	Jan 25	John Boyes	159
1893			Feb 18	Fred Pearcy	213
Jan 6	Tom Richard Brown	72	Mar 1	Josiah Dawson	45
Jan 10	Arthur Francis Burton	—	July 2	Charles Dawson	253
	William Harvey King	—	4	Daniel Langham	65
30	Andrew Hinds Archer	58	10	Albert Edward Daddy	103
Feb 22	Harvey Ross	174		Samuel Gall	133

When Sworn	Signature of Constable Sworn		When Sworn	Signature of Constable Sworn	
Aug 6	George Edward Petler	84	Apr 24	John Waines	268
Sept 28	Fred Wiles	129	May 22	Daniel Roche	140
Oct 10	William Brummitt Colbridge	99	June 26	John Robert Anscombe	160
			July 7	Frederick William French	291
12	Alfred Lee	114	Aug 26	Thomas Cornwell	110
15	Reuben Dalton	65	Sept 29	Mark Elgey Atkinson	64
23	Sydney Watson Phipps	114		Jonathan Bowran	160
Nov 5	Robert Shields	42	Oct 6	Arthur Edward Thurlow	184
6	Herbert Bean	88	16	Arthur Herbert Field	125
11	Michael Hynes	164		Walter Scott	201
Dec 6	Arthur Ridsdale	77	27	Frederick Robinson	239
	John Thomas Marshall	145		Edward Brown	258
	Arthur Andrews	179	**1897**		
	Alfred Amos Jackson	233	Jan 1	Alfred Bell	88
	George Arthur Fox	269	20	John Oxtoby	195
	Francis William Tregise	270	26	Ambrose Harrison	223
	William Fall	271	Feb 8	William Budden	116
	James Henry Woodhouse	272	Mar 24	James Pearson	97
	Jesse Lee Peart	273	July 5	James Henry Warren	269
	John Oxtoby	274	Nov 1	Constantine Kostrovitzki	270
	John Richards	275	9	Ernest Ely Bailey	280
	Alfred Cook	276	10	Henry Bryant	291
	George McDonald	277		William Pallister	292
	Arthur William Marshall	278	Nov 25	Thomas Arthur Sinclair	—
	George Alexander Burton	279		Charles William Ingham	—
	Fred J. Goundrill	280		Henry Wilkinson	—
	James Elston	281		Charles Reedson	—
	John William Hebblewhite	282		William C. R. Bentley	—
	William Thacker	283		William Pooly	—
	Septimus Bromley	284		George William Dugurd	304
	Henry Dowdes	285		Ernest Towse	—
	Osborne L. Cossens	286		Frankish Charles Kirby	—
10	James Leppington	287		Harry Wollas	—
	Nathaniel Allerston	290	Nov 29	Percy Hopgood	294
	George Dearing	288		Joseph Taylor	295
11	William Harland Bornfather	289		James W. Malton	299
				John Matthew Ezard	300
23	Herbert Wilkison	52		Frederick Norwood	306
1896				Thomas H. Harrison	307
Jan 1	Alexander Gray	274		Dorsey Ireland	310
20	James Ellerker	52		Richard Leppington	311
	Arthur Sanderson	240		Herbert North	312
Feb 17	William Sykes	200	30	Ernest William Farr	173
Mar 3	George Harry Musson	98	Dec 1	Robert Boyes	—
18	Fred Sonley	42		George William Cornell	309
24	William R. T. Jackson	99		Edmund Dales	—
Apr 13	Charles East	140		Charles Stainton	79
			15	Ernest Hartefan	107

When Sworn	Signature of Constable Sworn		When Sworn	Signature of Constable Sworn	
Dec 15	Richard Pearson	289	**1900**		
23	William Henry Shaw	275	Jan 15	Richard Cleveland	42
	William Faully	256	Mar 16	Daniel Tomlinson	
1898				Hudson	248
Jan 21	Robert Ward	223		Fred Hawkesworth	66
24	John Jefferson	248	22	Thomas Gibson	83
31	Walter Turrell Boanus	117	26	Frederick Hylderton	
Feb 15	Thomas Oats	208		Barber	160
Mar 17	George Drust	224	Apr 20	Ralph Tiplady	116
Apr 5	Thomas Edward Howden	33		Fred Jackson	261
7	John Burton	146		John Robert Stott	299
May 11	Robert Kilvington	169	June 23	John Jackson	157
June 3	Joseph Ralph	208	July 2	John William Hill	83
July 21	Joe Wrigley	303	3	William Thomas Andrews	275
Aug 3	Fred T. Goundrill	83	6	Frank Woodhouse	—
8	George W. Oldfield	307	Aug 2	Michael Digedan	52
Oct 7	Alfred Treacy	88	27	Willie Smith	242
10	John Binnington	195		Robert John Savage	62
Nov 1	Edward Butler	151		Edmund Crawford	113
28	Johnson Dent	86		Robert Longfield Traynor	107
Dec 6	Arthur W. Norris	109	Sept 3	Fred Addison	100
9	John William Thrower	72	12	Frederick Smith	131
14	Herbert Foster	260	22	Harold Dick	47
1899			Oct 12	Arthur Edward Shaw	133
Jan 10	John Warren Davis	158	18	Harrison Cocksworth	84
Feb 3	John William Hater	224		William Dalby Allerton	277
9	Walter Lee	88	23	Sidney Mason	274
Mar 13	Frederick Joseph Dewen	242	29	Richard B. Ashby	244
22	Edwin James Field	48	Nov 16	Fred Wright	272
23	Alfred Storr	51	19	Tom Arksey	260
Apr 11	John W. Duffield	275	**1901**		
May 8	Thomas Rodwell	289	Feb 27	Charles T. Bristow	167
16	Robert Scotter	81	Mar 23	Charles Gladstone	
	Joseph Vollans	287		Jackson	256
24	George Leggott	280	May 6	Charles Hopkin	223
	Charles Edward Stott	59		Harry Warters	247
June 6	William Galloway	314	Aug 3	James J. Brown	243
July 22	Ernest Fryer	132		John Edward Collier	180
Aug 3	Walter Walker	261	5	George William Metcalf	136
26	George Henry Hall	160	13	John William Slater	227
Sept 14	Harry Garthwaite	42	21	Thomas Young	262
Oct 12	David A. Nicklin	115	Sept 30	John Thomas Nichols	339
20	Charles Pearcey	314		John R. Hanley	324
	John Henry Hornby	40		Thomas Adamson	340
Oct 22	Harry Norton	48		Percy Hunt	322
Nov 1	Caleb Smithson Wood	75		William Hall Fawcett	323
Dec 4	John Winter	157		Ralph Sanderson	342
8	Arthur Webster	275		Edward Sherwood	343

When Sworn	Signature of Constable Sworn		When Sworn	Signature of Constable Sworn	
Sept 30	Thomas William Haigh	321	Oct 2	Richard Crawford	349
	Ernest Carrick	341	3	Herbert Bryden	352
	George Parker	320	6	Dick Clayton Havergate	348
	William Waller	344	13	Charles Frederick	
	Willie Walker	316		Lambert	351
	Fred Harrison	337		William Atkin	353
	Horace Austin	317		Ernest Bennett	354
	Arthur Jewitt	328	22	Frederick Charles Ware	350
	George Robert Evans	330	23	Thomas Birkitt	167
	Arthur T. Halliday	329	28	John Turner	355
	Herbert Rose	257	Nov 10	Thomas Tichiaz	356
	William Forth	334	**1903**		
	James Hall	338	Jan 12	Alfred Kingston	281
	Alfred James Foster	158		James Connaughton	332
	Lancelot Danby	336	23	John Timothy Oliver	112
	Albert Harrison Whitfield	32	Feb 20	Thomas Rhea	277
	Joseph William Hodgson	335	26	John Somerville	121
	Edgar Gilbert Lockwood	332		Joseph E. Hudson	353
	David Spittlehouse	333	Mar 2	William G. Swaby	37
	George E. S. Dent	318	4	Harry Duck	316
	Edward Dobson	325		William Ellison Maidment	355
	William G. Eaton	326	6	Frederick James Palmer	167
	Charles P. Moyses	319	28	John McDonald	159
	Samuel J. Mustin	327	Apr 21	James William Wattam	178
	G. E. W. Mulford	331	24	John William Morris	144
Oct 3	Sidney E. Pearson	315		Allison Rispin Saville	196
Nov 27	Walter Robinson	114		Albert Edward Snowden	311
1902			May 1	William Frederick Lyon	186
Jan 27	John R. Gardham	47	30	Smith Wild	175
Apr 5	Henry Dixon	198	July 3	William Austin Thacker	344
11	Arthur Hopper	209	10	Henry Isaac Hillier	328
18	Thomas Armstrong	226	21	William Haidlow	149
May 5	Walter G. Tomlinson	245	Aug 25	Edmund Brumpton	250
13	George Edward Fowler	44	Sept 5	William Albert Dalton	248
30	George Arthur Frederick		8	Frederick Shirley Young	89
	Condor	269		A. E. Stewart	98
July 25	Henry Statham	315		James Leonard Stanley	93
Aug 5	John Horatio Roberts	269		Arthur Poad Taylor	313
11	William Conneally	71		Henry Baldwick Ake	48
	Davis Norris	194	21	James Barr	171
Sept 1	Percy Harry Nixon	102	Oct 7	Edward Young Martin	206
18	Albert George Jefferson	37	12	George Ernest Rylands	121
	Cornelius O'Kelly	249		Edwin Fareham	327
26	Richard William Parrott	316	Dec 17	P. Malcolm	CC
Oct 2	Walter Bennett	193	**1904**		
	John William Pratt	345	Jan 11	George Henry Ripley	175
	Albert Edward Garbutt	346		Alfred Charles Every	233
	Charles Baker	347	13	Ernest Fisher	200

When Sworn	Signature of Constable Sworn		When Sworn	Signature of Constable Sworn	
Jan 19	John Anthony Barkley	161	Feb 11	William Elliot	363
20	John Arthur Hart	172	28	Henry Chilton	80
22	John Boyes	303	Apr 20	Joseph Wigglesworth	204
	Richard Walker	333	26	Richard William Prince	57
Feb 25	James Deighton Taylor	186		Hyma Watson	—
Mar 2	William Garton	147		Richard Henry	
9	George William Rouse	98		Richardson	364
	Thomas Binnington	253		Robert Jackson Caton	152
Apr 7	Charles Rainton	238	May 2	Alfred Ernest Newton	67
	Albert Knights	118	24	Francis Charles Greener	56
8	William Bennett	214		Thomas Tilburn	264
11	Joseph Blowman	263	26	James Hall	170
13	Fred Hargreaves	254		John William Buttery	253
	Thomas Wilson Watkins	94	June 12	John Blyth	107
26	James Frederick Bingham	78	July 11	Charles Archer	67
May 13	William Jemieson			Thomas William Nash	203
	Greener	253	Aug 2	Arthur Acey	206
	Walter Skinner	76	4	George Hall	47
18	Harry Downing	196		Arthur Savage	202
June 1	Herbert Simpson	148	14	George Arthur Reed	106
9	Richard Carter	308	Sept 9	Walter Sellers	114
29	George Henry		13	Thomas Arnott	113
	Woodmansey	126	19	Albert Drury	278
	Ernest Albert Hebaon	191	Oct 2	Ernest William Parnaby	199
July 1	Arthur Sergeant	355		Harold John Kirk	174
13	David Beattie	39	7	Herbert Fisher	310
	Frederick Edward Crack	265	27	Harry Robinson	206
Aug 23	Herbert George Duck	243	Dec 9	Charles Salt	212
Sept 13	Arthur Gresty	356	11	William Henry Sewell	155
15	John Henry Ford	357	12	George Douthwaite	180
	Walter Bradley	171	**1906**		
21	Simpson Hodgson	53	Jan 3	Ephraim Curzon	172
	George Alfred Crosby	114	16	Joseph Sidney Kettle	172
Nov 11	George Robert Newman	172		James Slater Drury	32
23	Henry Patrick Eam	239	20	Arthur S. Dickinson	187
Dec 7	Edmund Hilliard	185	Feb 9	Thomas Lincoln	108
1905				William Mann	313
Jan 10	John Bayley	216	21	John Alfred Pond	229
	Gilbert Waddington	359	23	Fred Grey	87
16	Arthur Rowson	358	Apr 19	Thomas Edward	
	Edwin Bell	360		Sanderson	118
23	Joseph Kilvington	37	27	Albert Crusie	
26	George William Foster	361		Hawkesworth	53
30	William Twidle	327	May 1	Stewart Witty	118
Jan 31	George Edward Farmery	47	29	John Coupland	313
Feb 1	John William Smith	59	June 1	Ernest William Edgar	
7	Jabez Clarke	138		Jesson	—
	Thomas William		7	Harrison Boothby	306
	Mackerill	362			

When Sworn	Signature of Constable Sworn		When Sworn	Signature of Constable Sworn	
June 7	Frederick Edward Stones	150	Sept 27	William Brown	162
8	Charles Frederick Pratt	284		William Harcroft	122
Aug 13	Frank Dales	74	28	Abraham Hawes	290
	Harry Hardwick	153	30	Horace Deyes	373
15	Ernest Roper Hickingbotham	205	Oct 29	Fred Wright	229
Oct 4	William Ernest Bird	80	Dec 27	Mathew Steadman	90
	James Arthur Nicholson	363		Albert Edwin Mee	316
20	Frederick Stone	356		Henry Conruth	357
26	Robert Milner	235		William Buttey	182
Nov 27	John William Nendick	179		Robert John Buttle	172
Dec 8	Robert Macnamara Paugher	136	**1908**		
12	James William Camp	227	Jan 16	Edward Thompson	191
17	John Charles Conyers	202	21	Albert Veasey	372
1907			Feb 25	Herbert Blyth	303
Jan 10	Henry Parsons	359	Mar 12	Joseph William Gascoigne	46
29	Frank Parker	49	17	Joseph William Cusworth	244
Mar 16	James Smith	216	26	William George Banks	176
23	John Bottomley Howgate	239	Apr 18	Joseph Colley	180
Apr 2	Henry Donaldson	356	May 16	William Oliver	244
3	David Percy Lamb	313	June 26	Joseph Moody	217
16	Percival Charles Markham	—	July 21	Thomas James Mullins	162
	Frank Lill Hodgson	—	Aug 13	Fred Bayley	105
18	Harry Willerton	90		Cecil Sheard Broughton	347
22	Charles Edward Tate	303		Arthur William Howard	375
May 11	Josiah Robert Fisher	98		Thomas Samuel Parker	376
13	Arthur Robert Haldenby	—		Frederick Joseph Brown	377
June 6	William George Benstead	365		William Warcup	378
	William Fox	366		Thomas Askham	379
	Arthur Harold Murrey	367		William Robert Bownes	380
10	Francis George Benson Arton	368		George Edward Dawson	381
	Charles William Fanthorpe	369		Robert Hamilton	382
July 4	John Wass Pallister	370	Sept 8	Herbert James Hewitt	366
30	Ernest Walford	119	29	Reginald George Hood	123
	Arthur Whittleton	163	Oct 29	George Albert Hempsall	153
	Harold Carlee	202	Dec 18	Richard Bezzant Wakefield	376
	George Henry Hardy	98	**1909**		
	George William Wilkinson	371	Jan 15	William Hector John Purcell	68
July 30	Thomas Booth	372	Feb 17	Fred Simpson	352
	Harry Weston	173	23	Robert Cox Heap	187
	John William Walker	365	Mar 4	John Edward Bird	293
	Frederick Waterson	235	5	Arthur Featherstone	165
	Sidney John Stanley	49		Walter Barnwell	383
			23	John William Walmsley	96
			Apr 7	William Grindell	345
			May 4	Archibald Hopkin	141

When Sworn	Signature of Constable Sworn		When Sworn	Signature of Constable Sworn	
May 25	Harry Hardwick	268	Jan 13	Benjamin Shorter	385
28	Harry Broader	161	14	James Malynn	386
June 14	James Thomas Fowler	215	16	Joseph Holmes	387
July 28	Henry O. E. Stubbs	218	Feb 10	Charles Gordon Anthony	201
31	Charles Henry Clift	228	16	William Large	135
Aug 24	Benjamin Acey	355	Mar 1	William Gosling	189
Sept 22	Frederick W. Hinch	355	14	Robert Whittleton	388
30	William Kay Northgraves	222	Apr 12	Harvey Stark	202
Oct 4	Thomas Graham	85	24	George Henry Brabbs	225
19	Puchard Pearson	177		Henry Wilson	268
21	John Richard Hewson	161	May 2	Sydney Shipley	137
26	Reginald Newall	355	8	William Henry Fenwick	377
Nov 9	Alfred Stow	353	16	Ralph William Briggs	390
	John Frederick Dickinson	177		Andrew Thomas Robert Long	268
16	Sydney Pearson	249		Edgar Lund	389
30	Henry Richardson	377		Sydney Mews	33
1910			June 8	Charles Thomson	391
Feb 12	Cyril Duck	252	9	Robert Johnson Durrands	392
Mar 7	Harold Roydhouse	384	12	Frederick Herbert Steadman	220
23	Elija Osborne Mason	161	July 27	Allan Vyse	266
30	Thomas Douglas	78	Aug 4	Harry Beckett	393
Apr 2	Herbert Peal Atkinson	143	17	Samuel Gossip	70
	Harold Scarff	191	24	Herbert Milner	394
9	David Hall	276	Sept 13	Reginald Hardgrave	58
May 6	George Luplin	249	27	Alexander Williams Tyson	391
19	Harrison Ingamells	128	29	William Gray	381
21	Herbert Brocklebank	219	Oct 3	Fred Pears Musham	39
June 14	John Thomas Bell	215		Harry Burgess	244
21	Harold Lewellyn Drewell	69	11	Sydney Warden	289
29	Albert George Cordock	230	12	John Robert Smith	302
July 8	Rupert Oliver	236	24	George Atkinson	395
26	Alfred White	46	Nov 10	Robert Coulson	397
	John Edward Williamson Smith	310		Charles Clayton Burton	396
Aug 9	Henry William Rowson	119	14	Henry Wilson	398
Sept 6	Robert Peele	232	18	Robert Holtby	399
29	George Morley D.C.L.	CC	20	Anthony Blazier	400
Nov 1	Edward Marson	228	Dec 5	Charles Walter Cook	401
9	Charles Herbert Curtis	205	18	James William Tuthill	187
15	Arthur Douthwaite	356	19	Thomas Lister	141
	John Thomas Moore	264		William Henry Noble	401
29	Henry Seymour Robinson	251	**1912**		
Dec 16	Fred Allan Lurder	266	Jan 24	Bertram Monk Wheeler	217
20	Ernest Bradley	187	Feb 1	John Thomson Scrimgeour	
1911			5	John Henry Gunson	402
Jan 9	George Andrew	260			
	George Metcalf Garland	384			
Jan 13	Charles Dowson	69			

When Sworn	Signature of Constable Sworn		When Sworn	Signature of Constable Sworn	
Mar 2	William Joseph Hunter	403	June 9	William Stockdale	314
14	Edmund Lowson Danby	62	24	Arthur John White	232
Apr 20	James Henigan	86		Thomas Waudby	363
	Richard Ralph	163		Frank Woodmansey	419
29	Frederick Titus James	302	July 1	Robert William Reed	312
May 1	Herbert William		22	Joseph Henry Steele	156
	Roughton	66	23	Thomas Pickering	31
8	George Bean	404	Aug 8	James William Boocock	41
14	George Edward Harvatt	69	Sept 2	Albert Hall	421
29	Francis Joseph Walsh	405		George William Whilde	284
June 3	Arthur Thompson	406		Archibald McKay	422
	Richard Gordon Ness	408	9	John Richardson	423
	Arthur Frederick Rose	407	Oct 4	George Robert Barker	251
6	Robert Kneeshaw		6	William Dosser Pawson	55
	Germain	409	9	John Holmes Edlington	424
	Arthur Pickering	411		Benjamin Hepworth	365
	John Ernest Porter	412	13	William Hairsine	426
7	George Robert Edkins	410	Nov 8	Thomas Sidney Smith	210
	John Tom Rose	413	10	Stanley Sowersby	425
11	John Richard Batwright	415	21	Pollard Hill	318
	George Alfred Stainton	414	22	John Lynas	223
Aug 3	Joseph Stanley Fully	72	26	John Edward Hird	237
19	Alexander Charlesworth	116	28	Harold Cooke	197
Sept 20	Robert Henry Daniel	290		Albert Harry Bradley	164
17	Sidney Charles Stanton	81	Dec 8	Albert Widdas	427
26	Arthur Carlill	11	19	Albert Clark	409
Oct 9	James William West	416	23	John William Wiffen	302
21	George Beales	246	**1914**		
30	Harold Frederick Lyons	60	Jan 1	William Edward Barford	207
31	James Garton	417	Feb 9	George Robert Irwin	211
Nov 26	William Benjamin Peam	388		William Marshall	212
	John Gibson	416		Herbert Mews	—
Dec 2	William Bilton	139		Ernest Harper	65
18	Herbert Dearing	310		Charles Arnold Stevenson	54
24	William Price	189	12	Arthur Robson	428
1913			17	George Kirby Dennison	429
Jan 6	Robert Johnson	377	23	Ernest Frederick Mitchell	430
13	James Robert Kell	108	Mar 16	Sidney Brown	432
Mar 28	Thomas Percy Wright	320		Leonard Dickinson	431
	Henry Wilson	374	23	Henry Burton	434
Apr 2	Nichol Foster	317		Ernest Leppington	433
8	James O'Sullivan	272	Apr 29	George Fred. Stonehouse	
12	Harold Priestman Cross	257		Porter	435
Apr 15	Thomas Henry Lanquick	251	May 5	Arthur Pinder	320
16	Robert Percy L.		15	William Lake	420
	Richardson	146	June 25	Fred Dennison Allerston	65
22	Bertram Frank Ashton	418	July 1	Reginald Johnson	72
June 6	Francis Joseph Watson	210	25	George Palethorpe	58

When Sworn	Signature of Constable Sworn		When Sworn	Signature of Constable Sworn	
Aug 20	Sidney Marshall Redhead	386	Apr 28	Frank Welton	165
	Frank Dennis	71		Arthur Wattam	48
Sept 8	Alfred Edward Reynolds	421	29	Fred Wilson	82
	Ernest Filby	430	June 10	Harold Harrison Lowis	139
10	William Graham Hill	249	11	Albert Edward Evans	197
15	Ernest Staples	175	12	Thomas Patrick Ryan	148
21	Albert Dann	84	16	Frederick William Albert	
	William Henry Peckitt	289		Krouse	199
Oct 9	George Massey	424	20	Thomas Henry Langwick	305
	Harry Jaram	436	July 14	Bernard Londsbrough	224
	Michael Mulchinock	404		John Edgar Huxley	57
Nov 17	Thomas Albert Sawdon	255	16	James Arthur Jordan	231
Dec 1	John William Davison	437	18	Arthur Broadhead	181
5	Charles Henry Wright			Harold Offen	158
	Dossor	51		Clarence Callan	188
10	Mark Hill	438	22	Frederick Victor Oliver	153
15	Fred Goodrich	439	30	William Nicholson	237
1915			Aug 25	Thomas Craven	60
Jan 5	Richard Francis Dearing	440	Sept 1	Thomas Henry Furniss	314
22	James William Boocock	41	2	Harold Gordon Aragreen	234
	James Edward Achmans	45	8	George Robert Allerston	315
Mar 2	Arthur Charles Dearing	275		John Henry Allerston	249
Apr 6	Frederick Barker	104	10	William Ewart Kirby	241
1919				Harry Jarvis	92
Jan 11	Thomas Henry Barker	142	16	Robert Johnson	262
Feb 12	Reuben Wilkinson	352	22	Harold Marriott	265
19	Harry Tessyman	365	29	Frank Jowett	213
27	Andrew Robert Kennedy	82	Oct 13	Angus William McLeod	120
Mar 5	Walter West	101	21	Robert Henry Yates	233
	Thomas Branton Ellarby	47	22	Horace Dale	381
17	Sydney Macfarlane	173	23	Walter James Spires	317
	William Wigglesworth	130	27	Harold Coctoby	329
	James Wiltshire	183		William Hayhurst	251
25	George William Green	219	28	Seth Jackson	161
	Harry Auther Thompson	134	Nov 7	William Percy Collins	259
	Nelson Hentall	92		Harry Tessyman	365
	Charles Twidale	88	Dec 9	Alfred North	286
31	Harry Field	111		Cecil Edmund Brenchley	184
Apr 7	John Douglas Parker	149		James Thomas Brooke	267
	Robert Garton	127		Herbert Woodthorpe	256
	George Henry Atkinson	150		Samuel Loft	102
14	George William Atkinson		10	Fred Hayton	55
	Thomas	138	15	Fred Pears Musham	39
Apr 15	William Nudd	54		Richard Dowson	
24	Percy Dogson	117		Moorfoot	364
28	George Bean	73		Charles Wilfred Swann	369
	Percy Goodfellow	124		Albert Bean	299
	Henry Bristow Wiles	137		Albert Broumpton	331

When Sworn	Signature of Constable Sworn	
Dec 15	Richard Wilfred Smithson	353
22	Robert Charles Rumsey	44
30	John Albert Shaw	310
31	John William Isbester	82
1920		
Jan 5	Albert Lawrence Clarkson	414
	Edwin Healey	406
7	Charles Sawdon	333
12	Albert Samuel Barnes	168
13	Hugh Sackville Bryant	347
Feb 2	Herbert Edwin Roe	167
9	Thomas Wilburn	311
Apr 9	David Hardbattle	332
	Joseph Stephenson	154
	George William Prince	166
20	Ronald Wallace Turner	383
27	Cyril Cockfield	50
June 9	George Richard Lowing	45
22	Fred Clarke	91
	James Cook	384
	Joseph Henry Walker	346
	Albert John Willis	169
23	Joseph Dennis	362
Aug 5	Harold Lister	251
10	Charles Winterbottom	97
18	George Mathew Perkins	131
23	Reginald Edward Appleyard Tate	244
	John Boon	184
31	Arthur Pool	406
Sept 6	Bernard Gawar Robinson	443
	Alfred Christopher Smith	304
	Ernest Frank Hargreaves	300
8	Frank Piggott	430
29	Harold Kirk	417
Oct 20	John Mylward Martin	395
	Joseph Kershaw	100
26	Harold Brown	403
Nov 10	Harry Boasman	440
18	Clarence Walter Day	424
1921		
Jan 20	Frank Reginald Long	305
24	Arthur William Mackay	402
	George Henry Tindall	91
28	Henry Robinson	412
Apr 12	William Charles Nicholls	441
June 8	Francis McDonald	—
17	William Henry Cook	175
June 21	Arthur Joyner	42
27	Frank Storey	99
	Henry Shepherdson	442
Aug 2	Herbert Arthur Durrands	103
	Harold Train	179
5	Frank Featherstone	112
8	George Clifford Byron Forgs	190
9	James Albert Armitage	291
	William Herbert Hancox	425
11	James Leonard Greenwood	98
15	Lewis Sheperdson	42
17	Arthur Joyner	443
23	Fred Chapman	444
Sept 12	Duncan Macrae	445
20	William Monkman Staveley	446
Oct 4	Wilfred Nicholson	447
8	Thomas James Graham	129
11	Bertie Ridley	140
31	Edward Patrick Buckley	394
	Matthew Dundas Bishop	167
Nov 3	Frank Johnson	448
1922		
Oct 19	William Alexander Woods Capt.	CC
1923		
June 4	Edward Bishop	64
14	John Bullas Kilvington	181
July 2	Henry Elston	313
Oct 1	John Edward Whitton	79
4	Edward Capstick	43
	Harold Kitching	56
	Hugh Kerr	68
	Michael Daly	77
	James Madill	93
	William Barnett Jordan	98
	Thomas Henderson Prince	125
	Charles William Ward	145
	Horace Johnson	148
	Arthur Green	150
	Joseph Edgar Johnson	160
	Thomas Sidney Gilbert	158
	Harry Kerslew	170
	Frank Green	180
Oct 20	George S. Jackson	214

When Sworn	Signature of Constable Sworn		When Sworn	Signature of Constable Sworn	
Oct 29	Walter Haywood	240	Jan 6	Norman Glew	287
	John Archer Ladigus	74		John Luther Clark	157
Nov 1	George Robinson	192		Thomas Walter	
Dec 11	Edward Stephenson	228		Sanderson	216
	John Ernest Nattriss	235		Ernest Oliver Walton	40
1924				Mark Slee Harper	285
Feb 13	Mark McCooey	316		William Johnston	288
Feb 22	John Hickmans	307		Henry Pollard	132
	Fred Daddy	295		Frank Bertram Simpson	252
	Thomas Henry Rumsey	292		Arthur Shand	227
	William Pearson	259		Roland Eaton Thistleton	36
	Ernest James Longley	324	Mar 2	John Farnsworth	62
	John Arthur Woodrow	300	Apr 13	Gilbert Underwood	412
	William Storey	297	**1927**		
	Richard Henry Clement	282	ᵀan 7	John C. Lessels	219
	William Robert Trowt	328		Sidney C. Archer	225
Mar 6	Alfred Leonard Barker	283		Frank Austin	274
Apr 29	Leslie Walker Robinson	147		Robert Clough	133
	Alexander William			Sidney G. Southard	296
	Guidell Anderson	251		Herbert Crammer	323
	Norman Newcombe			Arthur E. King	242
	Sewell	170		Frederick A. Page	338
Aug 19	Robert William Drewery	301		Thomas Y. Muddleyard	298
	Wilfred Lundy	39		Albert White	247
25	Arthur Bell	309		John Henry Miller	358
Nov 6	John Robinson	151		Robert James Powell	282
1925				George Tuplin	334
Apr 30	Thomas Milestone	93		Harry S. Falgate	348
	Leonard Rawlinson	316		Francis James Cuttill	83
	William Griffin	109	Feb 8	William Alfred Foyne	45
	John Alfred Holmes	228		Henry Thomas	
	Archibald Stark	294		Henrickson	337
	Charles William Tointon	138	Mar 2	William Robert Elston	321
	William Joseph Reeves	270	Apr 29	Herbert Dearing	309
	Ernest Cyril Berridge	350	Oct 19	Richard Berryman	339
	Henry Thomas James			Normal Daniel	107
	Edwards	195		Michael Boyle	165
	Wavel Theodore Ward	243		Ronald Cornelius Cockin	222
	Thomas Steele Paterson	162		Harold Beales	322
	Leslie Herbert Rose	282		Norman Stanley Bradley	326
	Gordon Tyson	208		Douglas Ross	335
	Harry Taylor	319		Benjamin Jones	362
	Albert Johnson Oldridge	268		Thomas Norman Drewery	361
May 11	Thomas Pickard	258		Alexander Smith	330
17	George William Cooks	279		Ernest Newton	342
1926				Dudley Tillotson	356
Jan 6	Harry Davill	115		Rupert Henry Shepherd	142
	James Arthur Bosman	38	27	Albert Edward Mee	387

When Sworn	Signature of Constable Sworn		When Sworn	Signature of Constable Sworn	
Oct 27	Charles Phillips	340	Apr 4	Robert Hall	341
Dec 14	Thomas Charles Stewart		9	Harry Rose	396
	Ewenson	316	18	Ronald Ellis Lawton	
1928				Glover	413
Apr 21	Stewart McArthur	198	23	Angus Hardy	336
May 14	Charles Ingham	209	**1931**		
July 11	Henry Llewellyn Bateman	309	Apr 9	Henry Atkinson	59
	Arthur Minshull	403		Walter Frederick Batty	327
	John William Thwaites	245		Norman Burton	201
	George Frederick Hulland	—		Cyril Downes	71
	Arthur Norman Todd	393		James Finch	435
	Herbert William			Stanley Jefferson	
	Woodward	90		Foreman	419
	Harold Victor Thompson	231		Albert Gibson	271
	Oliver Garnock Raper	316		Edwin Howe	308
17	George Richardson	261		Harry Burton Goodrick	171
Aug 7	Henry Elliott	168		Robert Match Morris	347
27	Charles Frederick Every	431		James Dawson Mundell	280
1929				Frederick Joseph Tait	118
July 4	Leslie Rogerson Webster	159		Edward Ashton	
	Stanley Fisher	317		Thompson	67
	Barnaby F. Baines	194		William Turnbull	196
	Robert Grainger	290		Jack Thomas Walter	152
	George Edward Younger	165		William Raymon	
	William Sampson Deyes	94		Duddington	204
	George Edward Kingston	218		George Graham	423
	Cyril Barton Todd	158		Maurice F. Healey	254
	Albert Edward Bugler	209		Thomas Ireland	126
	William Ness Garbutt	230		Charles William Todd	165
	Walter Robinson	122		Cyril Edward Cole	162
	Charles James Alfred			William Arthur Ingham	432
	Trott	178	**1932**		
	Robert Renwick Chilton	182	Jan 28	John Waldron	58
	James Jenkinson Irving	344		Geoffrey Corden Edwards	203
	George Robert Souter	277		James Reginald Hulby	174
	Vernon Keylock	179		Leonard Sampson Scott	185
	George A. Duck	263		Eric Robert Johnson	241
9	Frank Harman	408		George William Balmer	248
1930				Cyril Raper	249
Apr 2	Wilfred Baker	231		George Daniel	253
	George Butler Bell	354		James Crawford	278
	Alfred Foster	186		James Alexander Roberts	321
	Arthur Rumbalow Ollett	200		George Hastings	76
	George Albert Sutherland	250		Donald Taylor	84
	Fred Smith	357		John Lawson	315
	William Victor Thorp	144		Walter Braithwaite	106
	Robert Tiffin	121	Feb 3	James Cocksworth	206
	Art Frederick Webster	89		Frank Jackson	226

When Sworn	Signature of Constable Sworn		When Sworn	Signature of Constable Sworn	
Feb 3	Jack Trent Kirkwood	255	Oct 31	Gordon Meadley	20
	John J. Pickering	325	**1934**		
Oct 11	Arthur Salvidge	214	Feb 6	Stanley Harry Turner	7
1933				Herbert Henry Clarke	57
Jan 11	Sidney Taylor	404	13	Alexander Paterson	277
	Raymond A. Atkinson	207		Robert William Hather	380
	James Arthur Appleyard	193	Mar 18	John McDonald Banks	433
	John Henry Cooper	229		Norman Bricklebank	436
	Sidney Andrews	155		Bernard William Craven	372
	Eric Richard Pick	351	27	Ernest Lister	432
	George Henry Davy	273	Apr 10	Ronald Courtney Mawer	14
	Frederick Dickinson		May 29	Alexander Anderson	3
	Jeeves	306		Herbert Henry Hewitt	281
	George Patrick Feeney	284	June 11	William Edward Jacketts	25
	Walter Telford Gilby	289		Harold Craven Harrison	—
	Daniel Stuart	359	Aug 8	Benjamin Bell	49
Apr 3	John A. Hallett	212		James Sefton	2
4	Norman William Ness	11		Thomas William Shelton	176
	William Stewart	15	Sept 28	James Thirsk	345
	James Bowen	10	Oct 15	Herbert Hammond	373
	Percy Claude Collins	23		Strafford Allison	311
	Robert Lewis French	27	30	James Henry Maloney	53
	Alfred Arthur Turnbull	28	Dec 31	Harold Fairbank	57
	Richard Henry Allison	32		Frederick Gibson	19
	John Anderson	33			
	John Richard Ringrose	61	**1935**		
	Stanley Passmore	87	Jan 8	James Edward Waudby	203
	Clifford Ward Smith	113	Feb 26	Frank Taylor	61
	George Thomas Burton	114	Mar 5	William Leonard Seage	32
	Henry Simms	203	Apr 1	Albert Edward Baker	194
	William Kenneth Wilson	320	8	Stanley Lambert	226
	Richard Howard Smith	426	30	John Henry Edwards	258
1933				Joseph Charles Ralph	
Apr 20	Maurice Wilfred Lea	237		Craven	293
Sept 6	Michael Tudor Threlfell	367		George Herbert Savage	96
	Philip Smith	4		William Simpson	9
	Ronald Gordon Cameron	370		Alan Roach	366
	William David Ford	53	May 14	George William Maltby	368
	Cyril Edward Hoult	105	28	Robert Henry Foster	221
	Arthur Edward Whitty	136	July 24	Leonard Thacker	213
	Joseph Calvert Noble	371	30	George Haley Lister	291
	Ronald Bishop Gray	379	Aug 7	Frank Fisher	1
	Walter Horace Freeman	239		Harry Wilsher	375
Oct 9	Francis Boanas	30		Allen Bromley Johnson	78
23	Edward John			William Napier	52
	Winterbotham	194		Herbert Leslie Buckland	18
	Oliver Graham Souter	123	Oct 7	John Leonard Dickinson	239
	George William Goodwin	226	Dec 16	Norman Joseph Hobson	85
				Kenneth Barrett Colam	264

When Sworn	Signature of Constable Sworn	
1936		
Jan 13	Albert Hall	355
20	Rowland Holbrook Davy Baxter	—
Apr 21	Thomas William Piper	276
	John Charles Dickenson	143
	Stanley Clark	177
	John Etherington	6
	John Henry Donnelly	374
May 12	Geoffrey Leedham	377
June 16	Alan Herbert Dale	392
	Tom George Victor Thompson	46
	Albert Kitson	449
	Reginald Mitchell	450
	George Norris	438
	Richard Pratt	215
	Harry Edward Lee	378
	Robert Arnold Peters	439
	Frederick Davies	382
Sept 15	John Edgar Dobson	63
	John Ernest Leech	199
	Sydney Thomas Ablett	236
	Samuel Uttley Taylor	191
	Harold Hargreaves	70
	Jack Nicholson	376
	Gale Cuthbertson	266
22	Frank Denton	451
	David Lachlan McLean	452
29	George Henry Jackson Flick	454
	Stanley Rowland Flick	119
Nov 3	Ronald Nigel Joyce	13
Dec 28	Thomas Reynolds Bean	455
1937		
Jan 5	John Leslie Robinson	128
	Joseph Eric Walkington	458
	Herbert Hall	462
	Colin Arthur Wilkinson	8
	Harry Peel Tate	205
	Robert C. J. Harrison	85
	Stanley N. Wikner	457
	James Ferrier	456
	Brian Yeadon	459
	Richard Green	461
	Henry Martell Allard	460
11	Wilfred David Aitken	463
	Walter Thomas Gardner	260

When Sworn	Signature of Constable Sworn	
Jan 18	Howard Grainger	464
Feb 2	Joseph Alan Bessant	385
Apr 2	George Vincent McKenna	18
June 1	Thomas Skelton	389
	John William Appleby	180
	Leonard Lucas Tansley	391
	John Grieve	344
	Bernard Smith Spalding	202
	Dennis Lister	390
	Cyril Speak	197
	Harold Foley	104
	Charles Digby Davenport	465
	George R. Horner	466
	Douglas S. Hodge	215
	Roy Needley	81
	Carlyle Woodmansey	76
	Bernard Hilton Simpson	21
15	John Neldon	—
July 26	Joseph Christopher Ebsworth	—
Aug 9	Leslie Lynas	8
Sept 7	Charles Roland Featherstone	114
1938		
Mar 1	George Edward Jones	75
	Arthur Johnson	187
	Robert Thompson McMillan	233
	Richard Ayton	399
	Arthur Chapman	217
	John Robert Allerston	394
	Kenneth Hadley Hambler	468
	William Wollas Pybus	400
	William Arthur Robinson Newton	294
	Thomas Kenneth Stothard	397
	Eric Walter Barton	401
	Clive Monsey	373
22	Arthur Clayton	135
Nov 1	Robert Robinson	141
	Thomas Amos Grant	171
	John Edwin Ashby	458
	Donald Dixon	405
	John Douglas Reynolds	420
	Allenby George Nicholls	415
	George Herbert Searby	398
	Donald Fieldsend	407

When Sworn	Signature of Constable Sworn			When Sworn	Signature of Constable Sworn		
Nov 1	Lawrence Arthur Harvey		428	Jan 8	Annie Smith	PW	1
	Geoffrey Tenison		12	Feb 19	Dulcie May Davis	PW	2
	Walter Harry Dixon		66	Nov 5	Gwyneth Dobson	PW	3
	David Wilson		69	Dec 10	Edith Mary Boulton	PW	4
	Kenneth Barnes		22	31	Charles John Connolly		3
	George Henry William				Frederick John D'Arcy		5
	Taylor		80	**1946**			
	James Middleton		116	Jan 21	William Rees Evans		35
	Alan Lowey		163		Frank Newell		26
1939					Herbert Kemp		31
Mar 13	Duncan Crerar		188		Richard Bentley Eldon		7
May 16	Frederick Hamblett		246	22	Ernest Arthur Price		
	Michael Ganderton				Gallantree		48
	Tanicard		410	24	Herbert William Harry		
	John Edgar				Simpson		47
	Londesborough		388	25	Sidney Savory		51
	Richard Veuill Thompson		335	Feb 11	Elsie Kime	PW	5
	Cyril Martin		189	18	George Davies Hodgson		54
17	Sydney Fay		252		Barbara Marjorie		
	H. W. Merton		257		Mulligan	PW	6
31	Lawrence George			19	Rhoda Stevenson	PW	7
	Atkinson		135	25	Peter Donald Workman		58
	John Alfred Crawford		146	Mar 11	Robert Hudson Edwards		65
	John Theodore Howard			Apr 9	Henry Ferguson		67
	Woollons		223	15	Harry Storr Metcalfe		68
June 13	John Stanley Kemp		255		Frank Alvin		70
July 3	Thomas Arthur Stanley			16	Roy Farley		78
	Lockey		211	23	Betty Mary Lamming	PW	8
Aug 14	John William Morrell		459		Douglas John Duncan		80
	Thomas Ivor Rees		104		Dennis Frederick Watson		81
	Harry Stapley		108	26	Barbara Oliver	PW	5
	John Robson Taylor		17	29	Robert William Sharpe		82
28	George Hadnam		156	May 6	Alan Thomas Wall		40
	John Eric Bracken		24		Harold Warkup		50
Sept 25	Robert Cecil Cross		272		John Hoile O'Kane		88
	James Gunn Wilson		34	13	Roland Harper		93
	Thomas Camish		312	27	Roland Stanley		
1940					Middlewood		95
Dec 27	Jack Owen		—	30	George Alfred Raines		97
1941				June 6	Ivan Johnson		98
Feb 10	Charles Raymond Barker		72	7	Wilfred Scanott		111
May 10	Henry Edmund Pinnock		41	11	Frank Richardson		101
July 12	John Austin Dex		29	13	Frederick Harriman		116
Oct 2	Thomas Wells		CC	14	Bruce Snowden		405
Nov 4	William Charles Archer		10	July 1	Ronald Marshall Webster		126
	Gerald Jackson Calway		31	8	John Dawson		124
1945				15	John Ernest Grant		130
Jan 8	Jean Lyon Stewart	PW	Sgt		Alfred Owen Everton		127

168

When Sworn	Signature of Constable Sworn			When Sworn	Signature of Constable Sworn		
July	8	Joan Mablethorpe	PW 10	Jan	30	Harry Smith	363
	22	Kenneth J. Martins	—	Feb	5	Kenneth Green	364
Aug	6	Ida Kathleen O'Sullivan			17	George Norman	
			PW 11			Thompson	371
		Ronald Allen Griffin	—		24	Peter Fisher Chamberlain	382
	26	George Robert Tomlinson	139		27	John Green	377
	27	John William McGinnis	149			Thomas Edward	
Sept	2	Stanley Robert Peartree	156			Waterhouse	384
	6	Robert Charles Cook	163	Mar	3	Fred Barrett	386
	10	Arthur Barker	11		10	Edwin Austin Adcock	390
		Raymond Edward Wilson	73		17	Leonard Cawkwell	395
		Ieuan Thomas	34		24	Agnes Halliday	PW 15
	16	Walter Jennison	181	Apr	8	Ivor Stuart Bennett	397
	23	Joan Lilian Roper	PW 12		10	Alan Newley	398
		Joyce Merion Bailey	PW 13		16	Mavis M. Rudd	PW 4
	25	Dennis Holder	183		28	Ronald Tuton	402
	30	Alistair Seymour				Norman Ernest French	408
		Mackintosh	209		29	Donald Clark	409
Oct	7	Denis Charles Auchter-				William Lester	
		Lounie	210			Barkworth	411
	17	John William Ketley	211			George McDonnell	416
	28	George Gibson		May	8	George Fisher	418
		Willingham	223		17	Thomas Edward	
		Donald Sylvester	232			Tuxworth	421
		Donald Scrimgeour	240		27	John James Everitt	422
Nov	4	Herbert Isaac Richardson	241	June	9	Ronald Leslie Gardiner	425
		Frederick John Edward				Peter Mulligan	427
		Bradshaw	243		10	Leonard Bulson	
	5	Gerald Robert Wilson	257			Robinson	429
	11	William Wood	266		25	Peter Herbert Lamb	440
	18	Reginald Moulesworth	273		30	Peter Wilsher	434
	20	Arthur Eugene Azemar	266			Dennis John Smith	445
	26	Geoffrey Arthur Baskill	275	July	2	Edward Barnes	460
Dec	3	Henry Bevan	281		7	Philip Addison	454
		William Frederick			9	Maurice G. Harrison	—
		Tomlinson	293		15	Christopher Pound	43
	6	Arthur Robinson	278		25	Lily Brown	PW 5
	11	Edward Norman Harold		Aug	11	Ronald Elliott	44
		Long	297			Charles Kilvington	55
	31	Proctor Marshall William				Thomas Frederick	
		Steel	302			Gordon Peam	64
1947				Sept	8	Peter George Darley	161
Jan	6	Annie Howard	—		16	Owen Mervyn Sockett	159
	9	Frank White	92		22	Barbara Moller	PW 9
	27	James Arthur Holmes	318			Sydney Dearing	164
Jan	27	Eric Pearce	305		27	John Shears	159
	28	Donald John Sinclair	343			William Raymond	
	30	Albert Andrew Green	352			Munro	194

When Sworn	Signature of Constable Sworn		When Sworn	Signature of Constable Sworn	
Sept 29	Robert Clifford Smith	190	July 26	Richard Howard Smith	426
30	Frank Duffill	248	Aug 4	Gordon Hooten	420
Oct 13	Thomas Joseph Hargreaves	290	7	John Bean	433
21	Terence Patrick Edward Griffin	—	30	Robert Paterson McLean	436
			Sept 13	Ronald S. Barker	437
Nov 15	Leonard Oakes	267		John Wilson	442
17	Leslie Philip Dalton	262	28	L. Roscoe	443
22	Frank Hay	273	Oct 11	John William Kettleborough	449
26	Gordon Geoffrey Southard	276		Harry Holwell	450
Dec 1	Ronald Martin	274	15	Gordon E. A. Fisher	216
12	Peter Ezra Wigglesworth	277	19	Raymond Berry	459
24	Thomas Henry Jackson	281	Nov 1	Helen Gertrude Hobbs PW	16
29	Peter Hamilton Richardson	283	2	John Robert Cox	463
1948			3	Leslie Tabor	464
Jan 19	Gregor Duncan Macrae	7		Thomas Harold Cross	466
	Kenneth Hirst Ogram	10	8	Jack Wright	—
	George Anthony Hartley Densley	297	29	Stanley Ready	460
Feb 2	John Robert Sidebottom	302	Dec 8	Eric Wilson	21
16	Reginald Weston	303	13	John McLean	26
17	George Victor Rutherford	314	**1949**		
Mar 8	Horace Reginald Hill	325	Jan 3	Ernest James Corp	35
9	Rose Matchett	—		Stanley Greaves	46
	Charles Sidney Chapman	335	12	Jack Edward Smalley	34
15	Eric Stapler	338	31	Stanley Piggott	51
16	Donald George Nicolson	346		Herbert Bates	53
23	Gordon Whitworth	353		Betty Wilson PW	12
	Denis Lionel Bateson	358		Audrey Ireland PW	3
Apr 9	Bertram Stephenson	359	Feb 1	John George Pickering	20
May 3	Robert Barber	360	7	Bryan Callan	55
20	Thomas Peter Allan Ribee	369	Mar 10	Carlyle Woodmansey	76
24	Cyril A. Harrison	14	14	Geoffrey Roe	60
June 7	Eric Telfor	381	Apr 4	Michael Duck	72
14	James T. French	390		Frederick Raymond Hodges	61
	Walter Reed	398	May 3	Albert Reginald Richardson	75
	Joe Sidwell	383	13	Albert Bacon	98
17	S. Lawrence	CC	16	Albert Bean	73
July 5	E. W. Garton	408		Leonard Watson	100
	Bruce Watson	407	19	Leonard Eric Barker	102
	Jack Geoffrey Beech	404	June 13	Mary Forbes PW	14
6	Gordon Lythgoe	411	20	William Henry Rafton	112
	Kenneth Edward Kershaw	410	27	R. M. Janes PW	17
26	John Robert Goodwin	419	July 12	Colin George Edward Fernall	116
	Leonard Arthur Wilson	414	Aug 2	Ernest Albert Winter	127

When Sworn	Signature of Constable Sworn		When Sworn	Signature of Constable Sworn	
Aug 16	John McIvor De Boer	117	May 30	John Edward Cain	258
Sept 1	Dennis Christopher	120		Frank Henry Turner	254
	Alfred Knaggs	131	31	Frank Austin	267
19	John Eric Newlove	137	June 5	Ronald Morrison	284
26	James Arthur Atkinson	138		William Henry Harrison	283
Oct 10	Aubrey Harry Southam	134		Edward Mutchan	281
	Ronald Taylor	140		Jack Fox	270
17	Patrick Leo Unsworth	142		Walter Whittleton	285
	Charles William Sibley	144	12	Walter Alan Marsden	286
	Walter William Carmody	149		Arthur Ramsden	289
24	Henry Miller	153		Walton Sutton	290
	Alec Lock	151		Alec Kilvington	291
Nov 8	Donald Angus			Harry Wood	292
	Macdonald	154		Donald Edward Fulston	295
14	Clifford Jennings	155		James Higo	298
	Robert Trevor Lunnon	160	16	Maurice Downes	304
	Ronald Ernest Mackinder	161	19	Richard Robson	313
Dec 2	Jean Gertrude Ashton			Charles Raymond Jones	310
		PW 9		Alan William Grenderson	307
12	Peter Watson	163		Arthur Pearson	331
28	Albert Edward Naylor	164		Harry Pepper	319
	John Quail	166	26	Donald Hubert Slaughter	332
1950				Leonard Adams	333
Jan 2	Charles Ernest Garland		July 10	Albert Walker	335
	Wiles	175		Frank William Meanwell	343
30	Joseph Harrison Ward	179	12	Raymond Smith	349
	Frederick Arthur Sharpe	183	17	Kenneth Leslie Smith	381
Feb 13	John Collier	184		William Arthur Hodgson	360
20	Leslie Ernest Horne	191		Stanley Fieldhouse	362
27	James Arthur Davey	190		Charles Richard Spandler	387
Mar 6	Kenneth Peter Clark	192	24	Kenneth Richard Graham	390
20	Peter Gordon Young	202		William Nudd	396
	William Austin Nicholls	201		Charles Henry Paine	404
	Kathleen Allen	—		Jack Ransom	413
Apr 3	John Howell	203	31	John Haig Bolch	437
12	Albert Edward Taylor	207		Ernest Wilberton	447
	Gordon Dineley	206		John McGovern	470
24	Peter Bernard Morris	212		Dennis Ellerington	471
May 1	Peter Svenguard	224		John Spence	469
	Brian Butler	215	Aug 14	Charles Lewis Adams	472
	Peter Geoffrey Westoby	229		Frank Henshaw	473
15	Charles Rush	234		Harry Stuart Barron	474
	George Robert Jackson	226		Haydn Hugh Skeldon	475
22	John Henry Bean	245		John William Argent	478
26	John Thompson Porter	252		John Joseph Crawley	479
30	Aubrey Mettam Wells	264		Dennis Valentine Webster	480
	Norman Roe	265		Raymond William Ward	477
	Terence Tom Leathley	256		Robert Henry Boddy	476

When Sworn	Signature of Constable Sworn			When Sworn	Signature of Constable Sworn		
Aug 21	John Peter Lunn		481	Apr 30	Doreen Connor Robinson	PW	18
29	Jack Williamson		482		Dorothy Hockey	PW	19
	Gordon Naylor		486	May 21	Stanley Osgerby		519
Sept 4	George Edward Tull		483		Leonard Fergus		520
	Lawrence Edwin Armitage		484	June 5	Dennis Keith Williams		521
	Richard Moat		485	18	Robert Clough		522
11	P. Milburn Brearley		487	July 10	Kenneth Stanley Ostler		524
	Ronald Cyril Smith		488	23	George Robert Dodsworth		523
	Ronald Arthur Harris		489	26	Samuel Linford		525
	Herbert Terence Sorfleet		490	Aug 1	Frederick Arthur Edwin Taylor		526
18	Leonard Pearson		491	13	John Gavarini		527
	Norman Blanshard		492		Harold Alan Peacock		528
	Austin Hubert Ward		493	20	David Bryan Stark		529
	Barry Calley Wadsworth		494	29	Stanley R. Peartree		156
Oct 2	Antony Harold Coult		496	Sept 3	Mildred J. Ellis	PW	13
	Albert Kenneth England		495		June M. Frith	PW	1
9	James Arthur Robson		497		Angus Green		530
	Raymond Clark		498	10	Cyril Sharpe		531
	John Robert Bryan Williams		499		Stanley Risley		532
30	Owen James McCann		500		J. W. Mortinson		533
	Wilfred John Desmond Roach		501		Eddie Caswell		534
Nov 6	William Richard Francis Scholes		502	24	Brian Allsop Molon		535
	Leonard Coupland		503		Stanley Robert Atkinson		536
	Dennis Sydney Bielby		504		Robert Cundill		537
	George William Oliver Souter		505		Clive Harrison		538
Dec 4	Frank Hayton		506	Oct 1	Bradshaw Frederick John Edwards		243
11	Janet Christine Yardley	PW	10		Harry Raine Fellowes		6
1951					Norman Thomas		539
Jan 1	Henry Atkin		507	8	Colin Welbouen		12
	Edward Beedham		508		Leonard Eastbourn		540
	John Pearson Shaw		509	15	Kenneth Charles Craven		21
15	Ronald Bradley		510		Stanley Greenwood		22
22	Denis Ivor Billaney		511		Peter Gordon Gallant		541
29	Reginald Thomas Sims		512	29	Norah Hughes	PW	20
	Eric James Colbrook		513		Brenda Kettlewell	PW	21
Feb 19	Kenneth Charles Harbour		514		Charles Alfred Shepherd		39
26	Herbert Ernest Staples		515		Thomas Harry Hoult		40
Mar 19	Kenneth Hailstone		516		John Robert Woods		42
Apr 23	George William Lyons		517	Dec 3	Ramon Marshall Griffin		51
30	William Charles Dennis Boothby		518	17	Stanley Cawood		56
	Jean Neal	PW	15	**1952**			
				Jan 28	Thomas Henry Found		74
					Ralph Lomas		77
					Charles Eric Egglestone		99

172

When Sworn	Signature of Constable Sworn			When Sworn	Signature of Constable Sworn		
Feb 4	John Beadleson		103	Aug 18	Eric Walter Toyne		310
	Bernard Oakley		125		Ernest Smales		319
	Eric Smith		127	Aug 25	Horace Gerald Slater		344
	Cyril Reed		129		George William Tonks		345
	Mary Featherstone	PW	22	27	Ronald Douglass		340
	Isobel Cathaline Nicolson			Sept 15	Keith Arthur Cockerill		348
		PW	23		Gordon Holden		351
	Eve Ewbank Lightfoot			22	Frank Henry Johnson		365
		PW	108	29	Keith Frederick Callis		
	John Albert Tate		132		Krouse		366
8	Robert Lyon		137	Oct 13	George Charles Desmond		
	Walter Eric Kettlewell		139		Reid		368
	Harold Campbell		150		Leslie Vincent Wilson		376
25	Kenneth Barker		151		Ronald Ellis		381
	Norman Wilkinson		154		John Robert McNaughton		380
Mar 3	Michael Duck		72	20	David Wallace Dalrymple		400
	John James Hilditch		145		Peter Thomas Tattenfield		408
	Brian W. Hawker		160		Reginald Francis		
17	James Leslie Cherry		162		Cawthorne		413
	David Ernest Victor Field		166	Nov 3	Charles Alfred Allman		417
	Arthur James Robinson		167		Walter Charles Jackson		418
	Alan William Sampson		169	17	Arthur William Best		430
24	Albert Boardman		183	24	Bernard Briggs		432
31	Shirley Catherine			Dec 22	Peter Barnard Davy		441
	Margaret Hudson	PW	24		Mark Straker Harrison		444
Apr 29	Joseph Robert Unsworth		193	29	George Dent		448
May 5	Terence Frederick Asquith		203		Peter Gilbert Frost		453
	Dorothy Obridge	PW	25		Albert Newton Worrall		466
12	Norman Frederick Robert			**1953**			
	Beales		208	Jan 5	James Alfred Jacobs		473
17	Joan Brackbank	PW	11		Alan Page		474
19	Gordon Lamb		218	26	George Arthur Taylor		482
	Colin Alan Tyson		225		Eric Seabrook		490
20	Kenneth John Jones		226	Feb 16	Robert Dixon		492
26	James Harry Curtis		228	23	Jean Harrison	PW	15
	George Victor Lee		244		Marjorie Johnson	PW	19
	Arthur Ronald Deurance		247	Mar 16	John Walter Roland		505
June 9	Dennis Holmes		268	21	Brian Enevoleson		497
19	Dennis Henry Mews		279	30	Albert Collinson		531
30	John Naylor		284	Apr 27	John William Richardson		534
July 1	Dennis Arthur Mitchell		292	May 11	Allan Denton		535
7	Derek Ewart Haden		290		Alan Frederick		
	Stanley Roebuck		295		Cocksworth		536
21	Thomas Cooper		301	18	Leslie D'Arcy		542
Aug 5	John Taylor Blashull		—	June 15	Roy William Lindop		543
6	Barbara D. R. Wentworth				Peter Kyman Lord		544
		PW Insp		July 27	George Lambswood		546
14	William Kirkwood		339		Ronald Clark		547

When Sworn	Signature of Constable Sworn		When Sworn	Signature of Constable Sworn	
July 27	Patricia Margaret		May 21	James Black Patterson	145
	Middleyard	PW 4		Arthur Thomas Dearing	148
	Patricia Ramsay	PW 12	26	Henry Arthur Edwards	125
Aug 4	John Malcolm Beverley		28	Arthur William Heron	150
	Buck	548		Cecil Taylor	159
17	Robert Edwin Clarkson	545	July 15	John Duncan Martin	163
Sept 7	Keith Clark	549		William Bradshaw	167
14	William Smith	550		Joseph Morfitt	170
	Alfred Walter Ireland	551	28	Robert Derving	183
	Herbert William Close	552	Aug 3	Geoffrey Tullock	191
Oct 5	John David Wells	553		John Brian Wright	192
	David Edward Williams	554	9	Stanley Richards	201
12	Peter Ray Hyde	555	16	Richard Clive Beacock	202
19	Robin Anthony Scott	556		Sidney Bernard Saunders	205
	Jean Marjorie Marriott		Sept 6	Douglas Thomas Willey	214
		PW 14	Oct 6	Michael Fowler	226
Nov 2	Douglas Vernon			David Deighton	230
	Woodward	557	7	David Farmer	216
9	Jenny Werin	PW 3	25	Raymond Jackson	235
	Joyce Waites	PW 9	Nov 9	Eric Turner	244
	Peter Watts	558	15	Frank Bache Ledger	247
	John Thomas Jefferson	559		Herbert Smallwood	251
23	Allan Scruton	560		Peter Arthur Ollett	258
	Gordon Charles Wilson	561	22	John Bully	243
30	Harry Evison	562		Keith Herbert Allison	259
Dec 7	Bernard Vincent Kay	6		John Robert Sidebottom	302
	Geoffrey George Tindall	13	Dec 13	Brian William Barker	271
14	Robert William Currie	20		Kenneth Bourne	287
1954			20	James Barry Croft	282
Jan 18	Jeffrey Rose	29		William Bache Ledger	283
21	Richard Aylwin	399	**1955**		
25	Walter Overfield	36	Jan 10	Brian Clyde Gallagher	279
	Ronald Thomas Friend	37		Gordon Clifford Lee	288
	Joseph Rushby	39	17	Lois Worsnip	PW 15
Feb 15	Dennis Maw	42	24	Peter Morrison Nickson	289
18	Reginald Henry Kelsall	45		Eric Marriott	290
Mar 1	David William Cawkwell	54	26	Clive Frederick Naylor	291
Apr 1	John Edward Penn		Feb 9	Paul Bacon	292
	Haldenby	60		Michael Robert Parry	296
	Eric Allan Coates	62	14	Leslie Farrow	300
5	Eric Wilfred Dalton	74	28	Keith Charles Ernest	
	Kennether Archer	77		Asquith	307
14	William Keith Trezise	87	Mar 14	George Ronald Walker	316
	Leslie Milner	99	Apr 4	Ronald James Stinson	321
20	Kenneth John Long	103		Henry John Varney	324
26	Harold Trevor Skipsey	109	8	Henry Westgarth	326
May 17	Bryan John Bennett	110	25	Charles Roy Padley	317
May 17	Albert Strodder	127	27	Edwin Rodmill	328

When Sworn	Signature of Constable Sworn		When Sworn	Signature of Constable Sworn	
May 9	Leonard Hurst	329	Mar 5	Thomas Bryan Capper	526
16	Francis Reid	337	Apr 16	Clifford Jennings	155
	Terence Land	346	May 7	Herbert Bates	53
26	Peter Martin	347		Stanley Milbourne	526
June 2	Leslie William Love	350	14	John Henry Bean	245
	James Alfred Bottomley	351		Kenneth Leach	528
July 4	Francis Alan Cameron	354		James Robert Storr	540
	Terence Watson	361		Terence Peter Wilson	542
	Charles Peter Barrett	365		Bernard Harry Carr	547
	Kenneth Page	368	June 4	Ivan Richardson	548
18	Irene Whitehead PW	21	11	Mavis Whiteley PW	26
Aug 15	Ronald Arthur Marshall	373	18	Peter Stevenson	550
	Raymond Varey	380	25	Doreen Winifred	
	James Robert Harris	382		Ashton PW	27
	Dennis Leonard Davell	420	July 2	David Russell	551
29	Geoffrey Chamberlain	384		Leslie Holmes	553
	Michael Ivor Kirk	398	25	Anthony Robb	554
Sept 12	Margaret Ann Ward PW	22		Malcolm Alexander	
Oct 3	William Henry Baines	403		Baron	555
	Nicholas Barry Collins	404	Aug 13	John Henry Hordon	12
	Robert Frank Trilten	412		Ronald Lee	13
	Stanley Osgerby	519	15	Raymond Gould	14
5	Roy Gilder Live	413		John Thomas Frederick	
	Martin Gaulden	441		Knox	18
7	Brian William Cook	432	27	Ian Douglas Todd	34
10	Ivy Mary Hayes PW	13	Sept 3	Arthur Jenkinson	38
24	James Anthony Chick	431	Oct 1	Oscar Jackson	44
	Malcolm Henry Wiles	446	15	Mary Haques PW	28
	Paul Dent	447		Douglas William Dixon	
	Wilfred Henry Lamming	450		Kirk	74
31	Margaret Ann		22	Raymond Hill	85
	Berryman PW	18		Terence Frederick	
Nov 7	Lawrence Edwin Armitage	484		Asquith	203
14	Michael Richard Powery	453	24	Kenneth Michael Cherry	92
	Herbert Edward Simpson	457	27	Peter Burgess	90
	Dennis Sanderson	467	Nov 12	Frank Jewitt	102
Dec 5	Peter Dent	469		Allan Pick	109
	George Duncan Kitching	477	26	Colin Richardson	111
	Peter William Thomas	483	Dec 3	Brian Francis Ehlert	115
1956				Patrick Welsh	117
Jan 2	John Thomas Allenby	480		Mary Bowering PW	29
	Colin Brian Precious	487		Bertha Ducker PW	30
	Alan Gray	488	27	Michael Biglin	118
23	Norman Martin Helm	490		Alan Young	123
25	Walter McKinley	501	31	Gordon Ernest Bird	128
Feb 27	Leslie Poskett	504		Ronald Peter Sagar	129
	Robert Norris Carmichael	523	**1957**		
	Stanley Coates	525	Jan 14	Trevor Frank Spencer	133

When Sworn	Signature of Constable Sworn		When Sworn	Signature of Constable Sworn	
Jan 14	Ronald Withell	137	Dec 2	Peter William Slaney	354
	Brian Larcum Waring	138		David Arthur Hardwick	356
	Bernard James Curtis	145		Harry Minns	366
	Peter Johnson	152		Brian Marshall	369
22	Allan Plumtree	160	Dec 5	Charles Richard Beverley	
Feb 4	Brian Holwell	167		White	351
16	Frank Arthur Clarke	168	30	John Airey	385
Mar 4	Reggie Gibson	170	**1958**		
	Beryl Robinson PW	5	Jan 6	Irene Holland PW	28
25	Peter Colin Walsh	173	20	Barry Storr	393
	Peter George Ottaway	182		Terence Anderson	395
	Anthony Kempton		Feb 3	Rose Smith PW	4
	Cannons	186	10	Peter Jefferson Saville	398
Apr 1	Marie Janet Lee PW	31		Dennis Richard Downs	420
	Harold Wallis	187		Norman Ellwood	423
	George Sidney Mitchell	200		Eric Philip Scaife	424
15	Peter Johnson	201		Brian William Gillyon	432
16	Peter Welsh	216		Rowland Colman	435
23	Geoffrey Bartlett	205		Geoffrey Tunley	437
	John Harold Walker	227	Mar 3	David Fewlass	452
29	Irene Tyrer PW	32		David John Wildridge	463
	Valerie Henshaw PW	33		James Delaney	467
	Peter Giblin	230		Maurice Gibbons	487
May 13	Janet Christine Waugh			Walter Mulligan	490
	PW	10		John Amos Terry	504
	Leonard Tonkin	238	31	David Harry Williams	456
	Reginald William Skiggs	242	Apr 1	John Lawrence Higham	526
20	Arthur Well Beerst	231	21	Edward Moore	528
June 30	Terence James Bibby	244		Peter Frederick Redhead	540
July 15	Brian Reginald Baines	249		Anthony Maxwell	
	Neil Robert Berryman	251		Edwards	551
22	Brian William Camell	258	22	Robert McCall	12
	Barrie Sanderson	261	May 12	Geoffrey Albert Malletts	15
	Brian Jessop	269		Thomas Cross	18
26	Edward Ellis	280		George Keith Harness	20
Aug 12	Reginald Watson	283		Mary Jane Cowling PW	27
	John Stanley Ramsey	289	June 2	Barrie Andrew Johnson	27
Sept 18	Herbert George Cressey	296		Michael Anthony Clayton	36
30	Edward Gordon Spain	323	June 9	Anthony John Morrell	59
	Henry Ernest Hood	328	16	William Frederick	
	Dennis Kent	316		Tomlinson	293
	Anthony Victor-Large	309	30	Alec Samuel Birkett	71
Oct 3	Bernard Anthony Ostler	308		Bryon Davidson	75
12	John Fryer	329	July 5	Barry Lilley	67
21	G. E. Kemp	334	21	William Iveson	78
Nov 12	Ivor Barry Sutherland	341	26	Brian Harry David Lucas	85
Nov 12	Edward Martin Youell	342	Aug 11	Terence Michael	
Dec 2	Colin Chris Firth	346		Middleton	89

When Sworn	Signature of Constable Sworn	
Aug 11	Royston James Worthy	102
Sept 8	Eileen May Lunn PW	15
22	Colin Derrett	107
Oct 13	Maurice Garmston	110
20	Ian Keith McNeil	116
	Frederick Newmarch	122
Nov 8	Bernard Shepherd	143
10	Robert James Marshall	145
	John Richard Jameson	152
	Brian Sargeant	168
Dec 1	Ray Plummer	222
	Gordon Revell	238
5	Colin O'Grady	216
29	Leslie Charles Baker	170
	Roy Buchanan Barker	198
	Charles Edward Garland	231
	Jack Smith	245
	Dennis William Dean	262
	Gordon Hill	263
	Michael Henningson	266
	Christopher Robin Gray	272
1959		
Feb 2	Pauline Oliver Edwards PW	20
9	Trevor Knight	282
	Charles David Reed	283
20	John Edward Nix	320
23	Betty Dawson PW	25
Mar 16	Kay Raper	322
23	Brian Enevoldson	497
31	George Matchett	328
Apr 1	Alan Frederick Terry	330
May 4	Anthony Steadman	336
	Alan Dent	337
	Peter Saxby	338
	Thomas William Crombie	341
	Brian Malcolm Bellis	367
8	David John Whincup	369
11	Donald George Nicholson	412
June 1	Colin Stephen William Passmore	379
	Walter Charles Ashbridge	456
	John Keith Wilkinson	457
June 5	David Malcolm Austin	8
	Anthony Johnson	12
13	David Hanmer	16
29	Alan William Coulson	43
June 29	David Baslington	59

When Sworn	Signature of Constable Sworn	
June 29	Kenneth Woodcock	79
Aug 8	John Harrison	18
	Graham Walker	81
	Wilfred Henry Cooper	91
	Michael Train	94
	Keith Norton	113
Aug 17	Barbara Sandal PW	14
31	Thomas Garland Elvin	114
Sept 7	Helen Kathleen Luton PW	16
	Ian Fraser Brocklesby	147
26	Anthony John Cayle	152
Oct 2	David Victor Clarkson	156
12	Dennis Leonard Davill	160
Nov 2	Geoffrey Maxwell Hutchinson	167
	Brian Dibnah	173
	Graham Howard Watson	178
	David William Morris	179
Nov 16	Denise Shearwood PW	21
17	Clive Garbutt Cross	210
30	Gerald Allen Beaumont	207
	Gordon Richard Harrison	222
	Tony Barrett	225
	Terence William Atherton	237
Dec 3	Stanley James Hill	245
1960		
Feb 1	Robert Peck	252
	John Barry Train	258
8	Colin James Moore	261
29	Margaret Salridge PW	3
	William Liddle McLowchlan Laing	267
Mar 5	Kelvin Everett	272
28	Trevor Laycock	297
Apr 1	Kenneth Alan Oakshott	325
25	Michael Nolan	311
May 2	John Albert Evins	335
	Terence Denton	340
30	Brian Wilson	357
	Harry Vincent Whitewood	371
	Colin Hugh Smith	372
31	John Thomas Coulman	342
June 10	Malcolm Thompson	375
27	Richard Groke	354
29	Eric Hutchinson	385
	Peter Bell	422

When Sworn	Signature of Constable Sworn		When Sworn	Signature of Constable Sworn	
July 11	Elaine Margaret East PW	17	Aug 8	Stephanie Frances Ward PW	13
Aug 2	John Leonard Walmsley	451		Eva Reibleim PW	22
26	Geoffrey Eastburn	519		Patricia Kenny PW	3
29	Percy Wilson	2	28	William Ernest Shirley	262
	Terence Frederick Oliver	528	Sept 25	Keith S. Boyes	266
Sept 26	Charles Anthony Glanville	9		John Bradley	267
	Neil Harrison	10		Geoffrey J. Swain	275
	Harry Longworth	12	Oct 12	Roy Taylor	224
Oct 3	Barry James Anderson	14	30	Jeffrey Sidney Melhuish	303
24	David Hopwood	25		Trevor Pickersgill	312
31	Brian Austin	28		Malcolm Holtby	322
	Trevor Hare	33		Harold Branford	325
Nov 11	Walter McKinley	501		David Arthur Stanley Dudding	341
28	John Sugden	38		James Madrell	355
	Trevor Hesk	43	Nov 6	Patricia Jean Boulton PW	26
Dec 12	Frances Eileen Moses PW	14		Valerie Mary Nicholson PW	27
28	Colin Harper	51		Drewa Constance Towse PW	29
	Clive Wilson	62	20	Denis Charles Auchterlounie	371
1961			27	John David Hazell	375
Jan 4	Raymond Pallier	78		Peter Rowson Smith	398
12	John Milfred Taylor	80	Dec 1	Allan Douglas Jarvis	412
16	Peter Michael Cullen	85	11	Pauline Anne McIntosh PW	31
30	Harry Bullock	49	28	John Barrie Horsfield	370
	Geoffrey Adamson	99		Dennis D'Arcy	372
	Bryan Maxwell Dickinson	116	**1962**		
Feb 18	Josephine Nightingale PW	10	Jan 29	Harold Ian Alcock	422
27	Brian Jack Lawton	121		Robert Nicol Binnington	438
	Allan William Robson	122		David Harry King	439
	Alexander Stewart	130		James Ronald Wilkinson	443
Mar 21	Alan Thomas Holmes	143	Feb 26	Dennis Harwood	471
27	Alan William Lamb	132	Mar 3	Eric Melvyn Cookman	457
	John Newton Henry Hale	142		William Mercer	481
30	George Anthony Turner	152	26	John Ogston	19
May 1	Valerie Youngs PW	21		John Keith White	37
	Patrick Michael Phelen	158		Malcolm Thompson	33
15	Richard Charles Hargreaves	178		Alan William Grieves	3
29	John Neville Freestone	183		John Benstead	499
	Stanley Thomas Pegg	195		Kenneth Clark	514
June 26	George Walter Richardson	208		Michael McNally	10
	Michael George Sathcatt	213		Anthony Hardy	9
July 26	John Richardson	220	Apr 16	Barry Lord	51
31	David Norman Bartlett	230		Peter Ashton	66
	Kenneth Dusher	233			
	John Thornley	238			
	Roger C. Lee	250			

When Sworn	Signature of Constable Sworn	
Apr 16	Peter Cooper	78
	John Overfield	61
	Peter Hoyles	82
	Alfred Trevor Whitelam	94
May 11	Colin Harry Welburn	96
28	Ian Douglas Wilson	113
June 1	Adrian George Scott	151
25	Brian Albert Simons	152
	George William Bilbe	160
July 2	Richard Lee	165
5	Robert Walton	CC
9	Margaret Rose Duncan PW	21
16	Colin John Wright	174
	Ronald Walter Barrett	185
	Leslie Tye	204
20	Peter Douglas Baker	233
Aug 27	James Edwin Bird	222
Sept 24	Alan Reginald Crosher	236
	Norman Scholes	237
Nov 5	Roger Leslie Jackson	245
	John Arthur Tomkins	249
✳	Malcolm Russell Reed	251
	Geoffrey William Smith	253
26	Michael Richard Clarke Thornton	263
	Brian Norris Fletcher	302
	John Stuart Sanderson	327
30	David John Hughes	315
	Clive D'Arcy	283
	David A. Gowthorpe	322
Dec 31	Jacqueline Holmes PW	22
	Geoffrey Ogden	341
1963		
Jan 4	Andrew Thomas Helm	346
28	Peter James Lockwood	374
	John Michael Marsh	378
Feb 4	Brenda Catherine Emms PW	3
25	David George Hallas	382
	Stuart John Thacker	392
	Terence Verdun Waudby	462
Apr 1	Gordon Acaster	12
2	William Spencer	49
5	Michael Ian Phillips	84
8	Olive Chalmaine Joan Landen PW	13
10	Edward Barrie Davies	66

When Sworn	Signature of Constable Sworn	
Apr 29	John Dent	97
	Malcolm Ian Fowler	126
	Frank Heywood	183
	David W. Spaven	196
May 3	Frank Hornsey	221
	George Trevor Whitfield	238
May 31	Harry Edward Morgan	248
July 1	Robert Colin Frank	256
	David Staveley	290
	Keith Alfred Trott	291
5	Raymond Edward Blenkinsop	306
	Leslie Hope	353
8	Judith Smith PW	17
29	Allan John Tillotson	367
Aug 26	David Richard Hawkins	423
30	Trevor Stanley Whiting	438
Sept 30	Ronald Fraser Cook	1
	John Michael Holden	4
	Arthur Frederick Beach	463
	Terence Edward Farr	520
	John Lindsay Mathewson	37
Oct 4	Michael John Woodcock	23
Nov 1	Keith Eric Adams	78
	Ian Graham	105
	Stuart Rowbottam	312
4	Eileen Denford PW	12
	Phoebe Ethel Jorgensen PW	19
25	Frank Walker Bramham	313
29	James Malcolm Hunter	365
	Kenneth George Wood	378
Dec 30	Cyril Ellerby	57
	Brian Monkman	195
1964		
Jan 27	Trevor Terence Hewson	222
Feb 10	Alwyn Smith	43
Mar 31	Kenneth John Markham	49
Apr 3	Michael Alexander Butler	561
	Malcolm Frederick Donsworth	562
	Stephen Neil Madsen	563
	Jeffery Barrie Rawson	564
Apr 6	Mavis Christine Ackroyd PW	20
27	John Tyler	183
May 25	Cyril Paul Renton	273
29	Timothy Beckett	136

When Sworn	Signature of Constable Sworn		When Sworn	Signature of Constable Sworn	
June 8	Patricia Ann Ablett PW	23	Dec 28	Alan Stewart Thompson	188
29	Michael George Bell	275		John Roderick Heron	202
July 6	Gillian Derrel James PW	27		Leonard Bertram Hodey	206
27	Alan Precious	379		Denise June Turner PW	6
	James Wigginton	445		Beryl Kennedy PW	10
Sept 28	Stuart Ramsey	305	**1966**		
	Colin Clive Harrison	565	Feb 21	David Bradshaw	196
Oct 30	Stuart Hickson	566		Barry Frederick Cross	208
Nov 2	Miriam Scott PW	33	Feb 21	Ronald William David	
23	John Brown Arthur	567		Holland	224
Dec 7	June Randell PW	30		Michael Robert O'Grady	245
28	John Reginald Anstee	568		Clive Handey	256
	Robin Hudson	569	Apr 25	George William Davies	246
1965				Michael Christian	
Jan 1	Michael Beckett	570		Gunderson	290
	Kenneth Clark	571		George Alan Parkes	323
4	Margaret Tomlinson PW	32		Anthony White	365
25	Gerald Parker	572		Roy Stoker	367
29	Christopher Paul Erving	573	May 2	John Dent	392
Feb 22	Norman Moore	575	6	Dorothy Ann Taylor PW	11
	Geoffrey James Swales	576		Robert Alexander Howie	382
26	David Gamble	574		Douglas Peter Varney	385
Mar 8	Nina Clare Robinson PW	14	23	Walter John Gregory	423
29	Charles Frederick White	578	June 13	Keith Frederick Callis	
	Alan Moore	579		Krouse	426
Apr 2	C. P. Beadle	577	18	Gordon Frank Galloway	402
5	Carol Ledger PW	1	27	Roy William Hannam	429
May 3	Margaret Mary Dean PW	15		Gordon George Lythgoe	433
7	Bryan John Bennett	580		John Daniel How	544
24	Reginald Quance	4	July 1	David Moody	509
27	John Stephen Rignall	43	18	James Edward Sennett	555
June 28	David Hind	50	25	Graham Boynton	36
July 1	John Patterson	45		Paul Basil Thompson	539
30	David John Holford	51	29	Denis Wiley	51
Aug 23	Eric Spencer	57		Michael Tait	479
31	Michael Fox	86	30	David James Arthur	
Sept 27	David Everingham	97		Metcalf	439
Oct 1	Peter Bean	32	Aug 1	Colin Stephen William	
	Ian Graham	35		Passmore	547
25	Norman Scott	156	22	Gavin Middleton Brown	41
29	Michael Wilson	155		Lynn Hughes PW	3
	Graham Jackson	146	26	Pauline Challans PW	1
Nov 22	Ian Lambswood	174	30	Paul Douglas Walker	45
	Susan Mary Hickey PW	2	Sept 26	Keith Donald Harper	527
26	J. R. Nyde	157		Ian James Eric Oakes	70
	K. Sutton	172		Walter Overfield	94
	David Handley	176		Suzanne Holmes PW	4
Dec 28	Stuart Harold Dry	185	Oct 24	William Quinn	56

When Sworn	Signature of Constable Sworn			When Sworn	Signature of Constable Sworn		
Oct 24	Reginald Patchett		78	May 15	Marjorie Johnson	PW	32
	Barrie Keith Slater		88	22	Brian Taylor		176
	John Maxwell Pullen		155	June 5	Peter Graham Billam		185
	Donald Shoreland		165		Robert George Lund		208
	Stanley James Clark		177		Barry Edward Cundill		260
	John Shires		104		Robert James Abrahams		394
28	Philip Arthur Wilson		173	9	Susan Williamson	PW	11
Nov 21	Helen Margaret			24	Peter G. Sutton		579
	Greenwood	PW	14	26	Warwick Turner		
	Olive Mary Hogg	PW	15		Rawlinson		84
	Nicholas Michael			June 26	Barry Milkins		461
	Simminson		183	July 10	Sidney Albert Jacketts		581
25	Peter John Mounfield		199	17	George Melville Leeming		388
Dec 5	Alistair Robin Cooper		160	24	Robert Peter Sewell		272
12	John Thomas Porter		223		Howard John Martin		538
28	Gwynneth Jean Grinnell				Ian Raymond Bowsley		541
		PW	16		John Robert Seddon		582
	Susan Elizabeth Jones	PW	17		Michael Dowson		583
	David Walter Lewis		239	Aug 21	Christopher Stephen		
30	David Vaughan Ramsden		216		Doyle		224
31	Ian Malcolm Cookman		166		Colin Welks		584
1967					Peter Daddy		585
Jan 2	John Gordon Mitchell	CH Insp			Barrie Spencer Smith		586
6	Geoffrey Walter Cole		284		David Charles Gemmell		
23	Colin Ray Lewis		237		Garbutt		587
	Gordon Turner		275		Raymond Brierley		588
25	Anne Wooldridge	PW	20		Harold Earl Moore		589
27	John Lindsay Lamb		294		R. S. Webster		590
30	Leslie Hall		312	Sept 25	Kenneth Blythe		591
	Colin Alfred Bunnett		379		John Frederick Jacobsen		592
	Isobel Catholine Nicolson				John Edward Jennings		593
		PW	23		Paul Ernest Larkin		594
Feb 3	Philip Ruffles Woodcock		301		Michael Arthur Partridge		595
20	Philip Eric Thompson		427		Brian Andrews		597
	Eric John Wilmot		455		Bryan Victor Beever		598
	David John Fox		562		David Richard Clayton		599
	John Naylor		567		Christopher Scaife		600
24	Trevor Stanley Lummiss		367		Thomas Hawkesworth		602
Mar 6	William Ronald Jones		35	29	Rita Margaret Barley	PW	21
	Peter Graham Burdass		63		Kathryn Elizabeth Jebson		
	Michael Francis Dennison		119			PW	29
28	George Robert Rowland		156	Oct 2	David Harry King		596
	Pamela Anne Marshall	PW	30		Norman Graham Bason		605
31	Anthony Edward Deyes		4		Derek Hall		606
	Gavin Paul Hunt		26		Frederick Charles		
Apr 1	Eric Spaven		140		Willoughby		607
24	A. Dearing		121	23	David Edward Harrison		601
28	John David Parker		161		Robert James Carr		609

When Sworn	Signature of Constable Sworn	
Oct 23	Rodney Arthur Walter Kennington	610
27	Michael George Hobson Wardell	603
Nov 3	John Ridley	604
24	Angeline Rose Webster PW	34
Dec 4	Martin Graham Midgley	608
	Michael Kent	611
	Geoffrey Walker	612
29	David Brian Barrett	614
1968		
Jan 22	William Andrew Gordon	613
Feb 3	Alison Hart PW	35
19	John Michael Westaby	617
23	Desmond Inglestown	615
	Keith William Seward	616
Mar 29	Anthony Dickinson	618
	Stephen Piper	619
30	John Watt	620
May 4	Geoffrey Kitching	3
6	Douglas Raymond Mennell	35
20	Andrew Guy Ablett	31
	David Holmes	64
June 24	Edward Jefferson	114
	Kenneth May	134
28	Christopher Charles Pottage	83
July 1	Charles Michael Wray	159
22	David Owen	180
	Stuart Michael Allerston	194
29	Michael Norman Kennington	183
Sept 23	Sheila Riley PW	3
	Malcolm Harris	217
27	Roy William Robert Bly	197
Oct 25	Pamela Birt PW	6
	Victor Baldwin Jones	252
	Paul Christopher Foy	270
Nov 18	Barry Arthur Bignall	363
	John Charles Dains	375
	Thomas Derek Evans	376
	John Prosser	391
	Ian Leslie Adams	354
1969		
Jan 6	K. Rudd	418
	Leslie Adams	406
	John Lance Wilkinson	465

When Sworn	Signature of Constable Sworn	
Feb 3	Susan Mary Macbeth PW	15
	Richard Ian Green	539
	Ian Alexander McPherson	542
7	Andrew Nicholas Jarratt	565
	John Michael Redshaw	501
Mar 3	Brian Coulter	567
	Robert Russell Jones	389
	Peter Alexander Reed	399
	Robert Kenneth Brown C.Supt	
Mar 6	Paul Lawrence Barker	—
7	Peter William Nesbitt	—
24	Michael Robin David Graham	—
31	Geoffrey Connolly	625
	Bryan David Percival Symons	621
	Michael Dowsan	626
	Keith Crosby	627
	Peter Smith	624
	Frank Morrison	623
	Ann Taylor PW	17
	Elizabeth Skow PW	4
	Gordon Clarke	305
	Kenneth Walter Andrews	622
Apr 19	Alan Smith	17
June 2	Susan Elizabeth Costill PW	19
	Brian William Atkinson	26
	Barbara Lydia Benson PW	21
6	Roy Ian Seratom	45
23	Barry Foster	47
July 7	John Charles Winstone Morris	—
11	Jeanette Allen PW	—
Aug 4	Trevor Davidson	—
16	Janice C. Pool PW	22
	M. Higginbotham	111
23	E. Goodall	106
Sept 2	J. P. Beal	117
30	C. M. Holmes	176
Oct 1	Peter J. Boalton	171
4	Stephen A. Wilde	156
6	Susan Elizabeth Saul PW	27
	Ian Davidson	129
9	Garry C. Scaife	141
15	Alan Thomas Brocklebank	181
	John James Craig Watt	181
16	William Dennis Orr	214

When Sworn	Signature of Constable Sworn	
Oct 23	Richard Woodmansey	216
Nov 12	Roy Roebuck	230
17	Stephen Mathers	249
24	Graham William Hewitt	307
Dec 1	Michael Stuart Rollinson	300
	Edward Duncan Kershaw	315
20	George Edward Hodges	339
1970		
Jan 5	Richard Andrew Grantham	428
	Alfred Davidson	374
Jan 5	Michael Fieldhouse	427
	Dorothy Mary Kaiser PW	33
	Barbara Mann PW	29
10	John Ernest Parkinson	458
	Dennis Royston Ramsey	583
Feb 2	Barry Cross	589
	William Alan Barrett	586
	Stephen Williams	597
Mar 2	David Webster Rogers	599
	Paul Edwin Beardshaw	361
	Terence Harold Theakston	504
16	Robert Arthur Sanders	69
	Keith Sutherby	476
17	Margaret Anne Crawford PW	2
23	Edward Philip Alderman	483
25	John Newton Henry Hale	142
31	George Arthur Brocklebank	629
Apr 6	Malcolm Grange	10
18	Patrick John Costello	24
May 4	George William Fox	23
	Chris Dawber	628
14	Michael Francis Dennison	119
16	Grahame Cooper Bone	46
27	Gregory Holmes	101
June 1	Colin Geoffrey Simon	135
	Robert Thomas Peacock	43
2	Philip Leonard Blogg	108
3	Malcolm Stewart Garrison	136
3	B. G. Bland-Roberts	44
15	Margaret Brenda Chicken PW Insp	
20	Stephen Harman	121
July 1	Malcolm Stuart Russell	156
6	Ian Tute	149
Aug 3	Philip Hall	189
Sept 1	Barbara Ann Blunt PW	6
	James William Pearson	186
3	Kathleen Beardshaw PW	9
14	Frank Anthony Munns	194
	John Edward Midgley	197
Oct 5	Raymond Webster	217
	Ian Charles Taylor	255
	Roy Richardson	257
	Terence Harmer	272
Oct 5	Michael Pattison	280
	Gordon Hawkesworth	340
24	Stephen Graham Andrews	344
26	M. J. Bland-Roberts PW	12
Nov 2	T. A. Smith	453
	Mervyn Bishop	392
	Peter Verity	461
	Alec Edward Alexander	523
	Norman Laurence Appleby	492
	Bryan Francis Calam	415
	Alan John Baldwin	364
30	Hilda Elizabeth Calvert PW	31
	Keith Charles Walsh	535
Dec 1	Edna Sherwood PW	14
1971		
Jan 1	Christopher Boulton	567
15	David Bird	615
19	Brian Thomas Phillips	624
22	Rodney Humphries	630
Feb 1	Martin Johnson	592
	Michael Downs Claxton	587
	David Leslie Hirst	585
	Michael John Leonard	596
	Jacqueline Edith Spain PW	16
	John David Cummings	594
	Michael McLean	631
10	Stephen John Whiting	617
Mar 1	Rosemary Katharine Helm PW	36
	Malcolm Frederick Ablett	632
	Stephen John Boulton Smith	633
	Graham Hopkin	636
	Richard Ronald Connelly	623
29	Jennifer Diane Smith PW	37
	David Harold Bodecott	638

When Sworn	Signature of Constable Sworn	
Mar 29	Anthony Ingledew	637
	Edward Joseph Oldroyd	641
	Thomas William Lee	642
	Geoffrey Williamson	640
31	Douglas Gibson	639
	Glyn Thorpe Stephenson	635
Apr 4	Glynis Etain McGee PW	20
May 3	Maureen Madeleine Ashbridge PW	10
	Paul William Wain	111
6	Graham Robert Tate	634
8	Elizabeth Ann Slaughter PW	22
June 1	Stephen Gordon Southard	79
	Charles Andrew Selwyn Holt	158
	David John Diamond	176
July 5	Ivor Richard Marshall	442
	Roy Wilson	465
	Arthur Alan Beckett	525
19	Kenneth Leslie Smith	171
Aug 2	Barbara Greenland PW Insp	
	Kathleen Theakstone PW	25
	Ian Edward Hunter	583
	James William Clark	614
	Anthony Melville Cooke	182
	Michael Benjamin Cray	567
11	David Anthony Wright	621
31	Marilyn Cracknell PW	29
	Irene Adams PW	21
	Neil Geoffrey Woodward	645
	James Melvyn Hornsby	354
	Harry Leslie Remblance	312
Sept 1	Geoffrey Thomas Blunn	643
6	Dennis Michael Sims	401
	Richard Charles Wright	648
11	Steven Charles Powdrell	644
20	John Graham Morris	652
27	Andrew Mark Robinson	646
Oct 4	David Witted Atkinson	649
	Barry Edwards	376
	Philip Charles Windross	508
	Michael James Palethorpe	507
	David Michael Cropley	650
18	Noel Christopher Bennett	647
23	Sandra Dalton PW	38
Nov 1	Geoffrey John Clark	519
	Stuart Frederick Downes	651
Nov 1	Peter John McKay	653
8	David John Townend	654
29	Roger Booth	658
1972		
Jan 3	Brian Nickerson	655
	Christopher John Davis	657
Jan 3	Noel Francis Thornes	659
	Joan Beanland PW	39
26	Noel Horsaman	662
31	Philip Thomas Priestman	661
Feb 7	Jeffrey Day	656
14	Leonard Tabbitt	660
21	Robert William Brunton	664
28	Judith Smith PW	21
	John Eldred Robinson	663
Mar 13	Howard William Henry Lamb	665
	Roy George Whiting	666
23	Colin McVeigh	667
27	Stephen Leslie Ward	668
	David John Cooper	669
Apr 4	Roy Colin Greensill	12
17	Ian Michael Litherland Bell	23
	David Gordon Bell	24
18	Lyndis Avril Johns PW	16
May 1	Leslie Jeffrey Millar	57
13	Lynn Murray PW	19
25	Colin Roydon Walker	65
31	Brian Leslie Youngson	112
June 10	Keith Meadley	67
26	Fraser Higgins	159
July 3	Collinson William Other Wilson	131
	Philip Cockerham	149
	Richard Arthur Campey	137
6	David Francis Carrick	92
22	Graham Days	268
25	Alan Beck	209
Aug 7	Richard Charles Treece	329
21	Richard Graham Tinegate	289
29	Donald Barker	181
	Alan Knaggs	296
	William Arthur Templeman	226
	Linda Patricia Craig PW	7
Sept 11	Barry James Wilcox	514
Oct 3	Michael Harrington	340
	Peter Smith	355